THE HISTORY OF
MOTOR RACING

THE HISTORY OF
MOTOR RACING

William Boddy & Brian Laban

WHSMITH
EXCLUSIVE
· BOOKS ·

Juan Manuel Fangio

Acknowledgments
Photographs were supplied by: Autocar; Belli; W. Boddy; C. Briscoe-Knight; N. Bruce; Camera Press;
L.J. Caddell; Daimler Benz; G. Gauld; G. Goddard; P. Helck; IGDA; Keystone; L. Klemantaski;
London Art Tech; Mansell Collection; Mary Evans Picture Library; B. Mayor/Orbis; Mercedes Benz;
A. Morland; National Motor Museum; J. Overton; D. Phipps, C. Posthumus; Publifoto; Quattroruote;
J. Spencer Smith; J. Spencer Smith/Orbis; J. Tipler; M. Turner; I. Ward; N. Wright; All-Sport Photographic Ltd.

Special photography by J. Spencer Smith; additional text by Doug Nye.

This edition published in Great Britain exclusively for W H Smith Ltd by
Macdonald and Co (Publishers) Ltd
London and Sydney

A member of Maxwell Pergamon Publishing Corporation plc

Greater London House, Hampstead Road, London, NW1 7QX

© Macdonald and Co (Publishers) Ltd 1977, 1987, 1988

First published in Great Britain in 1977 by Orbis Publishing Ltd

ISBN 0-356-15122-0

Filmset by SX Composing, Rayleigh, Essex

Printed and bound in Hong Kong by Dai Nippon

Jackie Stewart

CONTENTS

CHAPTER 1

PIONEERS OF THE TRACK

THE CARS: 1894-1914

Motor racing is nearly as old as the motor car itself. The early motor races were contested over the ruler-straight *Routes Nationale* of France, and for a good reason. Firstly, the French received the emergence of the horseless-carriage as a practical means of transport with more understanding and far fewer restrictions than those it was plagued with elsewhere, particularly in England. Secondly, the pioneers were faced with the task of making carriages drawn by mechanical means (instead of behind horses or other suitable animals) prove that they could, in fact, represent an effective replacement. For this reason their primary concerns were making the new-fangled vehicles run with a modicum of reliability and safety and then to show that these autocars, automobiles, motor cars, as they were variously called, were able to cover a reasonable amount of ground and at far higher speeds than animal-propelled carts and carriages were capable of doing.

Thus, the best means of both proving these matters to a sceptical public and of improving the design and construction of the motor car itself, was accomplished by organising races, which were thus generally well supported by those who saw a big commercial future for the motor car and by those who, liking these new exhilaratingly fast vehicles from the sporting viewpoint, realised how essential it was for them to prove themselves, so that authority would not frown on them. In the next chapter we shall see how the then deserted, unfettered main highways of the European continent were ideal for such

Below: one of the 30 hp, 6.3-litre lightweight Renaults which competed in the ill-fated Paris-Madrid race of 1903; it was in one of these cars that Marcel Renault crashed and was killed, causing the race to be stopped. The maximum weight limit for the event was 1000 kg, so the chassis of the cars were drilled as much as possible in order to reduce the overall weight and allow for big engines; this process undoubtedly took away a substantial amount of strength. The optical phenomenon of the forward lean of the car, typical in photographs of this period, results from the use of a focal plane shutter camera. As the shutter moves across the image, the tops of the wheels, being recorded on the film slightly later than the bottoms, have advanced slightly – hence the 'crouch'

Above: the Peugeot Vis-à-Vis which passed the finishing line first in the Paris-Rouen Reliability Trial and shared the prize money with the second-placed Panhard; the car was driven by a Monsieur Doriot who is seen here seated next to Pierre Giffard, the organiser of the Trial

pioneer motor races, which were at first great town-to-town contests, regarded with awe by the horse-minded fraternity, but all the time teaching lessons to those who designed and built the competing cars. Because these grew rapidly ever larger, more powerful, and therefore faster, they made it plain that the horse had met its match and that even express trains might soon be unable to match the performance of these new petrol-burning motor vehicles.

The first proper motor race, contested in 1895, was the Paris-Bordeaux-Paris race, but the Paris-Madrid race of 1903 which was stopped at Bordeaux by order of an irate Government due to the many accidents which happened, caused future contests to be held over properly policed closed roads. But these were still public roads fenced off and guarded for the purpose, usually triangular circuits of considerable length. This continued to be the norm up to and even after World War I. The result was that cars were raced, and thus demonstrated, under normal road-going conditions, having to contend with hills, conventional corners, cambered road surfaces, dust and other natural hazards of the kind encountered by travellers. As time moved on, it became logical to institute classes for the various-sized vehicles that were avidly entered for such exciting contests of speed and endurance, and eventually to impose certain restrictions on the engineering factors of the motor cars

that were soon being specially constructed for racing purposes and growing ever faster.

From primitive things that were decidedly experimental and, in fact, mere horseless-carriages, they quickly became fast, then very fast, decently reliable and controllable by the standards of their time. For this reason, those long-ago, courageously fought motor races of the pre-1915 period were exciting to watch, and important to analyse after they had been run off. The cars that contested them, from the earliest Panhard & Levassor to those 4½-litre overhead-camshaft Mercédès which put up an all-conquering 1–2–3 victory in the 1914 French Grand Prix (to the consternation of the French on the eve of war), are now if immense historical interest, and the handful that have survived and have been restored to original condition and running order are fine machines to own and drive.

Before the first full-scale motor race was run in 1895 there had been the important Paris-Rouen Trials of 1894. The best performance in these was made by a De Dion steamer which was able to carry six persons. This was really a steam tractor and, although it headed the finishers, which comprised thirteen petrol cars and seven more steam vehicles, it was not given a prize. The important cars at the time were the Peugeots, which had Panhard & Levassor engines which were hung at the back of a low chassis frame made of hollow steel tubing, through which the cooling water circulated. Final drive was by side chains but the whole conception of the carriage was crude, to later eyes, with wheels of different sizes front and back, although some did have wire-type spokes, and steering by a lever atop a vertical column, as was then customary practice.

The 1894 Panhard & Levassor cars had already set the fashion others were ultimately to follow, in mounting their engines at the front of the frame. The engine itself in these cars was a V-type Daimler motor, the larger of the two sizes used being of 75 mm bore × 140 mm stroke. This power unit, which had its two cylinders angled at fifteen degrees from the vertical, developed about 3½ hp at 750 rpm. Ignition was by the prevailing hot-tube, obviating electrics, and a surface carburettor was used, although the Panhard engineers already had a float-feed carburettor on the stocks, which was fitted to one of their Paris-Rouen entries. The drive from the V-twin engine went through a double-cone clutch to a gear chest which gave three, or in some models four, forward speeds, it being notable that these gears were not always enclosed in any form of casing. Reverse was obtained by keying one of two gears to an intermediate shaft, from which the final stages of the transmission consisted of single or double chains. This short-wheelbase, high-perched Panhard was controlled by a left-hand steering lever that was said to transmit jolts from every stone or rut encountered by the front wheels. The driver had quite a handful to contend with, as the throttle and governor controls were before

him and with his right hand he worked the levers for changing gear, reversing and applying the side brakes. There were also the usual pedals, and foot and hand brakes were interconnected with the clutch. Radius rods tensioned the driving chains.

Thus, the first-ever competition cars! They had low-power governed engines with unpredictable carburation, and ignition at the whim of the wind, which could snuff out the burners on which the platinum hot-tubes relied. They were terrible to steer, and gear-shifting was a difficult accomplishment. But at least they pointed the way to better, and certainly far faster cars to come, and were just about practical, which cannot be said of those Paris-Rouen entries which proclaimed motive power achieved by gravity, hydraulics, compressed-air, multiple levers, pendulums or just the weight of the passengers! Indeed, most successful of these 1894 primitives, the Peugeot, covered the $78\frac{3}{4}$-mile course at an average speed of $11\frac{1}{2}$ mph.

By the year 1895, when the first real motor race took place between Paris and Bordeaux, Panhard & Levassor had progressed further. They had their own engine, which they called the 'Phönix', a vertical twin-cylinder power unit. Still a very crude, short-wheelbase machine, nevertheless, the advent of the ever-more powerful engine must be recognised. This successful 1895 Panhard & Levassor had solid rubber tyres and retained hot-tube ignition, although as it had its engine at the front the burner was less affected by the wind than those of the Peugeots, with their low-hung rear-placed engines close to the draught and the dust. The Panhard's steering gear was still direct-acting and reversible, thus calling for great strength and continual concentration. The winning Panhard & Levassor weighed 604 kgm, and its engine developed some 4 hp at 800 rpm, from cylinders of 80×120 mm, which was sufficient to give it a maximum speed of $18\frac{1}{2}$ mph. The gears were now enclosed to protect them against dust and road grit. It is interesting that at this stage of automobile development, although the pneumatic tyre for racing had made its appearance, it was quite unreliable and it was the solid rubber tyre, as used on the 1895 winning Panhard & Levassor, which ruled supreme, superior to the iron tyres which were employed on some of the competing vehicles.

Ever-more-lusty power units were the hallmark of these early motor races. The four-cylinder 8 hp Panhard & Levassor engine had appeared in that 1895 Paris-Bordeaux event and when this type of race was repeated the following year it was just such a car that proved victorious, averaging $14\frac{1}{2}$ mph over $1062\frac{1}{2}$ miles of decidedly indifferent roads, for the race was not only out of Paris to Marseilles but the competitors had to return to Paris. So, we find the monster racing car already in evidence as early as 1896, because in those days of insipid little cars of $3\frac{1}{2}$ to 4 hp, an eight-horsepower Panhard was indeed a monster. Yet, exciting as such giant racers seemed to the ordinary automobilist of eighty years ago, it must be remembered that they relied on crude brakes, a spoon on the back tyres supplemented by a contracting band on a drum on the transmission; that after dark they had to rely on candle-lamps for illumination of the tree-lined unlit roads they raced over, and that suction-opened

Left: the 4-litre De Dietrich of 1903, similar to the Charles Jarrott car which started first in the ill-fated Paris-Madrid race of that year

Below: it was a Mors like this which Henri Fournier drove to first place in the celebrated Paris-Berlin race of 1901. The drive chain broke as he was about to start the victory parade!

Below right: driving a borrowed 60 hp Mercédès touring car like this, Belgian Camille Jenatzy won the 1903 Gordon Bennett cup at Carlow, Ireland

automatic inlet valves were as commonplace as the solid tyres, tiller-steering and tube-ignition. Yet, it was these great town-to-town contests that were forcing the pace of design and evolution, both of racing cars and ordinary automobiles and were also making the name of Panhard & Levassor famous and France the premier country among the car-building nations.

From that time onwards, it was a case of increasing the size of engines to force more speed from these wooden-framed, cart-sprung racing *bolides*. Engines ran at virtually a fixed speed, so increasing the rate of crankshaft revolution, as was done later to obtain a gain in power, was out of the question. Instead, cylinders were made ever larger, the old adage that there is no substitute for cubic inches being very much to the fore, and big gilled-tube radiators were used to cool these enormous engines.

So much was this the case that by 1898, classes for the different-sized cars that were entered for races had been instituted. Starting with motor cycles of less than 100 kgm and then those two-wheelers of over 100 but weighing not over 200 kgm, the cars were divided into those of 200 to 400 kgm and those which turned the scales or tipped the weighbridge at over 400 kgm. That year

the 8 hp Panhard & Levassor had wheel-steering, its 80 mm × 120 mm four-cylinder engine making it a very fast car by the leisurely standards of the day. Electric coil ignition was taken up by Panhard, following the Peugeot fashion, and the power race continued. Mors stole the advantage from Panhard and by 1901 progress had dictated that equal-sized wheels be used at both ends of these racing cars. It was the 24 hp Cannstatt-Daimler racer of 1901 that set the ultimate fashion, that of using a radiator of honeycomb tubes. Mercédès pushed home their technical superiority, with a pressed-steel, channel-section chassis frame, the new type of radiator and a gate gear-change. This soon became the accepted format and it was then a case of engines becoming bigger and ever bigger in respect of the swept volume of their cylinders. The high-tension magneto replaced the low-tension magneto machine which had necessitated mechanically interrupted breaker-points within the actual engine cylinders, where they soon sooted-up (although Itala retained low-tension ignition for Grand Prix racing cars as late as 1908) and the automatic inlet valve gave place to mechanically operated poppet valves, with Fiat pioneering the placing of all such valves in the cylinder heads.

The speed of these racing cars must not be under estimated. By the time of the 1908 French Grand Prix, when giant power plants were being installed in flimsy chassis, over 100 mph was attained on straight stretches of the road circuit, in spite of the fact that wind-cheating bodywork was not normally resorted to. There had been attempts at so-called streamlining, notably with the inverted-boat type of body fitted to the Mors car which made the best, meteoric, showing in the ill-fated 1903 Paris-Madrid race until this was stopped at Bordeaux. But on the whole, it was power, the brute force of really enormous engines, that made these road-racing cars go so quickly. The 1902 racing season had seen the advent of the famous, or notorious, 70 hp Panhard & Levassor, which contrived to have a 13.7-litre engine in a wooden chassis weighing, to comply with the contemporary racing rules, under one ton. The engine may have been absolutely massive, with its great 160×170 mm cylinders, but it was not very highly developed, being of the constant-speed concept, in which 1500 rpm represented maximum crankshaft speed. There was no valve overlap in those days of suction-operated inlet valves (of which the Panhard had three per cylinder) and splash lubrication sufficed for the big-end bearings. The cooling water was contained in copper jackets surrounding the cylinders, with the usual big gilled-tube radiator on the nose of the car and, to reduce the weight of the cast-iron pistons, their skirts were drilled, and, like-wise, the connecting rods to which they were attached.

Above: the 1913 Peugeot racing car, seen here in the hands of Georges Boillot at Boulogne. Boillot started his career in the Targa Florio, retiring from the 1908 and 1909 events, but winning the following year's race. By 1913 he was one of Europe's top drivers. He won the French Grand Prix in 1912 and 1913 and failed to take his third successive victory only due to engine problems one lap from the end of the 1914 race. He finished fourteenth at Indianapolis in the same year and set fastest lap in that race. A pilot in the French Air Service, he was killed in action in April 1916

This huge engine was rigidly mounted in the chassis, instead of being given a separate sub-frame as previously, and metal plates reinforced the frame. Front springing was by a transverse spring of three leaves, whereas Panhard had previously had a fancy for semi-elliptic springs to tie the front axle to the car. It is said that this transverse spring on the Seventy was located by rods – the advent of the 'Panhard rod' so well known today. Final drive was by the accepted side chains, to a dead axle beam. This enormous racer was able to make some 90 mph with its engine running at 1200 rpm, and the iron pistons sweeping up and down the bores at a speed of 1400 feet per minute. It was able to run away from all competition, but smaller-engined cars were not too far behind.

The battle of the cylinders existed in the Napier's use of a six-in-line engine, which was to achieve great things on the Brooklands track from 1907 onwards. But for road-racing, the four-cylinder engine ruled supreme. When the first of the French Grand Prix races as we know them today was held at Le Mans in 1906, the winning car, a Renault, was able to show that the simple L-head side-by-side-valve power plant was still viable, but its capacity was 12,970 cc, obtained from four cylinders of 160 × 150 mm, the over-square configuration, ahead of the cooling radiator. Renault even made use of a three-speed (instead of a four-speed) gearbox and at this date detachable wheels were disallowed, so that punctured or burst tyres, of which there were many, had to be changed on the fixed wheels; Renault had had the foresight to fit his cars with the newly arrived Michelin detachable rims. The biggest

Right: what many early cars lacked in sophistication, they attempted to make up by sheer brute force. A classic example of the latter-day adage that there is 'no substitute for cubic inches' was the 1907 120 hp Itala. The four-cylinder engine displaced 14,432 cc, giving a top speed of just 100 mph at a leisurely 1100 rpm. This particular car won the 1907 Coppa della Velocita at Brescia in the hands of Cagno (National Motor Museum, England)

A pit stop in the 1908 Targa Bologna, with Trucco's Lorraine-Dietrich taking on fuel; Trucco went on to finish second in this race

engines in that race were those of the Panhard & Levassors, at 185 × 170 mm, giving a swept volume of 18,279 cc. There were also the 18.1-litre De Dietrich engines; the Itala, Fiat and Hotchkiss entries for the Grand Prix were all of over 16 litres, making the 7½-litre Grègoire look like a light car.

That was the trend for many years, and it was one that the race regulations, which at different times imposed a fuel consumption limit or a restriction on engine-cylinder-bore diameter, rather than the designer's whim, finally broke down. Even when the latter artificial limit was imposed for the 1908 Grand Prix at Dieppe, being set at 155 mm, with 127 mm set as the maximum bore in a six-cylinder engine, huge power units still prevailed. Biggest were the Clément-Bayards and the Opels, at just under 14 litres, but engines of well over 12 and 13 litres were commonplace and the victorious Mercédès was a giant of 12,831 cc. All this, of course, implied very excessive piston speeds and already the idea existed that power could be better weaned by having a short-throw crankshaft with thus more lightly stressed pistons and crankshafts. Then higher rates of revolution could be used, and power output boosted not through capacity but from efficiently running and breathing power units.

The adoption of overhead valves and an understanding of overlap in camshaft timing made this possible, and it was quite soon to be exploited, not only in the *formule libre* races but also in light-car or *voiturette* contests, in which the short-stroke four-cylinder engine was to oust the abnormally long-stroke twin-cylinder entries.

Racing for the Grand Prix was abandoned for political reasons between the years 1909 and 1911 when long-distance events were boycotted out of jealousy by the major French and German manufacturers. When it was revived in 1912 at Dieppe, Ernest Henry had brought about a revolution in racing-engine layout with his Peugeot Grand Prix cars. These had the epoch-making feature of overhead valves inclined in the cylinder heads and operated by two overhead camshafts, and the formula followed ever after for the majority of top-racing power units. By having a camshaft above each line of valves, the lightest possible operating gear could be applied to them, killing valve float; the use of inclined valves meant that the hemispherical combustion chamber of maximum efficiency could be used. The then existent problems of the noise of driving two camshafts situated so far from the engine crankshaft and the manufacturing expense of the whole set-up were not problems that governed the design of a racing engine. The Peugeot not only won the 1912 French Grand Prix with this new remarkably efficient engine of 7602 cc (from a Fiat possessed with a vast engine of 14.1 litres) but in voiturette racing a 3-litre Peugeot to the refreshing new Henry formula was remarkably successful.

Top left : a man and his car: Fritz von Opel in the four-cylinder, 12-litre Opel, one of the largest cars in the race, at the start of the 1908 French Grand Prix at Dieppe. Opel finished 21st and a similar car driven by Jörns came in sixth

Above and right : the 1908 Austin 100hp Grand Prix car was, like many of its contemporaries, loosely based on a road-going production car. Shown here is the impressive 9677cc, straight-six engine, which unfortunately lacked sufficient power for what was quite a heavy car (National Motor Museum, England)

Below: David Bruce-Brown and riding mechanic on a Fiat S 74 in the 1912 French Grand Prix, displaying a rudimentary appreciation of driver protection with masks and goggles to combat the dusty, stone-strewn roads of the day

Inset: Jules Goux *(left)* and Georges Boillot *(right)* were the Peugeot works drivers in the company's early days. They were a great asset for their considerable engineering talents as well as for their competition successes. The photographs were taken at the 1908 Grand Prix des Voiturettes

The twin-cam Peugeot racing engines were the product of this brilliant Swiss engineer Henry and the Peugeot racing drivers Goux and Georges Boillot. They used a still-excessive piston stroke for their 7.2-litre GP cars of 200 mm, in conjunction with a 100 mm cylinder bore, so that with these new high-speed engines running at a maximum of 2200 rpm and producing some 130 bhp, the piston speed was as high as 2900 feet per minute. But it all held together to give a race average speed of nearly $68\frac{1}{2}$ mph for this gruelling two-day 956-mile race of 1912.

This Peugeot advance set the fashion for the future but was not immediately taken up universally. While shaft instead of chain final drive was now the vogue and detachable wheels with centre-lock hubs had facilitated tyre-changing, there were those who went cautiously towards twin overhead camshafts. Certainly, for the 1913 French Grand Prix at the Dieppe circuit, run again on a fuel-consumption basis, the 5.6-litre Peugeots ruled supreme. But in the dramatic race of 1914, over the Lyons course, five single-overhead-camshaft $4\frac{1}{2}$-litre Mercédès racing cars dominated the scene. This was as much due to the Teutonic care taken to prepare for the race and the use of team

tactics, or at least of having sufficient cars in the race to break up any opposition, as to the design of the winning engine, which was of modest capacity partly because efficiency could now be gained from a comparatively small, fast-revving engine; also, because the race rules limited engine size to 4500 cc. And just as the result of this oft-quoted 1914 French Grand Prix on the eve of the war was no proof that the single-overhead-camshaft engine was superior to the twin-cam power unit, nor was it conclusive over the matter

Left: the aviation-type engine of the successful 1914 Grand Prix Mercédès had 115 bhp (20 fewer than the 1908 cars). However, the engine was powerful enough to help the cars to a 1-2-3 victory in that year's Grand Prix

Below: three of the famous Mercédès Grand Prix machines of 1914, complete with their distinguished drivers Lautenschlager, Salzer and Wagner (from left to right) celebrating their 1-2-3 victory in the French Grand Prix, on their return to Germany

Below: a 1912 Mercédès and crew wait in the pits prior to the start of a Belgian event; although the Belgian Grand Prix proper was not inaugurated until the 1920s, the Belgian automobile club had first held a handicap event at Spa in 1895

of racing-car brakes. The Mercédès team had rear-wheel brakes, of expanding shoes within rear-axle drums cooled by air fins, supplemented by a brake on the transmission, as was commonplace from around 1904; they won against cars with the latest front-wheel brakes, as used by Peugeot and Delage. That the Peugeot was able to outbrake the Mercédès in this event is indisputable, but this ability was no match for team tactics as employed very professionally by the Mercédès organisation.

After the Armistice, as we shall see, both twin-cam racing engines and four-wheel brakes ruled supreme; at first, servo assistance was used for the brakes, but it soon became unnecessary.

In the light of modern knowledge it is seen that Ernest Henry did not, in 1912 and the remaining pre-war years, exploit to the full his splendid new engines. The hemi-head that his properly actuated inclined overhead valves made possible was less suited to the comparatively low crankshaft speeds he envisaged than for quicker-running engines, and another pre-eminent aspect of his design, namely the use of four valves to each cylinder, was at the time more a concession to its ability to combat valve breakage than a serious endeavour to obtain optimum breathing through the additional, if smaller, inlet valve ports. But these comments notwithstanding, the advance was of great significance. Indeed, overhead valves were soon to become universal for specially constructed racing power units and it is worth remembering that when Fiat first used their push-rod overhead valves on their 1905 racing engines, they also had the valves inclined at 45 degrees and were able to extract a useful 120 bhp from these 16-litre 180 × 160 mm power units, even though the crankshaft speed was restricted to around 1100 rpm when flat out.

Ernest Henry added the refinement of a camshaft above each line of valves by 1912 and the previous remark that he used four valves to a cylinder to combat exhaust-valve failure requires the endorsement that he was apparently also anxious to overcome the then-prevalent unreliability of valve springs, designing special tappets that relieved his valve springs of the necessity of closing the tappet mechanism. His first 3-litre engine was not an extreme power producer, giving perhaps 90 bhp at 3000 rpm in its 1912 Coupe de L'Auto form, which was its first high-speed application and it was comparable to the side-valve Sunbeam cars which created a furore by finishing 3rd, 4th and 5th in the Grand Prix itself. Even though output was only around ten horsepower above that of the L-head Sunbeam's engine, and the Peugeots were hampered by not adopting the streamlining then in vogue thanks to the influence of track racing at Brooklands, Henry still went on to develop his design much more effectively for the 1913 Coupe de L'Auto competition. He inclined his four valves at 60 degrees instead of at 45 degrees for that race and drove his 'upstairs' camshafts by a train of gears instead of by a vertical shaft. No more power was claimed but the engine was now the epitome of efficiency, producing its 90 bhp at 3000 rpm on a compression ratio of only 5.6 to 1. For the still-born 1914 light-car race of the aforesaid title, Henry had a four-cylinder engine of 75 × 140 mm built to comply with the race limit of 2½ litres. This car did well after waiting for the war to finish, winning the 1919 Targa Florio race. The 1913 3-litre Peugeots were within 5 mph of the top speed of the far bigger 1912 full Grand Prix cars, and the 1914 version, giving 80 bhp at the customary 3000 rpm, was capable of some 92 mph. Thus, the most advanced racing engine design of this pre World War I period appeared, with great success, in 7.2-litre, 5.6-litre, 3-litre and 2½-litre forms. It was to be widely copied by Sunbeam and Humber before the war, and set

a fashion for the immediate post-Armistice era, until Henry advanced again, with his straight-eight-cylinder Ballot engines.

At this formative period of racing-car development, ball and roller crankshaft bearings were accepted as a way round lubrication problems that had been far from solved at this date, and castor-base lubricants instead of mineral oils were the norm. Valve gear was semi-exposed in many cases even though engine speeds were increasing. From driving on the ignition and governor controls, the racing driver for some years prior to the war had had to make full and proper use of his gearbox with, of course, no aids of the synchro-mesh kind. Indeed, he had to be able to change gear without the clutch if need be and the practice of heeling and toeing was rife, whereby the accelerator was pressed to speed up the engine revs to accommodate the gearbox, at the same time as the foot brake was being applied to slow the car for a corner, round which it would be driven in the lower gears. This need to change difficult gears constantly while braking with indifferent brakes, using outside hand-brake as well as prodding the brake pedal while changing gear, together with wrestling with insensitive steering and a cord-bound steering wheel that would kick and cut the hands, made driving these pre-1914 racing cars in the long engagements that were normal to them, a very tiring and tough proposition, suitable only for the very fit. But their worst feature in this respect was the hard springing, from leaf springs that scarcely 'gave'.

Below: a 1912 Coupe de L'Auto Sunbeam, built for a light-car race at Dieppe in which it was part of a British 1-2-3. After competition, this car saw road service until it was stored in 1930. 1958 was the year when it was retrieved from mothballs and renovated; it is still able to travel at 85mph, by courtesy of its 2996cc side-valve engine
(National Motor Museum, England)

Yet, all things considered, it can be said that in the two seasons preceeding World War I, the road-racing cars, whether restricted by race rules or not, were very fast, not too unreliable, and generally pleasant vehicles, pointing the way directly to a forthcoming generation of what were to be known as 'sports cars'. The W. O. Bentley-designed 3-litre Bentley of 1919/21 is proof of this. . . .

In the field of the *voiturette* or lightweight racing cars, the general trends followed those of the bigger cars. The freakish twin-cylinder Peugeots with very long stroke engines gave place to the beautiful little four-cylinder Hispano Suiza of 1910, which had a 65 × 200 mm engine that gave something in the order of 52 bhp and was the forerunner of another pioneer sporting car, the 80 × 180 mm Alfonso Hispano Suiza. From there, as we have seen, Ernest Henry of Peugeot went ahead, with immaculate twin-cam racing 3-litre motor cars.

Down all these experimental and exciting years there were naturally attempts to break away from the conventional progression of racing-car evolution. The two-stroke power pack was tried, and discarded, Gobron-Brillié got further

Right: Léon Molon is seen at the 1913 Gaillon hill-climb with his Hispano-Suiza. This Hispano used an ohc engine, of 85 × 130 mm dimensions, based on the supercharged unit which was to have been raced in 1912. The cars were more reliable in normally aspirated form. Due to their odd shape, they were known as 'Sardines'

Below: one of the unsuccessful cars built by Humber for the 1914 TT. This, like many other cars of the period, used a Peugeot 'crib' engine, being of the classic twin-overhead-camshaft, sixteen-valve, four-cylinder type

with engines in which the pistons moved in opposition and required two crankshafts, connected together. Marc Birkigt, who was responsible for the Alfonso Hispano Suiza and those magnificent post-war production models of this illustrious make, tried to perfect the supercharged engine but forced induction of the mixture was left to Mercédès after the war, and for Fiat to render practical on the race circuits. Up to the war, multiple carburettors were far from being fully exploited and Henry was content with a single instrument. This is explained by the fact that valve overlap was little understood at this time and was at first applied only to late closing of the exhaust valves, because the idea of opening an inlet valve early to apply some ram filling was quite foreign to contemporary thinking. But over-large choke tubes in the carburettors were frequently found on racing engines, which were not expected to pull properly at much below 2500 rpm. These aids to an unobstructed gas flow contrasted oddly with the tortuous inlet manifolds through which the up-draught carburettors invariably fed the cylinders.

Plain big-end bearings were possible, especially if dry-sump lubrication assisted the less refined oils of those times to remain decently cool. Petrol would be fed by air pressure, usually from a drum or bolster-type fuel tank set across the back of the chassis; in those days, a riding mechanic was invariably carried and he had to operate a hand air-pump as well as watching the oil gauge casting glances astern for overtaking cars.

When Brooklands opened in the summer of 1907 in Surrey, it forced the pace of race-engine improvement, because on a banked course the throttle is open fully, or nearly so, for very long periods. Thus 'run' bearings, through over-hot oil, burnt-out exhaust valves and seized pistons, were more often the cause of defeat than in road racing and the track tuners were soon to learn the disasters that resulted from running the fuel mixture too weak, of not allowing sufficient cooling air to penetrate to the sump or oil tank, and of trying to obtain flat-out speed with piston and bearing clearances too tight. But sheer maximum speed was of the essence down at 'The Track', which is why it was not long before very advanced thinking was applied to reducing the wind drag inherent in chassis and bodywork. Radiators were cowled in, leaving only a slit or hole through which cooling air could reach their tubes, thus, incidentally, sometimes improving their capacity in that important direction. Bodies with long tails of tapering or 'airship' shape were quick to appear, and to carry out this so-called 'streamlining' to its ultimate, a long undershield would enclose the bottom of the chassis, as was done on road-going cars to exclude road dirt and dust. The extremists even faired-in front axles and small protruding parts such as spring hangers and dumb-irons with carved wood and fabric, one droll sight being a certain 1912 Lorraine-Dietrich with a vast area of exposed flat-fronted radiator, beneath which was a carefully streamlined axle! All this attention to reducing the drag of the wind undoubtedly paid off, enabling more speed to be realised for less power.

From the first Brooklands racers which were virtually stripped chassis that had worn touring and even closed coachwork until their competition débuts, the trend swung away to these splendidly sleek specially bodied track cars. It was but a step from fully faired two-seaters to the genuine racing single-seater, because a riding mechanic was not so necessary on the wide expanses of the Weybridge concrete as on a narrow, dust-obscured road circuit. These monoposto or single-place racing and record-breaking cars were only wide enough at the cockpit to accommodate the driver, and further drag-reduction was achieved by putting discs over their wheels. An even more extreme idea, pioneered by the Sunbeam engineer who was so keen on racing his products to endorse their worth, namely the great Louis Coatalen, was to isolate the radiator from the engine compartment, so that drag should not develop beneath the engine bonnet. It was Coatalen who had first thought of using a large aeroplane engine in a motor-car chassis and his 1913 V12 aero-engined Sunbeam of 9 litres capacity, endowed with the typical slim single-seater long-tailed racing body of the period, was a successful experiment in this empirical age. Another experiment sometimes attributed to a much later period of automobile evolution was four-wheel-drive, tried out on the big Spyker racing car as early as 1903, and front-wheel-drive, as used a little later on the transverse-engined American Christie racing car.

The real lesson of racing as it was up to the outbreak of World War I was that power from the petrol-burning internal-combustion engine could be efficiently raised by using the twin-overhead-camshaft engine, which was superior in making high crankshaft speeds possible, which the side-by-side valve formation could not encompass. This is reflected in the fact that the 1912 Coupe de L'Auto Sunbeams were the last successful side-valve racing cars, apart from minor races, and the T-head valve layout, as used for the Alfonso Hispano-Suiza *voiturettes* (that is to say having the inlet valves on one side of the cylinder block and the exhaust valves along the opposite side, necessitating two separate camshafts in the crankcase), did not survive the war. The racing-car engine had paved the way for the powerful overhead-valve aeroplane engines of the war years and those Mercédès which dominated the last Grand Prix to be held before hostilities broke out had engines significantly similar to those in the first German fighters to appear over the Western Front. So, racing was improving motor-car design, which in those earlier years was its purpose.

Braking, roadholding, speed and streamlining being the main headings under which the fierce incentive of competition had forced the pace. By 1914, the then-current four-cylinder long-stroke twin-cam engines were good for 130 bhp in Grand Prix form, although this output of 30 horsepower per litre left room for great strides after the war; indeed, supercharging made such progress easily attainable.

In the emerging days, Panhard & Levassor had gradually been overtaken by Mors, which put up such a great performance in the Paris-Bordeaux portion of the 1903 Paris-Madrid race, although the Renault light cars of the time were almost a match for the Mors. After this, Napier made some inroads with big six-cylinder cars. But Fiat raced away with their overhead-valve (pushrod) racers, until Peugeot got ahead with the twin-cam sixteen-valve engine. During this pioneer period, Britain was out-classed, apart from Sunbeams making the simple design of side-valve power unit perform well, and developing the Brooklands type of pure track-racing car, a sphere where Sunbeam, Vauxhall and Talbot were to the fore, the last-named make being the first to cover over one hundred miles in one hour.

Racing continued for a while in America at Indianapolis where these pre-1914 racers were able to hold their own. But it is to the post-war era that we have to look for the next stages of racing-car development. Better fuels and improved tyres aided the effective use of the higher speeds made possible by much higher rates of crankshaft rotation and by the use of forced induction.

Right: Walter Christie of the United States driving one of his own cars, which featured front-wheel drive and twin front wheels. The radiator on this car is scuttle mounted, while on subsequent models it was positioned behind the driver

Below left: advertising on racing cars was already apparent in 1910, as demonstrated here on the last of the Christie racers, the 'Barnstormer' Showman, record breaker and racing driver Barney Oldfield is at the wheel; note the tow rope for starting purposes

Below: a streamlined 15.9-litre Diatto at Brooklands in June 1910. This model was not notably successful, but, after World War I, the marque became competitive in the hands of the Maserati brothers

THE RACES: 1894-1914

The motor-racing contests of that empirical period prior to World War I were regarded with probably more awe, excitement and possible alarm than we devote these days to space travel and scraping Mars for dust samples. The motor car was scarcely established as a decent form of transport before the turn of the century, and was the subject of a good deal of open hostility and official threats. Yet, in the midst of all this, here were the new-fangled motor-carriages actually racing one another in smothering clouds of dust, along the ruler-straight roads of Europe. By 1902, these petrol-carriages, which were certainly not to be encouraged, were attaining quite respectable speeds on the straight stretches of virtually unpoliced public *Routes National*: about half as fast again as you could travel in the comfort and security of the best express trains.

Yet all this frenzied obsession with speed in the new age of motors was to improve these vehicles quickly and surely, so that within a few years of these first motor races, the motor car was a quiet, docile and swift form of everyday transport. We owe the greatest respect, therefore, to those brave men, the conductors of the early, very primitive racing cars: men who drove furiously into the unknown, striving to leave one town and arrive as quickly as possible at the next. Unprotected by crash helmets, protective clothing or Armco barriers, over routes sparsely marshalled and unpractised, they raced, as Charles Jarrott put it, over the never-ending road that led to the unobtainable horizon. Speed, ever more speed, was then the order of the day, at the expense of safe controllability, and driver comfort. Yet, there was never any shortage of keen amateurs who were prepared to pit their strength and improving skills against the hazards of racing, if they could only lay their hands on the steering wheel of the latest racing monster from the Panhard & Levassor or Mors factories.

Above: Charles Jarrott and his mechanic Cecil Bianchi on board a 1904 Wolseley

Below: one of the works twin-overhead-camshaft 3298 cc Sunbeams raced at the Isle of Man, where Kenelm Lee Guiness won for the team; he averaged 56.4 mph over 600 miles of racing. The cars featured four valves per cylinder, hemispherical heads and roller-bearing crankshafts

It all commenced calmly enough. In 1894, *Le Petit Journal* had the initiative to organise a competition for *Voitures sans chevaux*, to be run from Paris to Rouen, a distance of 78¾ miles, which was to be judged by the paper's staff and a number of consulting engineers. This significant and historic event, which took place on 22 July, attracted the remarkably large field of 102 vehicles. The entrants included Pousselet, Pellorce, De Dion Bouton, Lemaitre, Roussat, Gautier, Hidien, Victor Popp, Scotte, Klaus, Tenting, Panhard & Levassor, Quantin, Rodier, Archdeacon, Le Blant, Periere, Letar, Gaillardet, Varennes, Vacheron, Coquatrix, Leval, Peugeot, Darras, Geoffrey, Gillot, Loubiere, Duchemin, Ponset, Lemoigne, Bargigli, Le Brun, Spanoghe, De Prandieres, Corniquet, Martin-Cudrez, . . . the list is seemingly endless and all these pioneers really deserve to be listed, for they were the true forerunners of every competition exponent who followed them. Suffice to say that, adventurous as they obviously were, with very few exceptions such as Peugeot, Panhard, Jeantaud, Landry et Beyroux, Bellanger, and De Dion Bouton, their names did not continue into the future of motor racing.

Indeed, this first run was not a race at all. It was a trial, and the ingenious means of locomotion announced by many of the entrants were too optimistic to persist and were soon to reduce to steam, electricity and petrol. But that Paris–Rouen Trial was what sparked-off the great motor races that were to follow. As has been said, these divide into clearly defined types. Up to 1903, when the Paris–Madrid race was stopped at Bordeaux by order of the French Government because of accidents that had happened along the inadequately marshalled public road, the important races were from one town to others, which were designated low-speed Control areas, the route either ending at one of them or turning back at the final town. Thus they were road races pure and simple. They might be divided into classes, with the competing vehicles defined by weight or other limits, but speed was the vital ingredient. After Paris–Madrid, such races were, with a few exceptions that persisted into post-World War II times, run over closed circuits, which were shorter and could thus be properly controlled. These road circuits were invariably formed of temporarily closed public roads, often provided with temporary safety fencing to keep spectators off the course, pedestrian-bridges or tunnels.

The second sub-division of motor races in this experimental period from 1895 to 1914 involves the purpose behind all the racing. The very earliest contests were mainly a proving ground for the motor vehicle itself, although the better makes gained notice by coming through victorious in this latest sport. The French makes led the way for a long time and then came the Gordon Bennett races, for which teams of three cars had to be entered by each competing country. The cars themselves, all the components used in their construction including the tyres, and the drivers were required to be of the nationality of the entrant. Thus motor racing became not a mere proving ground but a battle of the nations. Emphasis was placed on this by the ruling which said that the next year's Gordon Bennett race would take place in the country of the winner, which caused Britain to search for a course in Ireland for the 1903 contest. This series lasted from 1900 to 1905 inclusive, and the victors were France four times, Britain once and Germany once.

Other nations having tired of French supremacy, and the Gordon Bennett regulations being difficult to enforce, the nationalised series of races gave way to the French Grand Prix, first held in 1906 and won by Renault. Fiat were victorious in 1907 and Mercédès in 1908. This was the most important race of them all, until other nations followed suit and held their own Grands Prix. The idea was to vary the race rules from year to year to promote advance in racing-car design and construction and to stage great international contests in which *make* raced against *make*, instead of, as in the Gordon Bennett races, nation competing against nation. This was a great success until 1909, when the major manufacturers refused to compete in long-distance events through a suspicion that they might lose to a smaller concern like Delage or Bugatti. Thus, the French Grand Prix was abandoned until 1912 and small-car or *voiturette* races were held instead.

Following the 1894 Paris–Rouen Trial, which sparked off all this auto-

Left: Percy Lambert aboard his 1913 Talbot, 25/50hp seen at Brooklands; it was with this car, in February of that year, that he put 100 miles into the hour. Lambert was killed in the following November while trying to regain his record from Peugeot: he crashed on the Members' Banking at the Weybridge track

Below: the first Indianapolis winner was Ray Harroun, who took the flag in this Marmon 'Wasp' in 1911 (averaging 74.61 mph); according to legend, his was the first car ever to feature a rear-view mirror

motive activity, the first proper motor race was held, in 1895, in the form of the Paris–Bordeaux–Paris contest, organised by the newly formed Automobile Club de France. It was a struggle occupying three days, from 11 June to 13 June 1895, with a field of 22 out of 46 somewhat optimistic entries; eleven reached Bordeaux and nine ran the entire distance of 732 miles. Whilst this sounds unremarkable by today's standards, the distance alone on those primitive carriages over such difficult going defies imagination! Most epic was the drive of Emile Levassor, who insisted on conducting his famous No 5 Panhard & Levassor without relief for fear of losing his lead, pausing every 100 kilometres or so to take on fresh supplies, but his total stopping time was a mere 22 minutes, on a journey lasting 48 hours 48 minutes! At Tours on the return run back to Paris he had a lead of $4\frac{1}{2}$ hours over his nearest rival, a Peugeot. Immense enthusiasm greeted him as he drove to the finish by the Porte Maillot, where, in true Gallic fashion, a monument was later erected to mark the finish of the very first motor race. In fact, as Levassor carried but one passenger he was not awarded the first prize (31,500 francs), which went to Koechlin's Peugeot, a carriage which had been on the road for 59 hours 48

minutes. Whereas Levassor had averaged 15.0 mph, this Peugeot had run at an average speed of 12.2 mph and another Peugeot, not eligible for the first prize, at 13.4 mph. Of those which retired, a Serpollet steamer broke its crankshaft and the Jeantaud, the only electric car to start, had axle trouble.

From this first race came others, faster and better supported, over longer distances. In 1896, they raced from Paris to Marseilles and back, a little matter of 1063 miles, and the winning Panhard, driven by Mayade, averaged 15.7 mph, proof that the motor car was both fast and a stayer. Panhard cars, in fact, walked away with that one. In 1897, they tried shorter races, the 149-mile Paris–Nice–La Turbie going to the Count de Chasseloup-Laubat, whose De Dion steam-brake averaged 19.2 mph. The Paris–Dieppe race of just over 102 racing miles was divided into classes for motor tricycles, *voiturettes*, six seater, four seater and two-seater cars, and Jamin's little Bollée contrived to do 25.2 mph, whereas the fastest car, in the four-seater section, was Count de Dion's De Dion, with a speed of 24.6 mph. Finally, there was the 107.7-mile Paris–Trouville contest, won by a Panhard at 25.2 mph.

In 1898, the race was from Marseilles to Nice, the celebrated driver Charron getting there first on his 6 hp Panhard at 20.4 mph, followed in by two more Panhards. Charron then won the Paris–Amsterdam race, averaging 26.9 mph for the 889¼ miles, with Giradot's Panhard second.

Not only were speeds higher but the number of recognised events increased. The season opened in March with the 75-mile Nice–Castellane–Nice race, this new pursuit of motor racing having by now extended from the capital city to the fashionable Mediterranean watering place. An entry of 24 cars and fifteen tricycles had been obtained and Peugeot-Frères gave Lemaitre the new big Peugeot, the 140 × 190 mm two-cylinder engine of which was sufficient to give this driver victory at 26.0 mph over Giradot on the four-cylinder 80 × 120 mm Panhard, a smaller Peugeot finishing in third place. The racing motor tricycles were nearly as quick: Teste on a De Dion averaged 25.1 mph, but their riders were apt to be badly hampered, even involved in accidents, due to the dust flung up by the cars.

The Panhard drivers, Charron, de Knyff and Giradot, filled the first five places in the Paris–Bordeaux contest, the winner's speed for the 351 miles being almost 30 mph; a Mors finished 6th. Flag signals were used throughout the Tour de France, which covered 1350 racing miles and was again dominated by the Panhard Company's entries, the big 16 hp racer of de Knyff winning at

Left: the Paris–Rouen Trial of 1894. The most important cars were the Peugeots like this example of Kraeutler which averaged 10.1 mph over the 78¾ miles. These cars were fitted with Panhard & Levassor engines and chain drive; steering was by a single lever mounted on a vertical column

Below: in the last Gordon Bennett Cup event of 1905, Léon Théry repeated his victory of the previous year, accompanied in his Brasier by Muller, his mechanic; as an extra reward for this performance, Théry was made an honorary member of the Academie Francaise

30.2 mph. Note how speeds were for ever creeping up as engines increased in size. These *average* speeds are most impressive if you can imagine the conditions under which cars raced in 1899. On the downhill straights on their top speed (or gear) such racers were truly awe-inspiring. Gerald Rose, the first writer to chronicle the great motor races of that period, recalled 'the tremendous rush and roar of one of the big racers coming down the straight towards Dieppe at 100 miles per hour, the driver crouching under the wheel and the mechanic's head just visible above the high scuttle', a thrill modern racing cars and conditions can never repeat. He wrote that of the 1908 Clement–Bayards in the Grand Prix, but the spectacle must have been just as thrilling before the turn of the century as the higher, more unwieldy racing giants and their intrepid pilots battled over the long French highways at speeds of over 60 mph.

Back in 1899, there was the little jaunt from Paris to St Malo, accomplished by Anthony's Mors at 30.7 mph, while in the Paris–Ostend 201-mile race the forthcoming struggle between Panhard and Mors was beginning, Giradot and Levegh respectively on these rival makes both averaging 32.5 mph, with a Peugeot third for good measure. Then, in the Paris–Boulogne race, Giradot's Panhard & Levassor was the victor at 33.5 mph but Levegh on a Mors tailed

him home, and was only 0.3 mph slower. To give a sense of proportion, in 1899 came a novel contest, run between Paris and Trouville, in which pedestrians, horses, cyclists, motor cycles and racing cars took part, over a distance of $104\frac{1}{2}$ miles under a handicap to end all handicaps. Thus, the runners got an allowance of twenty hours, the horses were given fourteen hours, the cyclists five hours, the motor bikes $3\frac{1}{4}$ hours and the racing cars had to do the course with a start of three hours. It was rather a snub to progress, as they finished much in that order, except that two horses arrived first and second, and a motor cycle was two seconds ahead of the first car. The average speeds are interesting: runners, 4.9 mph; best horse, 8.5 mph; fastest bicyclist, 19.4 mph; best motor cyclist, 32.5 mph, fastest racing car, a Mors, 35.2 mph. Motor traction had justified itself, but perhaps the racing men were glad to return to normal contests.

Racing recommenced in February 1900 with the *Course du Catalogue* which was sub-divided on a chassis/price basis and which Girador dominated on a big Panhard. The season was one fought out between Panhard and Mors, until things changed with the advent of the first race for the Gordon Bennett cup. This trophy had been donated by Mr James Gordon Bennett, Paris-based proprietor of the *New York Herald*, maybe with the idea of getting America into motor racing and breaking the hold which France had established. The races were team affairs between the National Automobile Clubs, who had to choose their own teams of drivers and cars. They held eliminating contests for this purpose but much bickering resulted. The route of each race had to be of not under 550 km and the event was to be given its baptism in France on 14 June 1900. A course was found from Paris to Lyons, via Orleans, Nevers and Roanne. No very severe mechanical restrictions were imposed, perhaps because Mr Bennett was not an automobilist, but two side-by-side seats, occupied throughout the race, were insisted on and the minimum empty weight of each competing car had to be over 400 kg. As this was a nation-against-nation contest, national colours for the cars emerged, blue for France, white for Germany, red for America (which in later years became the Italian colour) and yellow for Belgium. At first, this novel race did not attract much enthusiasm but it is an important motor racing landmark in the period 1900–05.

The first race could boast only five runners: three four-cylinder 5.3-litre chain-drive Panhard & Levassor's representing France, a Snoeck-Bolide from Belgium, that had a 10.6-litre engine with its four cylinders horizontally opposed and final drive by belt and chain, and from America an antiquated single-cylinder Wilton with a piston stroke of 177.8 mm, driven by chain. The 24 hp Panhards had little difficulty in preserving their status for, although Baron de Knyff retired, having lost top gear as well as hitting several stray dogs, many of which were run over along the route, Charron came in the winner at 38.6 mph, and second place went to Giradot's Panhard at 33.4 mph. The American and Belgian entries both retired, so there were only two finishers.

Above: the enormously successful René de Knyff was always recognisable by his flowing beard and habitually worn yachting cap. Pictured here in 1907, the Panhard director listed among his victories the 1898 Paris–Bordeaux–Paris, the 1899 Tour de France and the Marseilles–Nice–Marseilles race of 1900. He went on to become President of the CSI from 1922 to 1946 and died in 1954, aged 90

Left: a contemporary illustration by Reginald Cleaver shows the finish of the Marseilles–Nice race in March 1898. The report read: 'The motor-car race from Marseilles to Nice was attended with very bad weather, the roads from the pelting rain were dreadfully wet, and both cars and occupants were covered with mud soon after starting . . . Many of the carriages broke down on the road from various causes, their occupants finishing the journey by train'

Above: Fernand Charron, one of the first successful racing drivers, who won the 1898 Marseilles–Nice and Paris–Amsterdam races for Panhard. He was also victorious in the first Gordon Bennett trophy race from Paris to Lyons of 1900, despite a dramatic off-road excursion

However, the race was not entirely lacking in drama. Charron hit a big St Bernard dog, which jammed the car's steering, causing the Panhard to career across the road, over a ditch, through a gap between two trees and across a field, whence it regained the road by taking another gap in the trees, ending up facing the wrong way. But it was the heroic age of the game and the luckless riding-mechanic, Fournier, later to become a great Mors driver, got down and cranked-up the engine; the car restarted with Fournier holding the now disorientated water-pump against the flywheel, from which its friction-drive was obtained. The Panhard had bent its back axle when striking a bump near the start, but everything held well enough together for Charron to take the coveted Gordon Bennett cup. Giradot was likewise not without trouble, as in swerving to avoid a horse near Orleans his steering had also been damaged. That was motor racing over the open roads of 1900.

Because of the small entry and comparative public disinterest in the 1900 Gordon Bennett race, the AC de France decided to take steps to improve the situation before the 1901 contest was due to be run. As victors the previous year, the French had, under the rules, to host the race. The great Paris–Toulouse–

Above: the Automobile Club de France's Paris to Bordeaux race in 1901 was won by Henri Fournier's Mors, seen here. He completed the 327-mile course in just over six hours, averaging 53 mph

Paris event of the previous year, in which Levegh's 24 hp Mors had won at 40.2 mph for the 837 miles, had made the Gordon Bennett look rather anaemic. To give it more of the big-time appearance in 1901, it was to be combined with the race from Paris to Bordeaux. Alas, it did not work out that way. The complete race of 327 miles had the usual good entry and was won by Fournier on a powerful 60 hp Mors. This completed the course in 6 hours 10 minutes 44 seconds, an average speed of 53 mph, staving off the might of the 40 hp Panhards, which came home in the next five positions, Maurice Farman's averaging exactly 49 mph; the day of the brute force racing monster had dawned! However, in the Gordon Bennett division the winner was a mere tenth in the race overall, this being Giradot, on another 40 hp Panhard & Levassor, at a speed of 37 mph, his race time being nearly three hours longer than Fournier's. But France had at least retained the right to hold the Gordon Bennett race in 1902, although neither of her other team entries, a Mors and a Panhard, finished the course. Britain should have been represented in the 1901 Gordon Bennett race by S. F. Edge on his enormous 50 hp Napier, but the car was so heavy that its British tyres would not stand the strain and with French tyres it was not eligible for the Gordon Bennett race. The green car started, however, but retired with clutch failure. Nevertheless, it thereby set this colour – Napier green, as the British motor-racing hue, not always copied very exactly for the future.

Before we look at the 1902 Gordon Bennett race, it is necessary to describe another great race of the preceding year; this is the one which took place from Paris to Berlin. There were 53 Controls to be arranged along the 687-mile route, where the competitors had to be accurately timed in and out and led through the towns, usually behind official cyclist-marshalls. Local persons of importance had to be appeased in this era of ever bigger and faster racers capable of raising ever taller columns of dust and making ever louder noises – their exhaust notes were likened to the sound made by Gatling guns! Soldiers had to be found to police the long course, augmented by experienced flagmen, and buglers were needed to proclaim the passage of a car racing at express-train pace. *Pavé* still existed in places; elsewhere, dust was the menace – apart from straying dogs and cattle – and to combat that proper exhaust-boxes were specified. M. Serpollet drove over the entire route to see that everything was ready for this three-day racing epic. There were the usual three classes – Heavy cars, Light cars and *Voiturettes*. A highly satisfactory entry had been received,

Left: many were the adventures experienced by the competitors on the 1902 Paris to Vienna event. Here is the eventual winner, Marcel Renault, with his 3.7-litre car; he surprised everyone by his early arrival, and he won everlasting fame for his company

Below left: Marcel Renault and his 30 hp car about to embark on what was to become their last race, the 1903 Paris to Madrid. He died when his car overturned at Coune-Verac (*below*). His brother, Louis, finished first on the road and second overall in the event, and later decided to withdraw the Renault cars from competition for a year

33, 27 and 11, in these respective categories, of such renowned makes as Mors, Panhard, De Dietrich, Serpollet steamer, the new very technically advanced Mercédès from Germany, and the lighter but very game Panhards, Gladiators, Darracqs, and finally the little Renaults. The smallest cars were now able to keep up speeds faster than the biggest motors of a few years earlier, so the interest in this race must have been intense and its usefulness to the new motor movement was inestimable. The winner was due to pull up in front of the Kaiser's tribune and the competitors who made the arduous journey successfully were to go in a great procession along the Brandenburger Tor and down the Unter den Linden. There was even a class for tourist cars, which took nine days to do the route, and one for racing motor cycles, filled with 7 hp 170 kg De Dions.

It was no wonder such races caused a sensation; spectators would wend their way out to the start in their thousands, the cyclists carried Chinese lanterns to probe the early-morning mists, and horse-drawn carriages mingled with the few touring motor cars. As the racers went on their headlong way, the police had great difficulty in forcing the onlookers back to give them passage. It was a foretaste of the 1903 disaster – and the route was marked in the

more populous places by flowers, flags, even triumphal arches, erected by citizens who knew of the official lunches, dinners, receptions and fêtes that followed in the wake of the big and important motor races. The Mors might now be superior to all other cars and the great Fournier at the height of his skill and fame, but as the racers became heavier and faster, their crude tyres became the great levellers. Punctures resulted in delay if nothing worse, driver and mechanic wrenching off the ruined cover and tube with their bare hands, in order to fit a fresh cover from those piled up behind their seats. This could give the less-powerful autos a chance, so the result at the finish-line over 680 miles distant from the Paris start, was very much open to conjecture. They were racing for the Kaiser's cup, the Grand Duke of Luxembourg's trophy and other fine prizes, not forgetting £500 presented by the City of Hamburg, so they were unlikely to waste any time! In fact, it was the bearded Maurice Fournier who came through triumphant, ahead of the Panhards of Giradot and de Knyff, with another Mors fourth. Fournier's huge Mors had averaged 44.1 mph and it is worth reflecting on how a modern family car would have fared, before the days of universal *autoroutes*, over this formidable route!

Right: S. F. Edge, who devoted thirteen years, from 1900, to the promotion, racing and sales of Napier cars, the most important of which were the six-cylinder vehicles, the first to be built in large numbers. As a driver, his first major success was in the 1902 Gordon Bennett Trophy, after which he became British team captain

Far right: Mme du Gast on her 5.8-litre De Dietrich during the infamous Paris–Madrid race; she finished at Bordeaux in a lowly 77th position, but she would have been much better placed had she not halted to extricate Stead from under his inverted De Dietrich

Below: De Bron's 9.8-litre 45 hp De Dietrich prior to the start of the Paris–Madrid contest; the sound of the cars' exhausts was likened to that of Gatling machine guns

Panhards took the first three places in the Light-Car class, Giraud leading them in at 35½ mph. The lightweight Renault of Louis Renault was beginning its great run of success in the *Voiturette* class, averaging a noteworthy 36.9 mph, while the best of the motor cycles was Osmont's De Dion, at an even more impressive average of 36.4 mph. That, then, was the form that open-road motor racing took, just after the turn of the century; enormously exciting it must have been, too!

The importance of the Paris–Berlin race of 1901 was that it showed the progress of racing-car development. In fact, glorious victors though Henri Fournier and his Mors were, a chain broke as the post-race parade was commencing: he had grasped his success by a very slender margin. 1902 marked further advances, both in racing *bolides*, built to the new 1000 kg weight limit but still very powerful, and in the persuading of the French Government (which disliked motor racing) to sanction the Circuit du Nord event, where the competitors would be running on alcohol fuel. This was for the most part a success for it was very well organised, with bombs let off to announce the imminent arrival of the racers, but very few spectators turned up to watch them. The

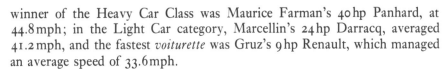

winner of the Heavy Car Class was Maurice Farman's 40 hp Panhard, at 44.8 mph; in the Light Car category, Marcellin's 24 hp Darracq, averaged 41.2 mph, and the fastest *voiturette* was Gruz's 9 hp Renault, which managed an average speed of 33.6 mph.

All this was a preliminary to the important Paris–Vienna race of 1902. This race very nearly did not take place, however, as the French authorities were reluctant to grant permission for it, even with the 1000 kg weight limit imposed to reduce the size of the engines that could be crammed into racing chassis. The Bavarians and the Swiss actually refused to have any racing on their territory and the route of this four-day, 615-mile race had to be continually changed. Nevertheless, the Viennese were keen to host the event and even put up special prizes. The climb of the Arlburg Pass, over which the route went, was the supreme test and resulted in two comic incidents. This section of the course was more like a trial than a motor race, with the snow just gone in time from the narrow unguarded precipices, where the ascents and descents were of startling steepness and torrents from the rivers had to be crossed on improvised bridges. It was here that Max, driving a small Darracq, struck a boundary stone, the car going some way over the edge and his and his mechanic's seats breaking away from the chassis. This left the former occupants safe a little way down the hillside, while the car itself plunged 100 feet further down. Max took a look at his wrecked racer, then climbed back to the road just as Barras arrived on the scene. The story circulated that Max had escaped death from under his car and he made excellent use of this dramatic story when he reached the finish. Then there was Derny, whose motor cycle ran away down one of the hills. All he could do was cry out in alarm, not knowing that De la Touloubre (whose real name was Captain Gentry) was up ahead in his Clément

car, and who, with the true racing driver's calm skill and reaction, would pluck him safely from the saddle of his run-away machine as it shot past the car. Or so legend has it!

Many cars had to be pushed up fearsome gradients but Teste's Panhard climbed at better than 23 mph. His was one of the new 70 hp Panhard & Levassors, which were enormously powerful for their light overall weight. Count Eliot Zborowski, father of the Zborowski who later thrilled English race-goers of the 1920s with his Chitty-Chitty-Bang-Bangs, did what he could to combat these fire-eating monsters from France, on his advanced 40 hp Mercédès. Even so he had to be content with second place in the unlimited class, behind Henri Farman's 70 hp Panhard. The other 70 hp Panhards of Maurice Farman and Teste, and the 40s of Pinson, de Crawhez and Chauchard filled the 3rd, 4th, 5th, 6th and 7th places in this class, with Edge's 40 hp British Napier beating the Mors Sixty of de Caters into 8th position. However, the hero of the Paris–Vienna event was Marcel Renault, whose little 16 hp Renault ran so well and so fast that he drove into the finishing enclosure, a trotting-track at Prater just outside the city of Vienna, long before the officials and spectators expected him. Indeed, Marcel made his circuit of the trotting track in the wrong direction and was made to go out and come in again the intended way, but he was still comfortably ahead of Zborowski's Mercédès and had vanquished no fewer than five of the 24 hp Darracqs. This excellent showing by a small car was a pointer for the future. Renault had averaged 38.9 mph, compared to Farman's 38.4 mph and Zborowski's 37.9 mph. The best of the 24 hp Darracqs had done 38.1 mph and the fastest *voiturette* was Guillaume's 12 hp Darracq which, averaging 30.6 mph, just turned the tables on the 8 hp Renaults. The winner was declared as Marcel Renault, and fame immediately engulfed the expanding company from Billancourt, on the Seine.

The 1902 Gordon Bennett Trophy race had been incorporated with the Paris–Vienna and appeared to have been taken by Zborowski on his all-German Mercédès but it was found that he had incurred penalties, so Edge and the big Napier were announced as the winners, after a drive of 11 hrs 2 mins 52.6 secs over 351.46 miles of the route, an average speed of 31.8 mph.

It was just as well that Britain had won the Gordon Bennett, because there was growing resentment over road racing in France and, had a French car won, it might have been difficult for that country to stage a decent race for the Trophy in 1903. As it was, the British now had this problem to face. In Belgium, the idea of racing over a closed circuit was instituted, with the Circuit des Ardennes race, on a pattern soon to be the accepted form. This 'circuit' consisted of a 53-mile route out from Bastogne and back, to be covered six times in the morning, before the motor cyclists had a two-lap race over it in the afternoon. The point, however, was that this race was devoid of 'controls' as it did not pass through congested towns. It was also primarily for amateur drivers and attracted great interest, the town of Bastogne being full long before the start. Britain's Charles Jarrott, an experienced racing driver of the day, equipped himself with one of the 70 hp Panhards and won at 54.0 mph, after taking the lead on the third lap. The celebrated driver Gabriel was second on a Mors Sixty, another of those fine cars driven by Vanderbilt finishing in third place ahead of Eliot Zborowski's 40 hp Mercédès. The fastest lap was turned in by Baron P. de Crewhez' 70 hp Panhard which came in 13th, followed by Baron J. de Crewhez on yet another 70 hp Panhard.

So, we come to the fateful year of 1903, which changed the very face of these early motor races. Even more ambitious than previously, the Automobile Club de France decided to have a massive contest from Paris to Madrid. They were, however, working in an atmosphere of restriction. The French Government had refused to authorise the Pau Week of Speed in February 1903 and permission was not granted for a race from Nice to Salon and back. King Alfonso was quite happy to allow racing on Spanish soil, however, so the section to Madrid was assured. Little was known about the route here but it was felt that the crossing of the Guadarrama mountains would present very little difficulty to those who had conquered the Arlburg Pass in the Paris–Vienna race. Eventually, even the French authorities gave in, and the great race was on. It

Camille Jenatzy working very hard to keep his 60 hp Mercédès ahead of René de Knyff's 80 hp Panhard on his way to winning the 1903 Gordon Bennett race between Carlow and Athy, Ireland

is significant that it attracted no less than 230 entries – which makes the support for classic races over seventy years later look rather poor by comparison. This excellent entry was made up of 98 Heavy Class cars, 59 *voitures legeres* and 35 *voiturettes*, as well as 38 motor cycles. That was the *early* entry-list, with over three months to go! Finally, with a few cancellations and many additions, Paris–Madrid had 314 runners, and these included sixteen Panhards, fourteen Mors, twelve Mercédès – but sadly lacking Zborowski's entry as he had been killed in a hill-climb at Nice – ten De Dietrich, seven Serpollet steamers, six CGVs, and even four Wolseleys from Birmingham. The new 90 hp Mercédès cars were the favourites, and the use of light chassis frames and light alloy in the engines had resulted in ever-more-powerful machines, now capable of some 100 mph on the open road, while carrying two persons and fuel for a long run.

The start of what should have been a stupendous race was as spectacular as ever. It was deemed too dark at 3.30 am in the morning to risk letting the racers go, but by 3.45 am, with thousands of onlookers pressing round the cars, which had to force a way through them, Charles Jarrott's huge De Dietrich set off towards Bordeaux, the spectators just opening up a path sufficient for him to get through. De Knyff followed Jarrott, then off went car-manufacturer Louis Renault. With hindsight, the tragedy can be seen staring us in the face. It was almost dark, while vision was later obstructed by

great dust clouds that made it necessary for the drivers to steer by looking at the line of the road-side tree tops. It was impossible properly to police this very long public-road course, along which cars sped at upwards of 90, even 100mph; the cars were top-heavy with poor brakes, and dogs, cattle and children were free to wander on the roads. News of fatal accidents began to come in and although, over the years, these have been exaggerated they were none the less appalling. Marcel Renault died when his 30hp Renault over-turned at Thery. Barrow's riding mechanic – they used to sit low on the side step – was killed when his De Dietrich ran so forcibly into a tree that it disinte-grated and one of its front dumb-irons was driven far into the tree trunk. Leslie Porter ran into a wall when cornering too fast and his mechanic Nixon was killed. In trying to avoid a child, Tourand shot into the crowd at Angoulême, causing the deaths of his mechanic and a soldier. There were many other acci-dents, but with less serious consequences it is important to remember, because history will tell you of *hundreds* killed. This *was* enough, however. The horrified French Government demanded that the race be stopped at Bordeaux, 342 racing miles from Paris. It would not even permit the racing cars to be driven to the station for their ignominious return to the Capital: they were dragged to the train behind horses. It was as disastrous as the Le Mans accident of 1955 and it was immediately to change the type of racing allowed in France. Through all this calamity, though, let us not forget Gabriel and the epic per-

The Panhard team poses before the 1903 Gordon Bennett event at Athy; Henri Farman and René de Knyff occupy the centre and right-hand cars

formance he put up in his 70 hp streamlined Mors. Starting No 168, he passed all but two cars, along this very demanding course. He won the Heavy Car class at 65.3 mph, after racing for more than 5¼ hours. But it was Louis Renault who had arrived ahead of everyone who had not either crashed or retired, his lightweight Renault averaging a magnificent 62.3 mph, which gave him second

place, a triumph short-lived when they broke to him the news of his brother's death. Salleron's 70 hp Mors was third, at 59.1 mph. Even Masson's Clément *voiturette*, an 18 hp machine which could be comfortably out-performed by a modern family car managed 47.2 mph, to win its class. Remember, that these are *overall* speeds and top speeds reached were probably half as fast again.

That was how it ended in 1903, most subsequent racing being on closed circuits. The Circuit des Ardennes was held again in Belgium and was a Darracq victory, and by charm and persuasion, especially among influential ecclesiastics, the British contrived an elaborate two-circuit course in Ireland for the fourth Gordon Bennett race, contested over 327½ miles. This time there were a dozen runners, including a team of three Napiers from Acton, London, with America, France and Germany against them. Alas, the Napiers failed and, rather surprisingly, so did the 80 hp Panhards. It was the red-bearded Jenatzy, 'The Red Devil', who brought his Mercédès Sixty (a stripped touring car used after a factory fire had destroyed all the intended 90 hp Mercédès racers) home the victor, at 49.2 mph. The Panhard aces, De Knyff and Henri Farman, had to accept second and third placings.

Although high quality racing was spreading to other countries, with the Florio Cup being held in Italy and the Vanderbilt Cup in America, the Gordon Bennett, with its unique rules making it a test of motor-manufacturing nation against motor-manufacturing nation, remained in the public eye. The 1904 race had to be held in Germany, the 87-mile course had to be covered for a distance of 317.86 miles and the June day of the race was declared a public holiday. Jenatzy tried hard to keep the Cup in his car's native land but it was the steady driving of Thery on an 80 hp Richard-Brasier which triumphed, his winning average being 54.5 mph to Jenatzy's 52.8 mph.

That took the Gordon Bennett back to France in 1905, the last time the race

was held. Entries had been increasing but, with the automobile now well established, its makers were anxious to race against one another and not be hampered by the Nationalistic GB rules. For this reason, the Gordon Bennett motor race (there were GB balloon and aeroplane races as well) lasted but one more year. In 1905 it was held over the great Auvergne circuit, in France, which incorporated such severe bends that it was said that at one corner the inmates of the houses could watch the racers pass from the parlour and then run across to their kitches to see them accelerate away! Once again, Théry won for the organising nation, on a Brasier, but a new challenge was rising in International racing, and two Italian Fiats followed Leon home.

47

Italy had held the mountainous Florio Cup race in September 1904, fore-runner of the very testing post-war series, and Lancia's Fiat had beaten the French and German entries. The 1904 Circuit des Ardennes had reached a satisfactory peak that year, a big entry and close racing ending with a win for Heath's Panhard, with Teste's Panhard (both of which were of 90 hp) only 1 min 55 secs slower, after battling for nearly 367½ miles. In 1904, too, the American Vanderbilt Cup race began, for a Trophy presented by W. K. Vanderbilt Jnr to the AAA. A triangular circuit was found not far from New York, on Long Island, using two time controls, through which the competitors had to tour for three and six minutes, respectively. Heath went over and drove to victory on a 90 hp Panhard, at 52.2 mph, and a Clement-Bayard was second. Third place went to Lyttle's 24 hp Pope-Toledo and other American cars racing included such makes as Packard, with the 'Grey Wolf' track racer, an S & M Simplex, with a big engine installed in a touring chassis especially for the race, and a Royal, which was just a tourer stripped for racing. It was the commencement of America's participation in road-racing events as distinct from track racing, however.

The Florio Cup was to flourish, too, and the 1905 race, held at Brescia, was won by Raggio in a gigantic 112 hp Itala, from a De Dietrich, with Vincenzo Lancia's Fiat third. America was taking enthusiastically to motor road-racing, the Vanderbilt Cup being over 283 miles in 1905, with no Controls to observe. Moreover, although it was won by a Darracq, with a Panhard second, an American 90 hp Locomobile, driven by Tracy, secured third place.

So, 1906 was set for the first of the great French Grand Prix races. There are historians who will prefer to regard the 1906 event as the ninth of the series, because, retrospectively, the Automobile Club de France called the eight pre-ceeding contests by this title. Thus, the first of these races, by this reckoning, was the Paris–Bordeaux–Paris race of 1895, followed by the 1896 Paris–Marseilles–Paris race, the Paris–Amsterdam race of 1898, the 1899 Tour de France, Paris–Toulouse–Paris in 1900, Paris–Berlin in 1901, the Paris–Vienna in 1902 and the Paris–Madrid (Bordeaux) race of 1903. Although the flirtation with speed, achieved by increasing engine size, continued unabated most of us prefer to think of the new type of race that followed the Gordon Bennett series in 1906 as the first of the Grands Prix. This was organised by the ACF, the leading French Club, and not to be confused with the Grand Prix de France, which was a less important event. The Grand Prix as staged in 1906 was clearly intended to ensure a French victory by simple preponderence of numbers. France was the biggest producer of automobiles at that time, measured in numbers competent to race, and therefore if she was not restricted to teams of three National entries, as she had been in the Gordon Bennett races, she stood an excellent chance of winning the greatest prize in the motoring world year after year.

So, the ACF went happily ahead with its plans: the Grand Prix was to be run under the same technical regulations as the Gordon Bennet, *ie*, there was to be a maximum weight limit of 1000 kg, or of 2204 lb, with a supplementary 7 kg if a magneto or engine-driven dynamo was needed for ignition. For the first time, it was stipulated that any repairs or adjustments required to a car during the race must be carried out only by the driver and riding mechanic. Such work was intended to be carried out at the 'pits' which, although taking their name from sunken replenishment depots, were, in this instance, at road level. They were on the outside of the course so as to be accesible to cars running on the right-hand side of the road, but the grandstands that overlooked them were on the inside of the circuit. Originally, it was intended to lap the course clockwise but, in the end, the rule which had applied since the days of the Roman chariot races prevailed and an anti-clockwise direction was used; a fine triangular course of 65 miles per lap had been selected just outside Le Mans. That races really were true tests of endurance and gave spectators and competitors perhaps more than their money's worth, in those times, is emphasised by the six laps that were required to be completed on two consecutive days, giving a race distance of a fraction under 770 miles. Another innovation was the absence of any form of 'control', whereby drivers previously had to run through danger areas at normal speeds or even behind bicycles. The closed circuit made this possible except where the course passed through St Calais, and this place was by-passed by a wooden road specially made for the purpose.

As had been intended and anticipated, the entry list was mostly comprised of French-built cars, of which there were 26, compared with six Italian and three German examples. Big engines also predominated, all being over 12 litres, with Panhard-Levassor using 18-litre power units. To reduce the time two men took to slash punctured tyres off fixed wheels, detachable rims were adopted by Brasier, Fiat, Itala and Renault.

The Grand Prix commenced at 6 am on 26 June when Gabriel on a De Dietrich was flagged away; in fact, he stalled his engine and it was Vincenzo Lancia whose Fiat crossed the start line first. Thereafter, the cars left at 90-second intervals. Barras on a Richard Brasier led the first lap, at the best speed achieved, 73.3 mph, but the Hungarian driver Szisz, on the big works Renault, took the lead after three circuits and, at the close of this strenuous day's racing, he was still in that position, having averaged 66.8 mph. He was challenged by Clement's Clement-Bayard in second place and the third man home, Felice Nazzaro who drove an Italian Fiat. The cars were to be started on the second day of the race in the order of finishing the first day's racing, but it is significant that Renault refused to hurry, Szisz taking twelve minutes in his pit having

new tyres fitted and the essential fluids topped-up. Clement, too, took five minutes over similar precautions, whereas Nazzaro went immediately into action. Nevertheless, as he completed his opening lap, Szisz found that eleven cars had still not been flagged-off and he was so far ahead of his rivals that he could drive comparatively easily. The coal-scuttle-bonneted shaft-drive Renault from Billancourt gave no anxiety and thus won the 1906 French Grand Prix race in the formidable overall time of 12 hrs 14 mins 0.07 secs, which represents a speed of 63 mph. Nazzaro took his Fiat into second place but was well over half-an-hour slower than the French car, while Clement was third: a convincing French victory.

There were but eleven finishers out of the 32 who had set off. It is interesting to note that, although Szisz did not have to press-on at fastest-lap speeds, the winning Renault was, nevertheless, the fastest car through a timed kilometre, at 92.2 mph, compared to Nazzaro's Fiat, which was clocked there at only 87.2 mph. After this very worthwhile success, Renault did not trouble to contest the 1906 Circuit des Ardennes event, but France retained her supremacy there, since Duray's De Dietrich won, and a Darracq made the fastest lap.

Right : François Szisz – his Hungarian christian name was Ferenc – entered competitions as Louis Renault's riding mechanic in 1900, progressing to chief tester and racing driver. After numerous successes, the unflustered Szisz retired in 1908, reappearing briefly in 1914 to contest the French Grand Prix in an Alda – an outclassed car – and a French road race at Rochefort, which he won in a 12-litre Lorraine-Dietrich. He died in Hungary in 1970, aged 97

Below : François Szisz and riding mechanic Marteau in the 13-litre, 90 bhp Renault, which won the 1906 Grand Prix at Dieppe, averaging 63 mph over 12 hours 14 minutes (two days racing). These cars could approach 100 mph and were fitted with quick-release wheel rims in case of punctures

All this activity on the part of the French encouraged Germany to stage an important contest in the Taunus Mountains, over a 73-mile circuit. However, to encourage more ordinary cars she restricted engine size to 8 litres, which seemed a good move as an entry of 92 was received. To Germanic regret, however, the winner of the eliminating rounds and of the final was Nazzaro's Fiat, although a Pipe and two Opels were next home.

It was the Grand Prix in the automobile-pioneering country of France that at this period held the greatest appeal and attracted the most attention, however. For 1907, the ACF moved the locale to Dieppe, and imposed different rules, the consumption of fuel being limited to 30 litres per 100 km. This works out at 9.4 mpg and, while this was a move to try to improve engine efficiency, it was not of great inconvenience to competitors, and big engines remained the norm. Renault had sold their successful 1906 cars (the winning one for an astronomical sum it was rumoured), but they built a set of replicas for this 'second' French Grand Prix. The race was to be over a flat, triangular 47¾-mile circuit, lapped ten times in a day, a single day's racing now being recognised as more convenient for everyone. National racing colours were also

insisted on for all the runners in this 1907 Grand Prix, whereas the previous year, as if to mark the end of Gordon Bennett Nationalism, they were not, the winning Renault being painted red, the hue of Italy.

Eleven teams of French cars were entered for the 1907 GP against one each representing Belgium, Italy, Germany, America and Great Britain. This worked out to 38 top-rank racing cars starting, and they were all the mighty four-cylinder racing monsters we can now scarcely visualise, although the Dufaux, Porthos and the Weigel entries were far in advance of their time in having eight-cylinder in-line motors. The first car was again dispatched at the early hour of 6 am, the rest going away at 60-second intervals. The previous Renault/Fiat duel again emerged, with De Dietrich well up. Louis Wagner led for three laps for Fiat, at a sizzling average of 72.1 mph. After he had retired

Above: Louis Wagner's 8-litre Fiat leading the 1908 Coppa Florio at Bologna, in which he averaged 90 mph

Inset, far right: Arthur Duray, born in New York but later taking French nationality, began racing Gobron Brilliés in 1902. After breaking the land speed record in 1903, at 83.46 mph, he moved to Darracq and in 1905 joined De Dietrich. It was in 1906 that he achieved his first success – the Circuit des Ardennes. Duray continued to race and attempt speed records until he retired in 1928

Near right: Felice Nazzaro was a Fiat apprentice, whose skill as a driver, mechanic and diplomat earned him drives in Vincenzo Florio's Panhard; in 1905, he graduated to the position of works Fiat driver alongside Lancia. In 1907, he won the Targa Florio, the French Grand Prix and the Kaiserpreis. Like Lancia, he went on to build his own cars, but mechanical failures precluded notable success. Nazzaro continued to race until 1929, having been appointed head of the Fiat competitions department in 1925

it was Duray who led, but eventually his De Dietrich seized its gearbox. This moved Nazzaro into the lead, with Szisz chasing him, but the red Fiat had an unshakable lead and won at 70.5 mph from the French car, with Barras' Richard Brasier third. It was a Fiat domination, although Duray had made fastest lap, at 75.4 mph. It was felt, however, that, whereas Fiat paid little heed to running out of fuel, which the petrol consumption limit made probable, Szisz may have been a trifle over-cautious in this respect. Fuel limits for racing were unpopular for this reason but this was still the golden age of motor racing for, if the great town-to-town contests were the ultimate, these enormous cars on the closed circuits, their big cylinders firing about 'once every telegraph-pole', must have been a most intriguing spectacle, as they battled for the *blue riband* of the motor-racing world.

The Grand Prix continued in much the same form in 1908 and the venue had not been changed, although certain improvements were introduced. By way of regulations, engine size was now limited to a maximum piston-area of 117 sq in, so that, at last, rather smaller engines were to be seen and, instead of a maximum weight-limit, it was decided to eliminate dangerously light cars by having a *minimum* weight-limit of 1150 kg, or of 2534 lb. On the Dieppe course, the inconvenience for the public, of having to get to grandstands on the inside of the circuit was changed by placing them outside it and, in consequence, the replenishment pits really were pits, sunk below the level of the road in order that the view of the spectators was not impaired. Moreover, the road to these pits was set back from the course proper, as was done as a safety measure in much more recent times. The surface of the road had deteriorated, so that much tyre-changing was the order of the day, the winning car stopping nine times for this reason and a Clement Bayard nineteen times. That speeds were rising is evidenced by the fact that of the 48 starters more than twenty were timed at over 100 mph through a flying kilometre. There were fewer French entries than before and French hopes were low when it was seen that it was a

German Mercédès that led on the first lap, and at a record 73.7 mph. However, this car failed to keep going and Fiats took its place; these in their turn retired and, after that, the race was a German procession, Lautenschlager's Mercédès winning at 69 mph from Hémery's Benz, with third position occupied by another Benz, this time of Hanriot.

This overwhelming German victory, coming as it did after the Fiat success of 1907, was a grave blow to the French motor industry. Design was by now advancing for, whereas the 1908 Mercédès cars retained the popular side-chain final drive, they used the honeycomb radiators which this manufacturer had pioneered, as did many other makers, and high-tension magneto ignition was normal, while inclined overhead valves and even the single overhead camshaft had arrived. The French manufacturers, however, found racing as a means of improving the breed and publicising their individual wares very costly and, after the Mercédès and Benz domination, they looked with very luke-warm interest on another Grand Prix in 1909.

The Automobile Club de France tried to persuade them to build cars for a race at Anjou limited to four-cylinder machines with a cylinder-bore not exceeding 130 mm and of a maximum weight of 900 kg. But the Club required an entry of forty cars at least to make such a race viable and, at the end of the year, had only nine entries. So, the idea was abandoned and the mighty French Grand Prix faded away for three years, to be replaced by a series of *voiturette* contests. There was a much less important Grand Prix held in 1910, at Le

Below: Lautenschlager's 12.8-litre Mercédès hurtles out of the pits past Jenatzy's 12.8 Mors during the 1908 Grand Prix at Dieppe. Lautenschlager inherited the lead after another Mercédès and the Fiats retired, and he went on to win, while the 100 hp Mors was unsuccessful

Right: Christian Lautenschlager joined Daimler in 1900, becoming foreman-inspector, and won his first major race, the 1908 Grand Prix. His driving style was steady and unspectacular, aiding the works Mercédès assault on the 1914 French Grand Prix, in which Lautenschlager took the laurels. He continued racing after World War I and remained in the employ of the Daimler concern

Mans, under the title of the Grand Prix de France, and even that was won by a 10-litre touring-type car built by Fiat. It was, admittedly, driven by Victor Hémery, but it did seem that, for the moment at least, the French could no longer win.

Meanwhile, these small-car races, organised by the influential French motor journal *L'Auto*, accelerated the efficiency of the current light motor cars, so that in the comparatively short period from 1909 to 1911 the ridiculously long-stroke, freakish, single-cylinder cars of Sizaire-Naudin (which used independent front suspension as a sop to progress) and Delage had given way to beautiful little four-cylinder racers, culminating in the 65 × 200 mm Hispano-Suizas, designed by the Swiss engineer Marc Birkigt and driven with verve and skill by, among others, the celebrated Zuccarelli. All this was too much for the French manufacturers of the bigger and more illustrious cars. If the Grands Prix were to be revived in 1910 or subsequent years they realised that such a great race might well be won by one of these newcomers to the motor-racing game, and, anyway, they were giving away publicity to them by not racing. It was an unhappy thought so, by the end of 1911, all arguments against the non-revival of the ACF's Grand Prix, were put aside and the race was held again, at the Dieppe circuit, in June. They even reverted to the ambitious scheme of having a two-day contest, to ensure maximum pressure, and thus, as the true Grand Prix cars again lined up, they were to race for a furious 954.8 miles.

Left: one of the four works 3-litre Sunbeams, which competed in the Coupe de L'Auto category of the 1912 Grand Prix. The car, driven by Rigal, took third place in the Grand Prix and won the 'L'Auto' cup

So, racing in the grand manner was on again and, to emphasise this, the ACF had imposed no restrictions on the entrants in the 1912 Grand Prix, apart from insisting that the competing cars carried bodies that were no wider than a maximum of 5 ft 9 in; and to this day no-one seems to know quite what they had in mind in so doing. A legacy of the light-car races that had flourished between 1909 and 1911, while the GP proper was in abeyance, was a separate section of the two-day race devoted to cars under 3 litres capacity, with their cylinders not less than four in number and with the stroke not less nor greater than twice the cylinder bore. To avoid freak entries, and no doubt with the new 'stick-and-string' cyclecars in mind, a minimum weight limit in this class of 800 kg (1763 lb) was insisted on and *L'Auto* gave the winner's cup. Surprisingly, this class was the more popular, for it attracted 42 entrants, out of a total of 56. Moreover, there were seven *Coupe de L'Auto* cars from Britain; four Sunbeams and three Vauxhalls. Naturally, all eyes were on the GP cars, from the stables of Lorraine-Dietrich, Peugeot, Rolland-Pilain, Excelsior and Fiat. The Fiat and Lorraine-Dietrich cars, with previous Grand Prix racing experience behind them, used enormous overhead-valve 15-litre engines and chain final drive.

However, the significance of the 1912 race was the appearance of the revolutionary new Peugeot four-cylinder, sixteen-valve, twin-cam, shaft-drive 7.6-litre racers. Whereas Fiat were claiming a developed horsepower of 200, these smaller Peugeots probably produced a genuine 130 bhp at 2800 rpm (they claimed 175 bhp) and the 'little' Sunbeams, still with L-head side-valve engines, around 80 bhp. Although the cars proved slower than those in the earlier races, the writing was on the wall – plain and easy for the knowledgable to read – that the day of the monster road-racing car was over. The Grand Prix resolved itself into a battle between the old-school Fiats, which were delayed by broken fuel pipes, and Georges Boillot's Peugeot of not much over half their engine size. The celebrated Boillot won, at 68.45 mph, from Wagner's big Fiat, which averaged 67.32 mph. The future was again underlined when one of the 3-litre Sunbeams, driven by Rigal, netted third place in the Grand Prix proper, at 65.29 mph, as well as winning the *Coupe de L'Auto*. Indeed, these Sunbeams, closely akin to ordinary fast touring cars, although having the benefit of Brooklands work behind them, came home 1-2-3 in the 3-litre race and third, fourth and fifth in the Grand Prix itself. As to top speeds, Boillot was timed at 99.86 mph during the race, Bruce-Brown on one of the gigantic Fiats at 101.67 mph, and Dario Resta in the fastest of the Sunbeam team-cars at 65.29 mph. The small car had arrived!

In competition with the great French Grand Prix, the AC de la Sarthe again held its GP de France at Le Mans, which was an opportunity for Boillot and Peugeot to show that their victory at Dieppe was no fluke. Boillot made fastest-lap, at around 80 mph, and Goux's sister Peugeot won the race, at 74.56 mph, both impressive figures over this course.

The Grand Prix proper was thus fully re-established. For 1913, the ACF set it on a new circuit, at Amiens, and, as before, reverted to a one-day contest, over a 19½-mile course to be lapped 29 times. A fuel-consumption limit was also re-imposed, twenty litres of petrol per 100 kilometres, or at the rate of a consumption of 14.2 mpg, the cars being required to carry regulation bolster petrol tanks, behind which streamlined tails were forbidden, either because they were thought dangerous or because they would have off-set the 'road' aspect of the racers. Each competing car had to weigh a minimum of 800 kg (1760 lb) before it was fuelled. They now ran *clockwise*, as contemplated by the organisers in 1906, enabling the grandstands to be placed outside the circuit, for easy access, and the replenishment-pits to be on the inside. Building a connecting tunnel and a concrete loop-road to avoid closing one main road that was near the course was nothing, now that the race was of such importance.

The shorter lap was nice for the onlookers but the new rules were not liked by the builders of racing motor cars and only twenty entries came in. Yet, design was very fluid; Peugeot had eared hub caps to enable the road wheels to be removed quickly with a hammer, and none ran out of fuel, with the 40½ gallons metered out to them before they were taken out to the start behind horses. New companies were now building special cars for racing, and Peugeot remained in the ascendant. Boillot won in a 5.6-litre car at 72.2 mph and was timed through the flying kilometre at 97.26 mph. His team-mate, Goux, was second, and one of the 3-litre *Coupe de L'Auto* Sunbeams came in third.

The GP de France, at Sarthe, had been reduced in distance and was of no great importance, except to Mercédès, who were using it before staging an impressive racing come-back, and to Bablot who won it in a fast Delage, at 76.8 mph for the 337½ miles, after recording the fastest lap at 82.5 mph.

So, we come to 1914, with Europe, about to be plunged into a holocaust of war, and Germany, in the form of the Mercédès Company, taking the greatest possible pains to dominate this last pre-war Grand Prix. It was run at Lyons, in the heart of industrial France, over an interesting course of over 23 miles to a lap, with a charming corner known as the *le piege de la mort*, to give a race distance of 466.6 punishing miles. The date was 17 July, 1914. Note the imminence of war! And it was the team of five white Mercédès, with slab petrol tanks and sharp-pointed radiators, white cars superbly prepared, which had the heels of all the others. For the first time, the race rules limited engine capacity to 4½ litres: quite small cars by previous standards! Mercédès elected to eschew the new idea of prodding overhead valves with two camshafts and used single-overhead-camshaft four-cyclinder engines with sixteen inclined overhead valves. They were shaft-driven chassis, but with only rear-wheel brakes, and their drivers were good solid testers rather than racing drivers, certainly not aces with the flair of Georges Boillot. They had to race against the might of Peugeot, with their front-wheel brakes and proven twin-cam engines, and cars from the Alda, Nagant, Delage, Fiat, Piccard-Pictet, Vauxhall, Schneider, Opel, Itala and Sunbeam factories, in the tense atmosphere of that far-away summer of 1914.

Boillot did his utmost. But the sorely stressed Peugeot retired with maladies mechanical, probably a broken valve but the exact nature of which historians still argue over. The white German cars from across the border had their troubles, too. But there were five of them, so they could afford a pacesetter to break up the Peugeot attack. It was Lautenschlager, victor back in 1908, who swept to victory before a dazed French crowd, he and his aggressive Mercédès having made a speed of 65.3 mph over the distance. As intended, Wagner and Salzer followed him in, at 65.1 mph and 64.6 mph, respectively. Spectators were only stirred from their troubled meditation of the proximity of a German war by Goux bringing his blue Peugeot into fourth place, at 63.9 mph, ahead of Resta's British Sunbeam. Eleven had retired out of 37 starters and only the coming war could reverse the result and its impact on French minds.

Above: Georges Boillot was to epitomise the 'Spirit of France' in the early days of motor racing. He was always linked with Peugeot, starting with the smaller rival concern Lion-Peugeot until the companies amalgamated, and he raced with some success in all categories, including record attempts and hill-climbs. His last race was his greatest: the 1914 Grand Prix at Lyons, where he fought the works Mercédès virtually single handed in his 112 bhp Peugeot

CHAPTER 2

IMPROVING THE BREED

THE CARS: 1914-39

Even though the war was ushered in with an over-whelming victory at Lyons by a team of 4½-litre Mercédès racing cars of outdated design (their single-overhead-camshaft power units being contrary to the thinking of the Peugeot engineers with their twin-cam method of valve operation, dispensing with rockers), the period of hostilities was a time for aeronautical rather than motor car advancement. Nevertheless, when racing became possible again, after World War I, it was seen that even the racing car power plant had evolved to a significant degree. The frenzied production and continually enforced improvement of aero engines during the war resulted in useful advances applicable to racing engines and indeed to the power units of ordinary cars. Improvements in the fields of detail design, metallurgy and production methods were obvious, but it was the use of smaller, multiple cylinders, however, in which another great advance lay.

That the two significant new racing cars of the post-Armistice period were straight-eights has been attributed to the use of such an engine by Ettore Bugatti for a powerful aeroplane motor during the height of hostilities. He also made an aero-engine with two blocks of eight cylinders set up side by side, with separate crankshafts geared together, to produce a really beefy sixteen-cylinder engine. But it was the straight-eight principal that endeared itself to the planners of racing engines for the revival of the sport after the war was over; the chief protagonist was again Ernest Henry. He added this multi-cylinder concept to his pre-war Peugeot twin overhead-camshaft valve actuation, when commissioned by Ballot to build him racing cars for the first big post-war American motor race, the 1919 Indianapolis 500 Mile contest. Henry enclosed the previously exposed overhead valve gear but retained his system of having four valves for each cylinder, two inlet and two exhaust, these being set at a sixty degree angle in the fixed cylinder head. Henry also relied on the long piston stroke of his earlier engines, the straight-eight post-war Ballot being a 74×140mm power unit, having a swept volume of 4894cc. This was adequate to comply with American regulations, which called for a maximum engine size of 300cu in, or 4917cc. The long crankshaft required for such an engine, on this Henry-inspired Ballot, ran in five main bearings of the roller type, and it was a complex piece of work, in four separate sections joined together by a taper-and-key arrangement. In contrast, the big-end bearings were plain, with split bronze bushes between the con-rod and journal, these had white metal inner faces with bronze-to-steel rubbing in the con-rod. Dry-sump lubrication was resorted to, in order to reduce oil temperature, but the engine was susceptible to big-end oil starvation and was limited to a maximum crankshaft speed of 3500rpm. While the big-ends were fed with oil through drilled crankpins, the main bearings were lubricated on the jet principle. Henry mounted this big engine on a sub-frame in a conventional chassis, with channel-section side members and semi-elliptic leaf springing. A cone clutch took the drive, through a four-speed gearbox, to the back axle via

an open propeller shaft. Like Bugatti with his in-line eight-cylinder aero-engine, Henry used a 4-4 layout of the crankpins of his long crankshaft. Ignition was by a Bosch magneto, and two Claudel-Hobson carburettors supplied the mixture. Ballot must have been well pleased with these cars, the two costing him, it is said, £30,000, even though they had pre-war chassis characteristics and bolster petrol tanks ill-suited to the flat-out racing which Indianapolis involved.

The American firm of Duesenberg had also prepared straight-eight racing cars for the 1919 500 Mile Race. This engine was more closely related to the Bugatti aero-motor, as it had a single overhead camshaft operating three inclined valves (two exhaust and one inlet) per cylinder via rocker gear, the camshaft being driven from the front of the crankshaft by a vertical shaft and bevels. The cylinder head was detachable and, to simplify the valve gear, a

Right: Maurice Ballot stands between the two 4.9-litre, straight-eight Ballots of Albert Guyot (*left*) and René Thomas in Paris, 1919. Ballot built motor engines prior to World War I, and engaged the brilliant designer Ernest Henry to build Indianapolis cars for the 1919 race. Thomas made fastest lap at 104.2 mph and Guyot took fourth place

Y-shaped cam follower prodded the paired exhaust valves. Again, a 'four-four' crankshaft arrangement was employed and there were but three main bearings, two plain at the front and a ball-race at the back. The gearbox provided only three forward speeds, but a nicely streamlined body was used. Neither of these two revolutionary new post-war racers did anything much at Indy, where the winner was one of the 1914 GP Peugeots (Henry could still afford to smile), but they set a fashion which lasted into the mid 1950s, that of in-line eight-cylinder engines for racing. The disadvantages of a long and therefore likely-to-be-whippy crankshaft were offset by such merits as the ability to dispense with a heavy flywheel, good balance (which brought reliability with it), an increase in piston area from small light pistons (thereby increasing combustion chamber efficiency and rate of crankshaft revs) and excellent low-speed torque, although Henry threw away the latter quality in his 1919 Ballot engine because of big-choke carburettors. The problems of feeding fuel to a long eight-cylinder in-line motor were solved by having more than one instrument and overcome completely in later years when supercharging was the norm.

When the 3-litre maximum swept-volume rule came in, in 1920, both these Ballot and Duesenberg designs were reduced in size and, subsequently, fared better. Peugeot, on the other hand, having lost Henry to Ballot and later to Sunbeam, were handicapped by an over-ambitious engineer who concocted for them a racing engine of 80×149mm and four cylinders which boasted five overhead valves each, three of which let the gas in, the other two being exhaust valves. There were three camshafts to operate this multiplicity of poppet valves, and eight sparking plugs; developing a claimed 108bhp at about 3000rpm, it was something to ignore, although it reflected the diversity of thought in racing-car drawing offices at this time. What this Peugeot and the 1920 3-litre Duesenberg did have in common was unit-construction of engine and gearbox, which pointed to a coming universal trend.

Another technical innovation which was, much later, to become universal

Right: the 3-litre straight-eight engined Duesenbergs took second, third, fourth, sixth and eighth places at Indianapolis in 1921. This is the car in which Jimmy Murphy won the 1921 French Grand Prix, and was the first American car to be equipped with hydraulic brakes all round

Below: the 1914 4.5-litre Delage Grand Prix car was fitted with four-wheel brakes, a twin-overhead-camshaft, four-cylinder engine, with desmodromic valve-gear, twin carburettors, and a five-speed gearbox. While the Delage was not particularly successful in the 1914 Grand Prix, W. F. Bradley took two 6.2-litre cars to Indianapolis and René Thomas won at 82.47mph

for racing and road cars alike, was the use of hydraulic operation for the brakes. Duesenberg had this for their impeccably prepared 1921 3-litre car which won the French Grand Prix, providing a nasty shock for European constructors. In fact, the fluid used for this then-exciting new form of brake actuation was a mixture of water and glycerine, retained within the single master cylinder by the ground-to-fit piston! This fluid actually passed along the tubular front

Right: originally entered in a Fiat, Louis Wagner drove a 3-litre Ballot at Indianapolis in 1921

Left: Fiat's 115 bhp, 3-litre straight-eight Tipo 802, built for the 1921 Grand Prix, had roller-bearing big ends fitted, but was uncompetitive

Below left: the 1.5-litre, four-cylinder Talbot-Darracq of Chassagne at the Brooklands 200-mile race of 1921, in which the team finished in the first three places

Below: Jimmy Murphy on his way to winning the 1921 French Grand Prix at Le Mans, where he averaged 78.22 mph to become the first American to win a major European motor race

axle and up through the drilled steering-pivot pins, to expand individual pistons that opened out the flexible spring-steel brake shoes. Other significant, if then individual, aspects of this GP-winning Duesenberg were torque-tube transmission, Delco high-tension coil ignition, and detachable wire wheels employing Rudge-Whitworth centre-lock hubs. The car was able to develop between 115 and 120 bhp at 4250 rpm and, with the help of its new-style braking system, this American Duesenberg took the European racing world by storm in 1921; the straight-eight racing engine was the fashion from then on. As others were to adopt the Ernest Henry twin-cam multi-valve cylinder head, so his pioneering of the eight-in-line cylinder layout was not disregarded, either. Ballot and STD used both for their engines of the new 3-litre racing formula, but for the latter cars (conveniently labelled Sunbeam, Talbot or Darracq, as and when it suited Louis Coatalen, who had built them, seven in number at a cost of some £50,000) a better bottom-end lubrication system was devised, using plain bearings for both mains and big-ends, again in conjunction with a dry-sump system. All these post-war racing eights, Ballot, Sunbeam and Fiat, were twin-cam engines of 65 × 112 mm in the prevailing long-stroke idiom. However, the Type 802 Fiat broke away from the Henry multi-valve school of thought, to set another lead in future design, as the engineer concerned, Fornaca, opted for two large valves per cylinder, set at 96 degrees: the classical hemi-head combustion chamber. He also used the cylinder and water-jacket construction, complicated but effective, which Mercédès had found practical in their pre-war racing car and war-time aeroplane engines, namely blocks of steel forgings, welded and machined with the water covers made up of sheet-steel welded in place. This notable Fiat engine had a single-

piece crankshaft instead of a built-up shaft, this being made possible by the use of split bronze bearing cages for the roller main bearings. The big-ends were of the same type and this all-roller-bearing power unit developed a useful 115 bhp at 4600 rpm. That was the norm for the 1921 Grand Prix season.

There was now a full appreciation of the value of four-wheel braking in the field of road racing. It not only reduced skidding but was almost as useful as good acceleration over a twisty course, in killing speed into the corners. To reduce the wear and tear on the drivers, servo operation of these mostly cable-operated brakes was usual, with the servo driven from the gearbox, which helped to apply the brakes when the pedal was depressed. This system was built into the great 37.2 hp Hispano Suiza touring-car chassis by the eminent Swiss engineer, Marc Birkigt. Racing bodywork, too, was evolving, into pointed-tail two-seaters, with decent protection for driver and riding mechanic in the prevailing long-road contests.

The influence of the big-time racers was handed down to the voiturette or 1½-litre class of racing car. Whereas the successful type immediately after the Armistice was the light-weight, four-cylinder, single-overhead-camshaft,

Below: Douglas Hawkes' 3-litre Bentley on its way to fifth place in the 1922 Isle of Man TT. Bentley won the team prize in the factory's second venture into competitions

sixteen-valve Brecia Bugatti, by 1921 and 1922 the twin-cam form of racing engine was supreme in this category. At first, it aped the bigger racing cars in having four valves per cylinder. In this form, the 1486 cc Talbot-Darracqs, another facet of Sunbeam Chief Designer Louis Coatalen's enthusiasm for racing, were producing no less that 50 bhp at 4000 rpm, which rendered them quite invincible.

We move now to the interesting 1922 racing season. This was run under the maximum capacity of 2 litres ruling. It was important because it brought some mixed design-thinking into the picture but it is remarkable that those companies which supported racing in the grand manner were willing to go to the expense of building entirely new racing cars every year; in recent times, of course, the 3-litre Formula One rule has remained unchanged to obviate this vast seasonal expenditure. Anyway, that was the position in 1922, with a minimum weight limit of 650 kg (1436 lb) to match this 2000 cc capacity ruling and the various manufacturers fielded many diverse configurations.

Ernest Henry changed from his straight-eight to a four-cylinder engine which he built for Sunbeam. It retained four valves per cylinder, now with the

Below right: Cushman's Brescia Bugatti prior to the 1922 200-mile race at Brooklands; basically a 1914 Type 13 model of 1.4 litres, the car was so named because of its surprising success in the 1921 Brescia event, the pre-war cars having been stored throughout the duration of hostilities

inlets at twenty degrees to the vertical, set higher in the heads than the forty degree exhaust valves, with two sparking plugs to each cylinder and twin carburettors. A plunger oil pump, a former Henry love, was used, feeding plain, white-metal, big-ends and the crankshaft ran in three ball-races, being the usual built-up affair. A cone clutch took the power to a four-speed gearbox and there were the expected mechanical gearbox-servo, cable-operated, four-wheel brakes. This was a retrograde design. The small piston area and restricted engine speed made these Henry-Sunbeams non-competitive, aggravated by a tendency to break their inlet valves. Yet, on ordinary petrol, these 2-litre compact 'four-potters' gave around 85 bhp at 4250 rpm.

Fiat countered the smaller engine-size by changing from the eight-cylinder to a six-cylinder engine and got 92 bhp at 4500 rpm – note that racing car engines did not rotate all that quickly – later increased to 110 bhp, which made Fiat the in-car of the 1922 season. If we accept this single-carburettor Fiat as the leading racing car of the period, we see it as a small 13½ cwt, staggered two-seater with a wheelbase of 8 ft 2½ in, its radiator neatly cowled, a full length undershield running beneath the wedge-tail body, and the exhaust pipe running for part of its length in a metal tunnel. The eight in-line engine still persisted, however, being used by both Bugatti and Rolland-Pilain, but Ballot had retrogressed to four cylinders. The lessons were plain to see. The future lay in light weight, multi-cylinders and roller bearings throughout the engine for high revs, with some attention being paid to low-drag bodies. There was Bugatti's plan of taking the exhaust-pipe out through the centre of a barrel tail,

and Grillot had gone to the terrible complexity of desmodromic mechanically closed valves on the Rolland-Pilain engines, a theme it was better to leave Mercédès to play with over three decades later!

The 1923 season was of less importance from the point of view of technical evolution, because supercharging was just around the corner, and would soon up-lift power output for a given cylinder capacity quite dramatically. In the meantime, what do we find? Coatalen achieved his burning ambition, that of winning the French Grand Prix, by the simple strategy of hiring Vincent Berterione away from Fiat to design for him a race winner. This Sunbeam six-cylinder looked outwardly and within much like the six-cylinder Fiats that swept all before them the previous year, for the Grand Prix formula remained at a top engine-size limit of 2 litres, as it was to do for a further two seasons.

Above: the 1922 Sunbeam Grand Prix team The drivers are Kenelm Lee Guinness, in number 16, and (Sir) Henry Segrave, in 21

Left: a 1922 Duesenberg; fitted with a Miller engine and rechristened the Murphy Special, Jimmy Murphy's Duesenberg won the 1922 Indy 500, while the car shown here finished second, driven by Harry Hartz

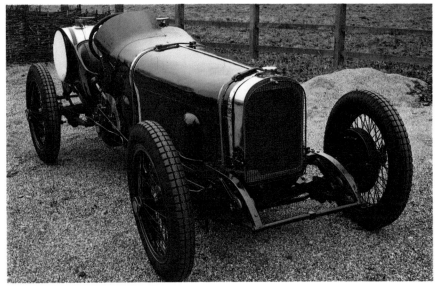

Above: the eminent Swiss engineer Marc Birkigt was responsible for preparing all competition Hispano-Suizas at the Levallois-Perret factory from 1911 until 1914

Above right: a 1922 straight-eight TT-type Sunbeam

Below: Sir Algernon Lee Guinness after winning the 1500 Trophy on the Isle of Man in 1922, with a four-cylinder, twin-overhead-camshaft Talbot Darracq

Below right: Sir Algernon on the famous Mountain course during his winning drive

Before we look briefly at other 1923 road-race designs, there were some racing cars built to compete in the rather odd 1922 Tourist Trophy Race to consider. This, belying its title, was for pure racing cars and was held over the well known Isle of Man course. The rules provided for cars of up to 3 litres capacity, with an additional 1½-litre race; the bigger cars had to weigh not less than 1600 lb. One of the straight-eight twin-cam Henry-style STD Sunbeams, based on the 1921 GP machines, but now with magneto ignition, twin Clauden Hobson carburettors, and a power output of 108 bhp at 4000 rpm, won a rather un-inspiring race, and a 1½-litre 16-valve 'invincible' Talbot-Darracq was victorious in the *voiturette* section. A very complicated TT Vauxhall was evolved for the TT event. Its engine was a twin-cam four-cylinder of 85 × 132 mm, with sixteen ninety degree valves in a detachable bronze cylinder head that sat on an aluminium cylinder block, in which there were removable liners surrounded by the cooling water. The camshafts were gear driven, and the built-up crankshaft had a central flywheel and ran in six ball-races; the big-ends used double roller-races. This was a good engine, of rigid structure, the ignition was by Delco coil with dual distributors, and one twin-choke Zenith looked after the carburation. Although the compression ratio was a modest 5.8 to 1, this fine if complicated power unit rewarded Ricardo with an output of nearly 130 bhp at 4500 rpm. Alas, the chassis, designed by King, was also very complex, as well as too heavy, and it was further hampered by novel compressed-air servo brakes with steering-column control, allied to separate mechanical linkage. The body was just as odd, being a slab-tank two-seater

with rather sexy scuttle cowls. At the time, this ingenious Vauxhall was a failure but its day was to come, in sprints, when it was subsequently developed into the multi-blower Vauxhall Villiers Supercharged Special and successfully used by Ramond Mays.

The TT also saw a British Aston-Martin endowed with a twin-cam engine which was pure Ernest Henry Ballot so far as its sixteen-valve upper half was concerned. Continuing with the 1923 Grand Prix entries: although, as has been said, Sunbeam won, the significant cars were the supercharged straight-eight Fiats. Similar in design concept to the 1922 successful Fiats, but with gear-driven overhead camshafts, they used a Wittig vane-pattern blower driven off the nose of the crankshaft and for feeding air into the carburettor under pressure,

Below left: the mechanical complexities of Raymond Mays' 1922, Amherst Villiers-supercharged, Vauxhall, which was rebuilt in 1931

which the mechanic is supposed to have been able to control. These were the fastest cars racing, which were said to produce an effective 130 bhp. Alas, for Italy, the new-fangled superchargers were not impervious to road grit, and they retired. But the writing was on the wall in big, clear letters – very much so, for Fiat with the new supercharged engine won the Italian Grand Prix before the year 1923 was out. Of the others, Voisin ran weirdly streamlined Knight sleeve-valve-engined racers; Bugatti was also mad on good air-flow over the car, with short-wheelbase straight-eight cars endowed with all-enveloping tank-like coachwork, and there was a lone vee-twelve-cylinder Delage which was also of future significance, among one six-cylinder and two straight-eight Rolland-Pilains; the latter were not successful in the Grands Prix. Their six-cylinder racer had a Henry-Schmid cuff-valve engine.

The 1923 season of Grand Prix racing had seen the greatest divergence of engine, chassis and aerodynamic design since the sport was resumed after the end of World War I. The next season was just as significant, but in a more stabilised fashion, as the supercharger had by now been virtually perfected. Although the engine capacity limit of 2 litres still prevailed, the use of a blower brought with it a very considerable power increase, which made the swept-volume ruling an arbitrary one and gave greatly increased top speed and acceleration.

The racing car which won most races in 1924 was the P2 Alfa Romeo. Like the Sunbeams before it, this fine racer owed much to the Fiat influence, in that it was designed by the talented Vittorio Jano who had served with Fiat from 1911. The Alfa Romeo used a straight-eight engine with its cylinder blocks in four pairs, their bore and stroke being 61×85 mm, giving an engine size of 1987 cc. In the style of the day both big-end and main bearings were of the roller-type; welded-up water jackets surrounded the cylinder blocks, a permanently-engaged Roots paddle-type supercharger blew air through a Memini carburettor via a long cast-conduit in the light-alloy base chamber and, naturally, the two overhead valves in each cylinder head were inclined and

Right : Campari and mechanic Ramponi after
victory in the 1924 French Grand Prix at Lyons

Below : Wagner's Alfa Romeo P2 in the same race

operated by twin overhead camshafts. This advanced, although conventional in
the racing sense, power unit was installed in a compact chassis with a wheelbase
of 8 ft 6 ins, using four-wheel-brakes with servo assistance. The cart-springing
which was normal at that time was practically overcome by the use of big-sec-
tion balloon tyres. Capable of well over 120 mph, the P2 Alfa Romeo became a
legend in its lifetime. The claimed power output was 135 bhp at 5500 rpm, which
was similar to the power developed by the 1924 Grand Prix Sunbeams, which
were simply improved versions of the Fiat-based 1923 cars, although now
supercharged, with a Roots blower compressing the mixture drawn from a
Solex carburettor within the supercharger casing. The Sunbeam six-cylinder
engine had dimensions of 67 × 94 mm and the very slight power advantage

made them faster than the P2 Alfa Romeos at the premier Lyons Grand Prix although they did eventually lose the race, due to faulty magnetos.

M. Lory had much improved his V12 Delage for the 1924 season, but it was not yet supercharged, as he had not yet perfected the layout of this car. This was not altogether a disadvantage, however, because it ensured reliability from the complex Delage power unit and netted the great French manufacturer second place in the Lyons Grand Prix.

The 1924 Grand Prix season is best remembered for the advent, although unsuccessful at first, of the new and extremely beautiful racing Type 35 Bugatti. It was as conventional in concept as the 1923 'tank'-bodied Bugattis had been unorthodox. With the shapely two-seater pointed-tail body and much-louvred bonnet behind the little Bugatti horse-shoe-pattern radiator, it blended well with the unusual wide-spoked aluminium wheels, whereby Ettore Bugatti sought to conduct heat away from the tyres and save unsprung weight at his axle extremities. These Type 35s were powered by a typical Bugatti straight-eight single overhead-camshaft engine of 60×88 mm (1990 cc) having three vertical valves in each cylinder, the cylinder block and head being in one piece. Bugatti was not only unconvinced at this period of time about forced induction,

Above: (Sir) Henry Segrave at the wheel of the 1923 six-cylinder, 2-litre Sunbeam Grand Prix car

Below: work in progress on the Alvis team cars prior to the Brooklands 200-Mile Race of 1923. The car in the foreground was driven by C. M. Harvey and went on to win the race when the Fiats expired. The Alvis Racing cars were based on the production 12/50 model

Right: the supercharged, 2-litre straight-six engine of the 1925 racing Sunbeam. This particular engine is fitted with the later SU carburettor in place of the original Solex unit

Right: the legendary Alfa Romeo P2, designed by Vittorio Jano and introduced in 1924. It earned a place in racing history in winning the first Grand Prix in which it was entered, the 1924 French race, with Campari at the wheel

Right: E. Friedrich in the 2-litre, tank-bodied, Bugatti, on his way to third place in the 1923 French Grand Prix at Tours

he was avidly opposed to it, so twin carburettors sufficed to feed his angular power-pack. This artistic engine had a built-up crankshaft turning in three comparatively small ball-races and two larger roller-races while the light con-rods had roller big-ends. The drive went through a Bugatti multi-plate clutch to a four-speed and reverse gearbox, the torque of the open propeller shaft being absorbed by side radius rods. The chassis was also well-constructed; the side members were carefully stressed and the back axle suspended on reversed quarter-elliptic springs of leaf pattern. The splendid appearance of the 1924 GP Bugatti was notably enhanced by the tubular front axle which possessed forged slots through which the front half-elliptic springs passed. All this contributed to the Bugatti's legendary road holding. The engine was scarcely competitive in terms of horse-power, giving about 100 bhp at 5200 rpm on its first appearance. Reliability and cornering prowess, however, made the Bugatti the most prolific race winner of the 1924–39 era. At its début at the important French Grand Prix it appeared that the ingenious wheels may have transmitted too much heat because the tyres gave continuous trouble. Incidentally, the brake drums were detachable with the alloy wheels.

Right : Kaye Don in the 146 bhp supercharged two-litre Sunbeam of 1924, pictured here at Brooklands in 1928

Below : the powerful 1925 Delage was designed by Albert Lory and won the French and Spanish Grands Prix

Below right : the V12 engine of the 1925 Delage used twin Roots superchargers and developed 195 bhp at 7000 rpm

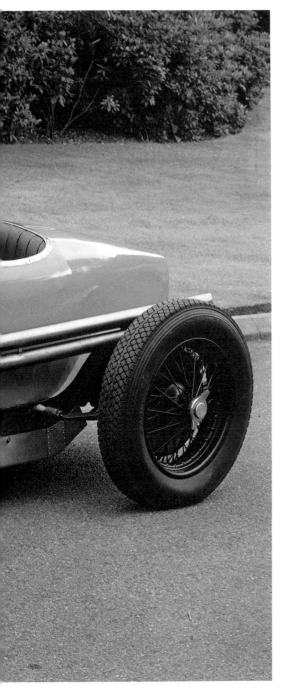

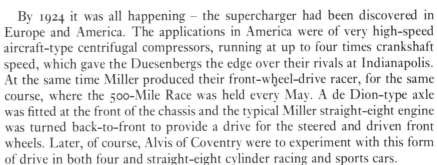

By 1924 it was all happening – the supercharger had been discovered in Europe and America. The applications in America were of very high-speed aircraft-type centrifugal compressors, running at up to four times crankshaft speed, which gave the Duesenbergs the edge over their rivals at Indianapolis. At the same time Miller produced their front-wheel-drive racer, for the same course, where the 500-Mile Race was held every May. A de Dion-type axle was fitted at the front of the chassis and the typical Miller straight-eight engine was turned back-to-front to provide a drive for the steered and driven front wheels. Later, of course, Alvis of Coventry were to experiment with this form of drive in both four and straight-eight cylinder racing and sports cars.

Mercédès returned to racing in 1924 with a Porsche-designed car, which followed the expected straight-eight cylinder configuration and had steel cylinders with Mercédès welded-on water jacketing, and dry-sump lubrication. The crankshaft ran in nine roller bearings, and other interesting aspects of the specification were four valves per cylinder, and a Roots supercharger blowing through the carburettor, in contrast to the sucking of air from the carburettor that Mercédès preferred for their sports chassis. Front springs passed through the axle although this was not actually a Bugatti preserve, as Fiat also did it. The Mercédès used sodium cooling for the hollow exhaust-valve stems and its engine was an impressive piece of work for 1924, developing perhaps as much as 160 bhp at the very high crankshaft rotative speed of 7000 rpm. Alas for German hopes, the poor road-holding made it highly dangerous, and it was in one of these Mercédès that the legendary Count Louis Zborowski of Chitty-Chitty-Bang-Bang fame was killed at Monza during the Italian Grand Prix.

The 2-litre ruling remained in force for the 1925 racing season but, as a change was suspected, new designs were not encouraged and the starting-grids were mainly composed of improved versions of the 1924 cars. Lory had done good work on his V12 Delage engine, which now boasted a notable power increase, through having twin Roots superchargers. These, and the large piston area, which the use of a dozen tiny pistons ensured, gave the potential of 190 bhp at 7000 rpm, nearly the dreamed-of 100 bhp per litre. However powerful the 1925 V12 Delage was, Alfa Romeo, with improved versions of the great

P2, was more powerful, and would undoubtedly have won the French Grand Prix at Montlhéry (over the artificial road-circuit) had they not withdrawn their cars as a mark of respect for their ace driver Antonio Ascari, who was killed when his P2 inexplicably overturned in a ditch when he was leading the race. Alfas ran on dope at this stage in their engine development, although ordinary petrol was still the norm for lesser racing engines.

Another important trend of 1925 was the elimination of the riding mechanic from the leading races. His chief tasks had been to warn his driver of overtaking cars, to maintain fuel pressure, to read the instruments and to keep an eye on the mechanics, while also assisting with tyre changes or similar operations away from the depot. The number of accidents in which the occupants of racing cars were involved now led the authorities to ban the riding mechanic, although for the time-being body widths remained of two-seater dimensions. Ettore Bugatti-the-Thoughtful faired over the passenger's seats of his Type 35s when he heard of this but, under protest, was obliged to have the metal cut away. In America, however, the centre-cockpit single-seater was already the accepted design for racing cars, and this was eventually adopted in Europe.

The 1926 International Grand Prix ruling for the maximum permitted engine capacity was $1\frac{1}{2}$-litres (1500 cc), which remained unchanged until 1928. There was also a minimum weight clause of 600 kg (1322 lb) – a reduction of 108 lb over the 1925 rule for 2-litre racers and, despite the elimination of the mechanic, the bodies still had to seat two, and not be less than 80 cm wide. Only one mechanic was allowed to get into the road to assist the driver at the pits.

In voiturette racing, the Talbot-Darracqs of the STD combine, under Louis Coatalen, were still supreme. New four-cylinder 67×105.6 mm (1481 cc) cars had been designed by Bertarione for this class of racing, based on the successful 2-litre six-cylinder Sunbeams. The Grand Prix cars themselves were now built to the $1\frac{1}{2}$-litre formula. The STD concern had more ambitious plans: they produced new, very low-slung, straight-eight supercharged racing cars of an interesting design. In compliance with the then-prevailing belief that fast cornering was enhanced by making a car's centre-of-gravity as low as possible, the Talbot's transmission was off-set in the frame, a gambit made possible because a mechanic no longer had to be accommodated. A double-reduction, back-axle final-drive lowered the actual height of these components and the driver sat on a cushion on the car's undertray. The chassis side-members were made of pressings, with vertical slots through which the back and front axles passed, suspended on semi-elliptic springs. The front axle of the 1926 Talbot was also a remarkable construction. It consisted of two tapering tubes, bored out almost to the steering pivots, bolted together at the centre, which was enabled, by the use of angled flanges, to be considerably lower than the front-wheel hub centres, and thus pass below the engine. This unusually rigid and very low chassis frame was enclosed by aluminium panels and nicely streamlined with a cowled sloping radiator. The engine had its steel 'pots' in two blocks with welded-on water jackets, as Bertarioni was responsible for the design. It was in accordance with mid-1920s practice, having twin overhead camshafts operating two inclined valves per cylinder and a nose-mounted Roots supercharger, twin Bosch magnetos, roller-bearing crankshaft, and a Solex carburettor for the blower to draw from. It developed some 145 bhp at 6500 rpm, and ran to 7000 rpm. A finned oil-cooler was fitted to the outside of the body. Transmission was now by torque-tube, and the front springs again passed through slots in the ingenious front axle. Top speed was in the region of 130 mph.

There was, at the time this 1926 Talbot was being tested, the popular idea that Grand Prix cars, intended to race over a road or artificial-road circuit, should be built as low as possible. This seemed to give them the ability to corner faster with a minimum of roll which, in those days of very hard non-independent suspension, could promote instability and skidding. It also brought with it the unfortunate factor that the driver was not always aware that forces were mounting to a point where his car would spin uncontrollably.

This notwithstanding, the Delage racers, which M. Lory prepared for the

Above: the accident which resulted in the banning of riding mechanics in racing cars. Kenelm Lee Guinness' badly damaged Sunbeam after he crashed during the 1924 Spanish Grand Prix at San Sebastian; his mechanic was killed

Above right: Robert Benoist on his way to winning the 1927 British Grand Prix at Brooklands. Delage took the first three places, their chief opposition coming from the Bugatti 35s, such as George Eyston's, being passed here by Benoist

Below: Rudolf Caracciola – *der Regenmeister* – on his lap of honour after his first major victory, in a Mercédès GP car, at the German Grand Prix, Avus, in 1926. Caracciola became known as one of the greatest ever Grand Prix drivers

new $1\frac{1}{2}$-litre Formula, were also very low-hung, albeit with a more conventional chassis frame than those of the Talbots, swept down to pass below the back axle. It was the engine of the 1500cc Delage which was a truly remarkable piece of engineering. Ignoring expense, Lory used the expected straight-eight cylinder configuration, with a bore and stroke of 55.8×76mm, which gave him a swept volume of 1484cc. Two overhead camshafts operated the valves, two per 'pot', angled at a hundred degrees. This, too, was conventional stuff, but the complexity of almost watch-making precision came with the details. The camshafts were driven by a train of gears, amounting to twenty in all, counting the drives for the auxiliaries. There were roller and ball races in abundance, each camshaft running in nine such bearings, so that the total used was in excess of sixty. The crankshaft was a forged one-piece counter-balanced affair, and was again fully-rollered. This marvellous little racing power unit was given the required power output by means of twin superchargers mounted on the near side and driven by a shaft from the timing-gear train; they sucked from one carburettor apiece. There were two oil pumps for the dry-sump

system, a water pump and a Bosch magneto. All this complexity gave Lory more than 160bhp at the now acceptable engine speed of 7500rpm. But what he had not allowed for was the difficulty of getting excess heat away from his wonderful power unit. This passed, via the exhaust pipe, too close to the driver's footboard and cockpit side, so that feet and torso were roasted in long races, like a loaf in a fierce oven.

This was unfortunate as these $1\frac{1}{2}$-litre GP Delages were as fast as they were aggressive looking. On the low-height theme, the rather whippy chassis was so low that the tops of the front tyres were on a level with the top of the vertical radiator. The driver could touch the ground easily if he put a hand out of the car, and the height to the top of his scuttle was a mere $35\frac{1}{2}$in. The wheelbase measured 8ft $2\frac{1}{2}$in, while suspension was by short, very stiff half-elliptic leaf springs and there was a powerful servo braking system, with large ribbed drums behind the wire wheels. The front axle was a three-piece tubular one

Above: the Amilcar C6 of 1926, some 35 of which were produced. Designed by Edmond Moyet, the works cars won 74 events in the voiturette class during that year, outclassing the rival Salmsons

Top: the 1100cc, dohc, six-cylinder engine of the Amilcar C6, which ultimately produced 108bhp at 6000rpm, powering the car to a top speed of 125mph

Above: the magnificent V12 Sunbeam Tiger was the last World Land Speed Record car to be raced on a circuit. Only two of these cars were built, based on the 1925 2-litre Grand Prix model. Using a supercharged, 4-litre, V12 engine, this car took (Sir) Henry Segrave to a new record of 152.308mph, at Southport in 1926, and subsequently went on to race at Brooklands, Boulogne and San Sebastian. Its Brooklands' record included victory in the Mountain Championship for Sir Malcolm Campbell in 1932

Top: the 3976cc, V12 engine of the Tiger was based on two of the 1925, 2-litre, Grand Prix engines, mounted in a 75-degree vee on a common crankcase. The supercharged engine developed 296 bhp and was versatile enough to be used for both racing and record breaking

and Delage, in the face of a general change over to torque-tube final drive, retained an open propeller shaft.

By the time the start of the 1926 racing season had arrived, it was apparent that to build a competitive $1\frac{1}{2}$-litre road-racing motor car had become an exceedingly costly process, and this sadly reduced the number of different makes who could afford to participate. The celebrated Welsh engineer and racing driver, J. G. Parry Thomas, had decided to come in when straight-eight racers were using his now-famous conception of a single-overhead-camshaft engine, with inclined valves opened by a common inlet/exhaust cam per cylinder and closed by leaf valve springs. He was even more extreme in hanging his chassis low on its springs (the frame passing below the axles and being only 5 in. from the ground) which were of the quarter-elliptic type at the rear and semi-elliptic at the front. The bodywork of these Thomas Specials was so low and flat that it is said the mechanics, when in playful mood, would turn the cars upside down and roll them along on their wheels just as easily as when

they were upright. As a result, the Thomas creations became known as 'Flat-irons'. However, they had early gearbox troubles and were only competitive for outer-circuit racing and class-record breaking.

Ettore Bugatti was at last forced, by the 1½-litre Formula and the ambitious designs of his rivals at Delage and the Sunbeam/Talbot/Darracq combine, to resort to supercharging. Thus was created the 1½-litre Type 39 Bugatti. This was the straight-eight Type 35 that had made its début in 1924, endowed with a Roots blower on the side of the engine and with its stroke reduced from 88 to 66 mm, thus getting it down from 2 litres to the required 1½. The supercharger was driven by a train of gears and a short shaft and it 'puffed' at around 10 psi. Because of the oven-like propensities of the Delage cars and the hasty preparation of the new Talbots, they only just scraped a victory in the JCC 200-Mile Race at Brooklands at the end of 1926, so Bugatti began to reap the benefit of a simple, proven design.

The 1½-litre ruling continued for 1927 and the Delages then became the World Champion racing cars. Lory had cured the drivers' objection to staying in them for the length of a race unless they could douse their scorched feet in cold water, by the simple, if technically expensive, expedient of turning the cylinder blocks round, so that the exhaust ports and off-takes were on the opposite side of the car. This was not such a simple alteration as it sounds. It necessitated removing the twin blowers; a single Cozette supercharger was substituted. The engine and its five-speed gearbox was then off-set 4 in to the left of the chassis centre line, to give more space in the cramped cockpit; the radiator was slightly inclined and the steering improved. By using dope fuel, a blend of straight petrol, benzole, alcohol (for cooling the engine internals) and ether (to aid starting up), this fine power-unit was now producing some 113 bhp per litre, and a maximum of 170 bhp without revving above 8000 rpm, which was not to be sneezed at. It enabled the 1927 Delage to win every Grand Prix race in which it started. Even so, with a supercharger pressure of only about 7½ psi, this engine had much in hand, as Ramponi was to prove to Dick Seaman ten years later, when he challenged successfully the new ERAs with one of these by-then-ancient Delages. In contrast, money was running out for Talbot and this STD design was never fully developed.

Although Delage dominated the 1926/7 1½-litre Formula, there were a number of notable experiments at this time, which deserve mention, though they were unsuccessful. Itala made a V12 racer with two banks of cylinders at sixty degrees and horizontal valves, two per head, prodded from a central camshaft between the V of the cylinder blocks. There was a supercharger that blew air into ports uncovered when the pistons got to the base of the cylinders. This novel Itala not only had front-wheel drive, but independent suspension using transverse springs and rubber blocks. Built in 1100 cc and 1500 cc forms, this ingenious confection was never raced. Then Fiat returned, with a six-cylinder two-stroke racer possessing twelve pistons, as there were geared-together crankshafts one above the other, and common combustion chambers. This car was never raced . . . but the great Fiat Company did win at Monza with another remarkably ingenious design. It was a twin-six of 50 × 63 mm with its cylinder blocks side by side and the crankshafts geared together as on the two-stroke. Three twelve-cam camshafts were needed to operate the overhead valves and Fiat managed with plain bearings. This exciting swan-song of Fiat should have produced more victories, as the engine was giving 187 bhp at 8500 rpm on the bench. Known as the Type 406, this Zerbi-planned power unit was put into the light Tipo 806 chassis and, had it been developed, it might have offered a powerful challenge to the Delages. A team was said to be coming over for the 1927 British Grand Prix, but the Fiats were withdrawn and never seen again on a race course. In Britain, however, Alvis entered the field, with front-wheel-drive straight-eight cars, at first with horizontal overhead valves actuated by vertical rockers. The bore and stroke of the Smith-Clarke-designed, Coventry-built engine was 55 × 78¾ mm (1497 cc); later, conventional twin overhead camshafts were substituted.

All this 1½-litre 'F1' activity, led so ably by Delage, who showed that if sufficient time and money is spent, success should be comparatively easy to

achieve, reduced the former Talbot-Darracq dominated *voiturette* class to 1100cc, and sired the beautiful little Roots-blown twin-cam Amilcar Six and the less successful straight-eight Salmson, which was likewise supercharged.

So far as pure Grands Prix were concerned, the rule makers recognised that the very expensive small racing cars made artificially powerful (by dint of supercharging), would cease to be built, largely due to Delage's domination and the impending financial slump. Consequently, a period of free formulae was introduced, in which the older GP cars, stripped big-engined sports cars, like the Mercédès and the Bentley, and a few new large racing cars, too like Sunbeam's 4-litre V12 and the immortal Type 35B supercharged 2.3-litre Bugatti, all had occasional success. Then, for 1931, proper racing cars were back in vogue. At first, the rules were peculiar, insisting on two-seater bodies but no riding mechanics, under the agreement that had been in force for some years, and races were to run for at least ten hours. The period of racing was notable for the arrival on the circuits of the Tipo 8C, or Monza, Alfa Romeo, a straight-eight, twin-cam, Roots-blown sports car stripped for racing, and of the 2.3-litre, double-overhead-camshaft, Type 51 Bugatti. After looking closely at some twin-cam American Miller racers, Ettore had at last gone over to that form of valve gear in this car. From the Monza Alfa Romeo stemmed the invincible Tipo B, P3 or *monoposto* Alfa Romeo, call it what you will. This was a genuine, though rather wide, single-seater, using Vittorio Jano's Monza engine which

Above left: a classic design unclothed: the 1927 Bugatti Type 35B is a masterpiece of engineering and, even without its bodywork, is one of the world's most instantly recognisable racing cars. The car is powered by a 2.3-litre, supercharged, straight-eight engine and features the distinctive Bugatti, alloy-spoked, wheels

Above: the 1931 Bugatti Type 51 was a logical progression from the 35B and in this car Ettore Bugatti finally adopted twin overhead camshafts. In 1931 it raced to victory in Monaco, Montlhéry, Spa, Tunis, Morocco and Czechoslovakia and maintained its domination for two more years, until Alfa Romeo and Maserati finally brought their efforts to fruition
(Donington Collection)

Below: Vittorio Jano's masterpiece was the Alfa Romeo P3, a direct descendant of his Monza design. The P3 was technically very sophisticated, using twin propeller shafts, to allow a lower seating position, and a chassis-mounted differential to reduce the unsprung weight. The car was virtually invincible
(Donington Collection)

Below right: the adjustable friction dampers of the P3 and one of the huge, finned brake drums
(Donington Collection)

had, along the years, been increased in size from 2.3 to 2.6 litres. The chassis, at first sprung on half-elliptic leaf springs, was only 26 in wide and was swept up compactly over the back axle. The clever thing about the *monoposto* Alfa Romeo was its transmission. Jano used twin propeller shafts, splayed out thirty degrees from a chassis-mounted differential, that was itself behind the gearbox. By doing this, he was able to sit the driver lower than in other racing cars where the seat was above the single propeller shaft. There were other advantages, too. The twin prop shafts with a drive on the chassis meant that, if the gear-ratios had to be altered quickly to suit a given race, they could be conveniently changed without stripping the back axle. Even better, by putting the differential unit up on the sprung chassis, unsprung weight on the back axle was reduced, with a beneficial effect on rear-wheel adhesion over bumps. Unfortunately the twin-bevel drives in this clever design made the axle somewhat heavier than if a single final drive had been used.

As the P3 Alfa Romeo was improved further over the years, it became one of the most famous racing cars of all time. The gear drive to the twin overhead-camshafts was taken up between the two separate cylinder blocks, which enabled the twin superchargers set beside the engine to be easily driven from them. Improvements in lubricants and bearing materials had given Jano faith in plain bearings for mains, big-ends and camshafts. The 2.6-litre engine of the P3 gave 180 bhp at the modest engine speed of 5400 rpm, a further reason why those plain bearings were adequate. In a car which tipped the weighbridge at just over 15 cwt, dry, here was a winner indeed. Moreover, the *monoposto* Tipo B Alfa Romeo was able to stand much development. Over the years its engine was increased to 2.9 and finally to 3.2 litres. It was made to handle better by using Dubonnet independent front suspension and, finally, in the period when the makers had retired from the racing game and *Scuderia Ferrari* was racing these splendid Alfa Romeos, the engine capacity went to as much as 3.8 litres. For a time, reversed quarter-elliptic rear springs were also tried. Nuvolari was able to defeat the German cars (of which more anon) on their home ground with one of these Alfas, at the 1935 Nürburgring German GP, in spite of a refuelling delay. In 1934, 68 × 100 mm, 2905 cc guise, this, the first of the European single-seater road racers, was capable of 145 mph.

The gambit of increasing the size of an engine was then universal. The Maserati which had evolved from the Diatto sports car into a straight-eight 2½-litre GP car by the 1930s, was later enlarged to 2.9 litres and was helped by hydraulic brakes, which Maserati had been quick to adopt around 1933.

Bugatti had gone to 4.9 litres for Formule Libre races, apart from making a fabulous four-wheel-drive sprint car, just as Alfa Romeo made two twin-engined *Bimotore* cars. Maserati also built, in later years, a 4-litre V12 and an earlier twin-six racer. Likewise, Alfa Romeo had, in 1929, put two 2-litre eight-cylinder power units side by side to form a sixteen-cylinder, 4-litre Formule Libre racing car.

All was changed in 1934, by the new 750 kg Formula. This was aimed at preventing the overdose of absolute power which the authorities who governed motor racing felt the free Formula had dangerously encouraged. They reckoned without the strength of Hitlerian Germany. Hitler wanted propaganda through motor racing and was able to divert enough money towards Mercedes-Benz and Auto Union to enable these Companies to produce quite extraordinary racing and record-breaking cars. The employment of expensive light alloys defeated the new maximum-weight ruling, while by mixing fuel-brews of the most advanced nature, enormous power was developed by their big engines, which were at the same time sufficiently light to enable the complete car to pass the weighing-in ceremony. It was a new era of racing, which produced

Right: a picture that tells the story of the German domination of motor racing in the late 1930s. The Mercedes pit crew at the Swiss Grand Prix, at Berne, in 1937 shows their own team cars of Caracciola, Lang and von Brauchitsch in the leading three places, with Stuck – in the rival Auto Union – lying fourth

Below: in the hands of Tazio Nuvolari the 2991 cc, supercharged, eight-cylinder Maserati 8CM became a race winner. The wide lower half of the bodywork complied with the minimum body width requirement of the 1934, 750 kg formula, leaving the upper half in narrow, wind-cheating form. Although the car was very successful, it had a reputation for being extremely difficult to drive and cost several drivers their lives
(Donington Collection)

some of the most exciting cars of all time. They were so light and powerful that only a handful of the most skilled racing drivers could safely unleash them and Hitler (contrary to expectations) had to invite foreigners to drive for him. Englishman Dick Seaman and the top driver of them all, Italy's Tazio Nuvolari were thus signed onto the driving strength.

By now, independent suspension was better understood and softer springing mediums, permitting greater road-wheel movement, were possible, which enabled these great cars to hold the road rather better than the older, harshly sprung, racing cars had done. Even so, the sight and the sound of these new 750 kg-Formula cars were astounding, as were the smell and the eye-watering-propensities of Mercedes-Benz methanol fuel! The cars, especially the rear-engined Auto Unions, tended to oversteer. It took a driver with very quick reactions to cope with this by adding opposite steering-lock and using just the right amount of throttle for the conditions, which varied with every type of corner, road surface, car weight and weather condition. It was truly the Age of Giants – of both men and machines.

In the end, as another war loomed large, the Germans dominated motor

Left: one of the most picturesque circuits ever to be used for Grand Prix racing was at Tripoli, set amidst palm trees and sand dunes. Hermann Lang's Mercedes is seen leading the 1937 event past the impressive pits and control tower

Below right: 'B' Bira in his 3-litre Maserati at the 1939 JCC International Trophy at Brooklands

Below: by 1937 German domination of motor sport was bringing magnificent machinery such as this W125 to the circuits. The 5.66-litre supercharged eight-cylinder engine gave a massive 646 bhp at 5800 rpm, making it the most powerful Grand Prix car of all time

racing. Mercedes-Benz topped everyone else. However, in spite of the enormous amount of finance available and the great armies of mechanics, spares and racing cars that the two Hitler-inspired teams brought to every race, these revolutionary new designs took time to perfect. For a short time, Mercedes-Benz were in trouble technically and Auto Union had the edge over them. The rest – Maserati, Alfa Romeo and Bugatti – did what they could, by opening-out obsolete engines, toying with independent front suspension (except for Bugatti, who was never to adopt it for racing, apart from a slight permitted movement in the centre of the tubular front axle of his last GP cars) and by taking, while they could, the top racing drivers. In the end, Germany gained complete ascendancy, up to the outbreak of war.

Mercedes-Benz quickly developed their W125 until, by 1937, it was the ultimate in the brute force field of thinking, as well as a perfect piece of road-racing machinery. It had, in this form, a Roots-blown, twin-cam engine of 94×102 mm for its eight, in-line cylinders, giving the power unit a swept volume of 5.66 litres. It developed no less than 646 bhp at 5800 rpm, and at only 2000 rpm gave as much power as most of the earlier 1930s racing engines had available at peak revs! Prior to this, Mercedes had raced the W25 cars, which had gained performance by continual increases in engine size. With the know-how they had attained from these, they applied not an independent system but a De Dion rear axle to their W125 chassis. They had already learned how to defeat wheel-spin out of corners by placing the final-drive and differential unit on the chassis frame, thus obviating the lifting of one wheel under torque, as suffered by a beam back axle. Now, they were able to combine this desirable characteristic with driving wheels which remained vertical as they rose and fell over road undulations. This gave them a much better driving force and killed the inherent oversteer of the swing-axle rear independent suspension systems. A skilled driver could now spin the car's wheels to promote oversteer when required, in a car that was otherwise neutral or deliberately set up to understeer. A very rigid chassis of oval tubes was used, in accord with these suspension arrangements, the front wheels being given coil spring and wishbone ifs, while the De Dion back-end used torsion bars. With a sleek aluminium shell of a single-seater body, these W125 Mercedes-Benz were classic cars, able to reach a top speed of some 195 mph, depending on the gearing in use.

Deciding that God is on the side of the Big Battalions, and that a maximum weight limit had entirely failed to hold racing-car speeds down, the authorities brought in a 3-litre maximum engine capacity ruling for 1938. This gave some consolation to the other European racing teams who had almost wilted away under the German onslaught. Even Ettore Bugatti's very handsome 3.3-litre GP car with its piano-wire-spoked wheels, the Type 59, had achieved little, even when given a 3.8-litre engine; Bugatti's last fling before the war centred around a 4.7-litre single-seater, again to no avail. Maserati tried to hold the German supremacy under the new Formula with their 3-litre cars, again without much success, and Alfa Romeo fared little better, although they experimented with three engines of this size: a straight-eight, a V12 and a V16. The last-named gave about 350 bhp, which was no match for the 3-litre Mercedes-Benz cars' 420 bhp. Mercedes achieved this by designing a new 67 × 70 mm, V12 engine of 2.96 litres, that gave the aforesaid power at 7800 rpm. It followed the general specification of the engine used in the W125 Mercedes-Benz, with twin overhead camshafts actuating four valves per cylinder, roller-bearings, Roots supercharging, fixed cylinder heads, and welded steel water-jacketting. An important advance was the employment on the 1939 version of the W154 of two blowers in series, driven from the nose of the crankshaft, to provide two-stage supercharging. One blower fed the other and remarkably high boosts were obtained satisfactorily, to an ultimate 34 psi. The mixture was sucked from the Mercedes-designed carburettor, a system to which they had changed their W125 engines in 1937. The 3-litre W154 in its final form gave 485 bhp at 7000 rpm.

Mercedes-Benz proved themselves masters of racing-car design and construction at this period, just as they had in the past and were to do again. Apart from their significant successes in the Grand Prix field, when the 1939 Tripoli GP was deliberately limited to 1½-litre cars to encourage the Italians (who were on top in *voiturette* racing at the time). Mercedes-Benz very quickly built two cars of this capacity using V8 engines, and won again. The car was designated the Type W165. Its ninety degree vee engine had dimensions of 64 × 58 mm and, from these 1.49 litres, the excellent power output of 260 bhp at 8500 rpm was realised. The twin superchargers, five-speed gearbox and De Dion rear suspension were like those of the full-scale Mercedes-Benz GP cars and, eventually, two-stage supercharging was adopted, when 278 bhp at 8250 rpm was spoken of for this 1½-litre engine.

Going back to the commencement of the 750 kg Formula, Auto Union, who were to oppose the Mercedes-Benz entries throughout the 3-litre Formula up to the outbreak of war, used a completely different approach. Dr Ferdinand Porsche had been encouraged by Hitler to design world-beating racing and record cars and, as he was engaged in giving Hitler his 'Peoples' Car' in the guise of the rear-engined Volkswagen, he put the engine of the Auto Union at the back. It was a very different proposition from that in a VW, however, being at first a V16, supercharged, 6006 cc power-pack developing a rumoured 600 bhp, and driving through a five-speed gearbox. This was enough to cower the opposition from the start, as stories of the fabulous performance of these secretly constructed P-wagons on early tests, in March 1934, filtered to the rest of Europe and to Britain. Dr Porsche had provided all-round independent suspension for his new racer, using trailing arms and torsion bars at the front (with which every VW Beetle owner will be familiar) and swing axles and torsion bars at the back. The chassis was made up of tubular members, the main tubes of which conveyed the cooling water from the nose radiator to the engine (and which tended to leak), and the engine had a central camshaft and push-rods to operate the inclined overhead valves. These A-type Auto Unions – the name was based on the Audi, Wanderer, Horch and DKW amalgamation – were difficult cars to drive. Their swing axles led to oversteer which was aggravated by the big 6-litre engine in the tail. However, while Mercedes-Benz sorted out their new straight-eight, 32-valve racers, Auto Union got their cars home first in a number of races.

For the 3-litre Formula, Auto Union put in De Dion rear suspension and

Top: the Bugatti type 59 first appeared in 1933 with a 2.8-litre engine, subsequently enlarged to 3.3 and 4.7-litres. This was the last Bugatti racing car produced in any quantity, and despite wins at Spa and Algiers the works cars were sold to private owners at the end of 1934

Above: the supercharged V12 Mercedes W154 developed 420 bhp and won five Grands Prix in 1938. Auto Union, the chief rival, scored two

Above right: the original 4.4 litre V16 Auto Union A type Grand Prix car of 1934, the development of which was fostered by the German Government

used a 65 × 75 mm, V12 engine, with two-stage Roots supercharging and inclined overhead valves, worked from triple overhead camshafts. The engine was still mounted behind the driver, but in this model the wheelbase was two inches shorter than in the C-type cars, at 9 ft 4 in, and the cockpit was further aft. Even so, it took Nuvolari, soon to be *the* crack Auto Union pilot, some time to get used to the handling characteristics of this 3-litre, 185 mph car which gave him 400 bhp at 7000 rpm to control, which was not surprising since the daring driver could provoke wheel-spin at 150 mph on a dry road.

Before we leave these outstanding contributions to motor-racing history, let us note down the principal engineers responsible for each car. They were as follows.

Mercedes-Benz: W25, Nibel and Wagner;
                   W125, Max Seiler, Wagner, Hess and Uhlenhaut;
                   W163, Wagner and Hess, under Dr Seiler;
Auto Union: A-type, Dr Ferdinand Porsche and Adolf Rosenberger;
                   B-type, Dr Ferdinand Porsche;
                   C-type, Dr Ferdinand Porsche;
                   D-type, Dr Werner, Dr Feuereisen and Professor Eberan von Eberhorst.

While all this intense top-formula work was going on, with the most exciting cars and racing of all time, the *voiturette* class had not been neglected. Raymond Mays had been instrumental in creating the ERA – its initials stood for English Racing Automobile – by using a supercharged, six-cylinder, short-push rod engine, based on that of the Riley Six, and a high 'cart-sprung' chassis, designed by the land-speed-record engineer, Reid Railton, to take a single-seater body. In 1½-litre form, these ERAs, which were sold to private owners, were decently successful. However, Dick Seaman had a 1927 straight-eight Delage, developed to give a reliable 195 bhp which, by virtue of needing fewer stops for refuelling, could beat the works ERAs. The Continental opposition came from 1½-litre Maserati and Alfa Romeo cars, but these were to have a greater importance after the war. Had hostilities not intervened, some very interesting 1½-litre racing must have resulted, because Auto Union were known to be working on a car to compete against the W165 Mercedes-Benz. It was thought to be capable of giving 327 bhp at a rousing 9000 rpm from a V12 of 53 × 56 mm bore and stroke, using a higher compression ratio, in conjunction with supercharging, than Mercedes-Benz had yet dared try.

THE RACES: 1914-39

Although World War I stopped European and British motor racing, it did see some of the valuable lessons of competition converted into effective aeroplane engines, at first by Mercédès and then later by Rolls-Royce and others. Until America became involved in the hostilities, it was able to continue an indulgence for the world's fastest sport. There was, however, still a strong European flavour, even across the Atlantic, because many successful pre-war Grand Prix cars were shipped there to continue their track careers. The Peugeot and Sunbeam 1914 Grand Prix cars appeared in the USA, and Ralph de Palma, the great American driver, secured one of the 1914 French GP-winning 4½-litre Mercédès racers. With the Peugeot, Dario Resta won many titles in 1915 and 1916, but de Palma took the important 500-mile race on the oval Indianapolis track (a race which started in 1911) in 1915 at an average of 89.8 mph; he also set the fastest lap at 98.6 mph.

Four 1914 GP Delages arrived for the 1916 Indy 500, but this was won, in the absence of the Mercédès, by Resta's Peugeot which averaged 83.26 mph for 300 miles, at which point rain stopped play. The Mercédès/Peugeot but de Palma also changed to the Mercédès, to win at Omaha.
rivalry, originating at Lyons in the eve-of-war Grand Prix, was continued at the Chicago board-track for the 300 Mile Chicago Derby which ended in a victory for Resta's Peugeot at 98.6 mph when, right at the end, after four hours of intense battling, a plug cut out on the Mercédès and the car was forced into the pits. Incidentally, the Peugeot proved able to lap at 109 mph.

These Henry-designed cars won many other American war-time triumphs, but de Palma also changed to the Mercédès, to win at Omaha, averaging

Howdy Wilcox won the Indy in 1919 with a 1914 4½-litre Peugeot, now privately entered, at 87.95 mph. One of M. Ballot's new, Henry-designed, straight-eight cars, built in remarkably quick time, was taken to Indy by René Thomas where he set fastest lap at a record 104 mph.

A varied assortment of pre-war, Henry-engineered Peugeots turned up when the Targa Florio was run over Sicilian mountain roads late in November 1919, with the 2½-litre car of André Boillot leading the team. The Targa was a punishing race over atrocious road surfaces, but André triumphed, although he crossed the finish line backwards because spectators had run onto the course and caused him to spin under braking. It was M. Ballot, however, who advised him to drive back down the course, turn around and finish with his car facing the proper way in case of disqualification. After this, it is said, Boillot collapsed over the steering wheel and cried 'C'est pour la France'. His car had been off the road six times but he had averaged 34.19 mph for the 268 eventful miles.

With racing on the Continent moribund through 1920, it was at Indianapolis where the action returned. The Americans had now imposed a 3-litre engine capacity limit, so new straight-eight, twin-cam Ballots had been built, ready

Far left: the engine of the C type Auto Union, a 6.1-litre, 520 bhp, supercharged V16 which produced enormous low-speed torque. It was said that wheelspin could be provoked at 150 mph on a dry road

Left: with the change of formula for 1938, Auto Union produced a supercharged 3-litre V12 engine for the new D type chassis

Above: the ERA B type, number R10 of 1935. This car belongs to Jack Williamson who raced the car in its early days; his son Jonty campaigns the car in vintage events today

Below: André Boillot, younger brother of Georges, in a 2.5-litre Peugeot of 1914 at the start of the 1919 Indianapolis 500 Miles race. Tyre trouble precluded success

for the résumption of Grand Prix road racing; at Indy, they met the straight-eight Duesenbergs. The Ballots were fast, with de Palma's car dominating practice. However, in the race, his car caught fire and then ran out of petrol. The race was, however, won by another 'Henry crib', in the form of a Monroe, the engine of which was outwardly the same as a 1913, 3-litre Peugeot. The Monroe was driven by Gaston Chevrolet and averaged 88½ mph for the 500 miles; de Palma and the Ballot had to be content with fastest lap, at 99.15 mph. Thus, for the time being, a four-cylinder engine had triumphed over the new, small multi-cylindered units.

Racing resumed its former significance in 1921, with the return of the French Grand Prix, run to the same 3-litre formula as Indianapolis. Firstly, however, the Americans had their traditional Indy 500 again and this time the straight-eight motor car was in the ascendant. However, Tommy Milton's Frontenac, yet another crib of a four-cylinder Henry-type engine, won, at 88.16 mph, from half-a-dozen eights, three Ballots and three Duesenbergs. After this, it was to the Grand Prix, run at Le Mans over a course that was soon a sea of jagged stones, that attention was directed. Inspired by what it had done during the war, America decided to go for the road-racing 'blue riband', and sent over their left-hand-drive, three-speed, straight-eight Duesenberg cars, with hydraulic four-wheel brakes.

The state of the course, which used part of the pre-war circuit, was most unfortunate, as much work had been done to prevent dust, and to bind the surface. However, puncture-promoting flying stones did not stop Jimmy Murphy from beating the European runners, his Duesenberg finishing the 322 miles with its driver bruised and dirty and the car's straight-eight engine ready to seize after a piece of rock had holed the radiator. Nevertheless, Murphy was comfortably ahead of the Ballots of de Palma and Jules Goux. It was a convincing victory, in a race mostly of trouble for the Ballot and STD cars. The winner had averaged 78.10 mph and achieved fastest lap at 84 mph. Of the rest of this first post-war GP field, Guyot, Dubonnet and Joe Boyer made up the four-car Duesenberg team; Mathis drove a tiny Mathis more to demonstrate than race it; Guinness, René Thomas, Segrave and André Boillot drove the Anglo-French STD (or Talbot-Darracq) straight-eights and Chassagne and Wagner had the remaining Ballots. Boyer retired with a seized big-end bearing, because, like Murphy, he had had a stone puncture the car's radiator which let out all the cooling water; Chassagne went out when the bolster fuel tank of his hastily prepared TD came loose; Guyot had a slipping clutch and a difficult-to-restart engine; and the STD entries were continually changing wheels due to defective tyres. Incidentally, Murphy had had the rigours of his great ride made more severe because he was driving with broken ribs.

This was an interesting commencement of post-war road racing, even if a devastating one for the European entrants. Fiat had entered but had non-started in this Grand Prix, and any hope of the Duesenbergs being matched against the new Italian cars at Brescia was dispersed by the news that they were returning to America. In this 3-litre contest, the Ballots at last came into their own for, although the Fiats were quicker and Bordino's made fastest lap, it was now the Fiat's turn to be delayed by tyre troubles. So, Goux's Ballot won, at 89.9 mph, from Chassagne's similar car, which was one mile per hour slower; Wagner's Fiat was a poor third.

For 1922, the governing body of the sport brought in a 2-litre engine-capacity limit, which meant that all the carefully conceived designs had to be scrapped and new ones worked out. The French Grand Prix was taken to a fast circuit at Strasbourg in 1922, where the local authorities were so keen to host the race that they contributed Fr350,000 towards the organisational expenses. The new ruling evolved the slowest and dullest racing cars for some time, with only Bugatti and Rolland-Pilain staying with straight-eight units. Sunbeam had the celebrated Ernest Henry design new four-cylinder, sixteen-valve, power units for them, but it was Fiat, with their sixes, who were the successful entrants. The wealthy Count Louis Zborowski was anxious to get into real motor racing and was sponsoring Aston Martins with twin-cam

Henry-pattern engines (it would be fair to say that Henry dominated racing-engine design during this period) but they were 1½-litre cars, and hence out-classed. Zborowski, however, had realised his ambition, but was to die for it two years later after having survived the Chitty-Chitty-Bang-Bang escapades at Brooklands without injury.

The Grand Prix, over a triangular course, started at 8.15 am, spectators being keen enough to rise early for their sport in those far-away days; they were to see both triumph and tragedy. Triumph, when the veteran driver Felice Nazzaro brought his Fiat home the winner, at 79.2 mph for the 500 miles, after he had been driving for 6 hrs 17 mins 17 secs, and tragedy because these Fiats had weak back-axle shafts. When one broke and let a wheel detach itself on Felice's nephew's car, the young Biaggio Nazzaro was killed. The third Fiat also suffered this alarming malady but Bordino, who had driven very fast in the opening stages of the race, survived. Thus, what would have been a Fiat 1-2-3 walkover was a lone and hollow victory for 'old-man' Nazzaro. Behind him, a long way back, two of the Bugattis, driven by de Viscaya and Marco, unexpectedly found themselves in second and third places. Another Bugatti, handled by Maury, finished outside the time limit; every other starter retired, the Sunbeams dropping out with valve-stem faults. So ended a dull Grand Prix that Bordino was apparently intended to win, and which his team-mate Nazzaro had walked away with (at mostly 4100 rpm and never exceeding 4500 rpm).

The rapidly built Monza Autodrome was used in 1922 for the 2-litre European Grand Prix and supporting 1½-litre Italian GP. Because the organisers were able to charge all spectators admission-fees, and 150,000 of them are said to have attended, it was possible to award prize money amounting to the equivalent of some £6000. A dismally dull race was run off in a drizzle of rain, with the Fiats dominating a miserable field of eight: everyone else was entirely outclassed. Bordino won from Nazzaro, averaging 86.9 mph, with the only other car still motoring at the end being de Viscaya's Bugatti which was flagged off. It is, however, interesting that Maserati had started in a Diatto, which he had driven so fiercely that he crashed and wrote it off.

Mercédès returned to racing in the 1922 Targa Florio. Moreover, their cars were supercharged. Ironically, it was Masetti who was the victor, driving a much revamped 1914 GP Mercédès, of the kind that had proved invincible at Lyons on the eve of war. Behind him, Jules Goux drove a great race to take second place in a 2-litre, twin-cam, four-cylinder Ballot, more a sports car than a racer. The Frenchman had had victory snatched from him because loss of brakes had caused him to crash and he had to complete that last, long Sicilian lap with a bent chassis and very bald tyres. He finished only 1 min 47 secs behind the Italian in his German 'veteran' Mercédès, however.

Above: the start of the 1919 Indianapolis 500 Miles race. The leading cars here are Packard, Peugeot and Ballot, and the race was won by American Howdy Wilcox in one of the 1914 model Peugeots at 88.05 mph

Below: Jules Goux pictured in 1926, the year he won the French and Spanish Grands Prix for Bugatti. He began racing for Lion-Peugeot in 1907, and won the Indianapolis classic in 1913 in a Grand Prix Peugeot. Goux was regarded as a good long-distance driver, and he excelled in events like the Targa Florio. He joined Bugatti in 1925, and continued to work for that company until 1955

Left: Le Mans in 1921. André Boillet's eight-cylinder Talbot Darracq at White House on its way to fifth place in the French Grand Prix

Right: in the 1922 French Grand Prix at Strasbourg Giulio Foresti's Ballot is chased through Duttlenheim corner by the two-litre, eight-cylinder Bugatti of Pierre de Viscaya, which ultimately finished second

The year 1923 was to see the ACI continue the 2-litre engine-capacity limit, in spite of the retrograde happenings of the previous season. However, things improved and the French Grand Prix, held at Tours, was notable for its big and varied entry. Coatalen, of Sunbeam, as was his wont, had secured the services of the Fiat engineers, and his cars resembled nothing so much as the previous year's highly successful Fiats, but painted British racing green instead of Italian red! They had the same unblown, six-cylinder, twin-cam layout that had recently carried Bordino and Nazzaro to such great success. Henry Segrave had, by now, become an accepted driver in the STD racing team and it might be thought that he would have easily won the GP at Tours. It was not quite so easy as that but, when the faster supercharged straight-eight Fiats had trouble with stones and dust, making short work of their new-fangled blowers, Segrave did in fact manage to win. He was helped by a clutch that had slipped in the early stages of the race, leaving his engine unstressed, as he could not use maximum revs. The other Sunbeams were having a great deal of trouble: Guinness with his clutch and Divo with a jammed fuel filler-cap that delayed him as he could only continue by putting petrol into a small reserve tank every lap. The Fiat drivers had a bad time, Salamano thinking, from the behaviour of his engine, that he was out of fuel, whereas the blower had quit. His riding mechanic was dispatched for more fuel, but was told he had to run and not borrow a bicycle as he had done. In the midst of all this drama, Segrave realised he had taken the lead. He went on, with his mechanic Dutoit by his side, to win the first Grand Prix to fall to a British-built car although, as has been said, its design was really Italian. Segrave had averaged 75.31 mph, his race-time being 6 hrs 35 mins 19.6 secs. The luckless Divo, French driver of the other green Sunbeam, did not cross the finishing line until 19 mins 6.2 secs later! Following came Friedrich's Bugatti, with its odd tank-like body, and the Guinness Sunbeam, a sick car that lost a further two minutes on the final lap after its engine had stalled. The only other finisher in this 1923 Grand Prix, a race that had opened with such promise, was Lefèbvre, in one of the odd, ultra-streamlined, sleeve-valve Voisins.

In the wake of the open and technically advanced 1923 French Grand Prix was the Italian Grand Prix at Monza. Alfa Romeo had a new P1 model, but it was unfortunately withdrawn after one of the drivers, Sivocci, had been killed in practice – the car was never seen again. Germany had been refused an entry for the French race but produced a revolutionary rear-engined tear-drop-shape Benz for the Italian event. America, in the absence of the

Below : Henry Segrave, 1896–1930, was one of Britain's best drivers of the 1920s. He joined the Sunbeam-Talbot-Darracq works team in 1921 and drove brilliantly in virtually every race he entered. In 1927 he shattered the World Land Speed Record in a 1000 hp, 44.8-litre, aero-engined Sunbeam, travelling at 203.79 mph. Vying with Malcolm Campbell, Segrave raised the record in 1929 to 231.44 mph with his Napier-engined Golden Arrow, for which achievement he received a knighthood. Sir Henry had latterly become interested in speedboats, and died on Lake Windermere when his boat struck a log during record attempts

Bottom : Segrave's victory in the 1923 French Grand Prix was aided by Kenelm Lee Guinness, who drove his Sunbeam flat-out to break the opposition and, when Guinness fell back, Segrave went on to win

Right: the Benz of 1923 anticipated modern Grand Prix design by 35 years, being mid-engined. Here, Minoia's fourth-placed car visits the pits during the Italian Grand Prix; the streamlined body, fitted with side doors, was seen only at this particular race meeting

Below: Veteran Fiat driver Felice Nazzaro, who won three classic races in 1907, took first place in the 1922 French Grand Prix at Strasbourg driving a 2-litre six-cylinder Fiat

Bottom: the supercharged, 2-litre, straight-eight Fiat which Carlo Salamano, wearing the linen helmet, drove to victory at Monza in 1923. Nazzaro was second in a similar car

victorious Duesenbergs, was represented by Indy-type Millers, but they presented little menace to the European cars, which had better gearboxes and brakes more suited to a road circuit. Fiat had at last got their superchargers functioning properly and fielded a team of three effective cars, to be handled by Bordino, Salamano and the ageing Felice Nazzaro. Bordino broke his arm in a practice crash but insisted on competing, with his riding mechanic doing the gear-changing for him. The Fiats were the vastly superior cars on the course but, in the race, Bordino had to confess that he could not continue, due to fatigue. Salamano and Nazzaro finished in the first and second positions, the former having averaged over 91 mph and set a new Monza lap-record of 99.8 mph. Third place went to America, with Jimmy Murphy's Miller; he was followed in by two of the unconventional streamlined Benz projectiles.

In *voiturette* racing, the revised supercharged Darracqs (or Talbot-Darracqs)

Below: Monza 1923, and the two leading supercharged eight-cylinder Fiats of Salamano and Nazzaro pass the Benz of Minoia

Left: programme cover for the 1924 Brooklands 200 Miles Race, which was won by Kenelm Lee Guinness in a Darracq. For the first time silencers were fitted to appease local residents

Far left: Malcolm Campbell's supercharged Fiat expires in the Brooklands pits during the 1923 200 Miles Race. Salamano, with goggles, whose Fiat also retired, looks at the engine

maintained their 'invincible' reputation but so feared the new blown 1½-litre Fiats that they abstained from running in the Junior Car Club's 200 Mile Race at Brooklands in October 1923. The irony of this was that soon after both Fiats retired with dramatic mechanical failures. Salamano and Malcolm Campbell had not expected this, and a track-racing 12/50 Alvis, based on the well liked Alvis sports chassis, won instead. This shows how supercharging was now dominating both classes of motor-racing, for the 1923 Italian Grand Prix had been the first International race to be won by a supercharged car.

The racing season of 1924 opened with the Targa Florio and was won by a 2-litre 1923-pattern Mercédès improved in detail by Dr Porsche. Alfa Romeo had their effective new P2 racers ready for the Cremona event and their obvious superiority in this race, which Ascari won at a speed of over 98 mph, being timed at 123 mph for ten kilometres, must have made the Milan concern feel very confident about the forthcoming French Grand Prix at Lyons. Once they arrived there, however, they discovered that the 1923-type Sunbeams, which now had supercharged engines, were the faster cars. Rumour has it that this was so obvious that the Alfa Romeo personnel offered to let

Sunbeam win, without harassing the new cars from Wolverhampton, if they would, in turn, allow Alfas to come home in second and third places. Whether or not this was true, it seems that Louis Coatalen would have refused and that the great French race was as much an open battle as ever. In fact, Sunbeam chose to change to new German magnetos on the eve of the contest and, as a result, suffered from chronic misfiring. Thus, the newly evolving great P2 straight-eight supercharged Alfa Romeo had the considerable distinction of winning the most important motor race of the year on its first appearance there. The driver to pull this off was the portly opera singer Campari, at an average speed of 71 mph. The V12 Delage cars of Albert Divo and Robert Benoist followed the winning Italian home. Segrave in one of the stuttering Sunbeams had to make do with fastest lap, at 76.7 mph; the Bugatti drivers had lost out with continual tyre trouble and the Fiat pilots with braking maladies.

The circus – although it was not called this in 1924 – then moved to Monza for the Italian Grand Prix, which Alfa Romeo absolutely dominated while, in San Sebastian, Sunbeam had, to some extent, atoned for their French Grand Prix disappointment by Segrave's success there. However, while Henry Segrave had had a tough time winning in Spain, Zborowski had been killed driving one of the unpredictable straight-eight 2-litre Mercédès cars at Monza, leaving Clive Gallop to bring the Count's body back to England and disband the great stable of racing cars at Higham, much to the detriment of racing at Brooklands.

Everywhere, the increasing cost of racing was causing manufacturers to wonder if they could afford to continue to participate and drivers to question whether the low prize money made it worth their while continuing this risky profession. One solution seemed to be to concentrate on racing at specialised circuits, where maximum admission money could be extracted from the spectators, which it was not always possible to do at a closed-public-road course where the spectators were scattered about. Thus, the 1925 French Grand Prix was run over the combined track and road circuit at Montlhéry, where high attendance figures were expected.

It was not a particularly impressive affair, however. It began as an Alfa Romeo/Delage procession, with Antonio Ascari ahead of his team-mate Campari but, after setting up the best lap speed of 80 mph, the experienced Alfa Romeo driver who was in the lead, somehow misjudged a long fast bend and his car tangled with the wood-paling fencing and overturned in the ditch. When the news reached the circuit that Ascari had died in the ambulance, the other Alfa Romeo cars were withdrawn, as a mark of respect, and Delage, next in the lead with Benoist and Divo, gained a rather hollow victory, at 69.7 mph, with a Sunbeam in third place, followed by a host of Bugattis. Prior to this, Bugatti, with an unsupercharged engine, had won the Targa Florio and the European Grand Prix had been run off at the Spa road course in

Top: the Robert Benoist/Albert Divo 2-litre V12 Delage pursues a Bugatti, passing close to the edge on its way to victory at Montlhéry, Paris, in 1925 Grand Prix. In this race Antonio Ascari caught his Alfa Romeo's hubcap on the chestnut fencing and was killed when the car overturned into the ditch

Above: Giuseppe Campari, who gave Alfa Romeo their first racing victory in 1920 at Mugello. He owned one of the P2 Alfas which he raced independently, winning the European Grand Prix of 1924. Campari also drove works sports cars, winning the 1928 mille Miglia; he was killed in an Alfa P3 at Monza in 1933

Right: the Le Mans 24-hour race, 1924. This was the first time the classic was won by British drivers; here the John Duff/Frank Clement 3-litre Bentley races an Alfa Romeo at Mulsanne

Belgium, resulting in another 1-2 Alfa Romeo P2 success, Ascari winning at 74.56 mph, after the Delage entry had retired.

By now the greatest credit was due to Alfa Romeo, for their success with their beautiful P2 racers, but this made racing rather monotonous. For example, they had very little difficulty in winning the Italian GP at Monza, the No 1 driver in the team on this occasion being Count Brilli-Peri but at the end of this 1925 season, Delage won at San Sebastian only because the P2 Alfa Romeos were absent.

In 1926, however, the new 1½-litre Formula appeared. This marked the beginning of a Delage domination as great of that of Alfa Romeo's in the preceeding season – but not at first, however. Bugatti was by now reaping the benefit of outstanding roadholding and reliability and this enabled Jules Goux to win the French Grand Prix at the dull Marimas oval but, as the only runners were all in Bugattis, this race came to be known as the most ineffectual French Grand Prix of all time. Indeed, this impossibly dull race which was 500 kilometres in length, had only Goux as a finisher, the other two Bugattis having retired. He averaged a mere 68 mph, driving alone for the final fifty miles. The Talbots were unprepared for the European Grand Prix at San Sebastian, and, as the new straight-eight Delage cars were still addicted to roasting their drivers, it was Goux and the Bugatti that won again. The Delage cars had been stationary for something like an hour during this race but eventually the Bourlier/Sénéchal car was able to make up for lost ground and finish second, with Costantini, whose Bugatti developed last-minute trouble, in third place. This strongly reflected on the wide spacing of GP cars of that time and on the patience of the 1926 spectators. Racing was enlivened, nevertheless, by a 'free-for-all' ruling that prevailed for the Spanish Grand Prix, which enabled Segrave to run with a 4-litre V12 Land Speed Record-type Sunbeam and for 2.3-litre Bugattis to mingle with the 1½-litre and 2-litre cars. However, Segrave's front axle caved-in and the Delage entries also struck trouble so a Bugatti won again, with Costantini finishing ahead of Goux, at a speed of 76.8 mph for the 374½ miles.

The 1927 season was again for 1½-litre cars in the nature of a triangular battle between Delage, Talbot and Bugatti, with the emphasis on the superb little straight-eight Delages. Indeed, the experienced Robert Benoist, who lost his life in World War II working for the French resistance movement, won four of the 1927 *grandes epreuves*. He was first to receive the finishing flag in the French GP at Montlhéry, in the Spanish GP run at San Sebastian, and in the European GP at Monza, while he led the British Grand Prix, which was run at Brooklands Track over a course made into a parody of a road circuit by the use of a few sand-bank chicanes. Delage had managed to win this race the previous year in spite of their cockpit overheating, but it had required two drivers with Sénéchal helping out Wagner on that occasion, and, whereas the average speed had been 71.61 mph, Benoist averaged 85.59 mph for the 1927

race. Bugatti decided not to compete in either the French or Italian (European) Grands Prix, and it is typical of Delage superiority that only one of these cars was run in the latter race, with which Benoist made the fastest lap at 94.31 mph, winning easily at just over 90 mph for 50 laps of a wet course. Fiat managed to win just one race, the Milan GP run at Monza, on an identical circuit to the European GP, with their odd twelve-cylinder twin-crankshaft concoction, which was entrusted to Bordino.

Racing after 1927 became more complicated. Many new events were instituted and this, together with the free-engine-size formula resulted in a situation whereby sports cars mingling with pure racing machines competed for different honours. Picking out some of the more significant events, there was that notorious occasion in the 1928 Targa Florio when Mme. Junek was ahead of all the male drivers for a time, until her Bugatti finally dropped back, leaving Albert Divo's 2.3-litre Bugatti in the lead.

1928 also saw the emergence of Tazio Nuvolari, who is regarded by many authorities as the greatest and most versatile racing driver of all time. That year his Bugatti took first place at Alessandria in a race called the Bordino

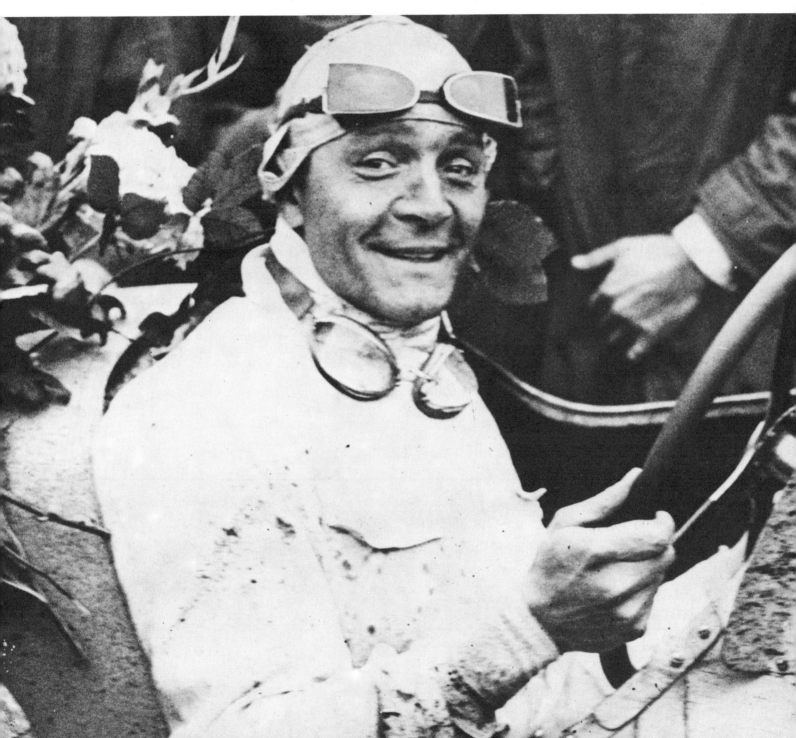

Left: car No 15 is a 1½-litre, twelve-cylinder Fiat Tipo 806, the last of the racing Fiats, with which Pietro Bordino won the 1927 Milan Grand Prix at Monza. Talking to Bordino is Felice Nazzaro

Right: from the cockpit of a Bugatti, following a Delage and a Sunbeam

Top: William Grover-Williams, who raced as Williams and was domiciled in France. He owned and raced Bugattis, and won the first Monaco Grand Prix in 1929. Williams joined the SAS during world War II, but was shot by the Gestapo in 1943

Above: the great Achille Varzi, who grew up with Nuvolari on racing motor cycles. The pair began racing Bugattis, but Varzi, feeling outshone, bought an Alfa Romeo P2 and enjoyed a great run of successes, culminating in the 1930 Targo Florio. From 1931–1934 Varzi returned to Bugatti, beating Nuvolari's Alfa P3, winning seven races, and the Mille Miglia. In 1935 he went to Auto Union and won his first race at Tripoli. After World War II he rejoined the Alfa Romeo team but at Berne in 1948, he was killed when his Tipo 158 overturned

Prize, after Pietro Bordino. Louis Chiron, the volatile French ace, won the 1928 Rome, Marne and San Sebastian Grands Prix for Bugatti and clinched a fine successful racing season by taking first place in the European Grand Prix at Monza, at a speed of just under 100 mph. Arcangelli, who competed in a revised edition of the 1927 Talbot, was a fast challenger, and he won the Circuit of Cremona race at the high speed of 101.31 mph. He also set fastest lap, at 103.2 mph, at Monza while a Talbot driven by Materassi won at Montenero. The German Grand Prix, held at the Nürburgring, was nominally a sports-car contest. However, this arduous race was won by Rudi Caracciola in a 7-litre Mercedes-Benz at a speed of 64.6 mph, with two similar cars following him home, having vanquished the road-equipped Type 35 Bugattis, which would normally have been expected to out-handle the big and heavy Mercedes cars on this mountainous circuit. Count Brilli-Peri was now Bugatti-mounted, but could only average a speed of 62.2 mph. Altogether, 1928 was very much a Bugatti year, with drivers of the calibre of Chiron, Nuvolari and Caracciola much in evidence.

The trend continued in 1929. The International season commenced with

a new, but now very respected street circuit race, at Monaco. It was won by the French-domiciled Englishman, W. Grover-Williams, in a Bugatti, at 50.23 mph, giving the well established professionals a nasty shock, as he made the fastest lap of this winding circuit, where drivers wore their hands to blisters continually changing gear, at 52.7 mph. The pending Alfa Romeo/Bugatti duelling was forecast when Achille Varzi, a dour driver who was to become an arch-rival of Nuvolari's, took the Bordino Prize at Alessandria at 68.24 mph, lapping a little faster than his average speed for the race. Divo again won the Targa Florio, over the Little Madonie circuit; his Bugatti averaged 46.21 mph

for his trip over the Sicilian mountains; driving adjacent to ravines, over stones and around hairpin bends. His car caught fire, until his mechanic used a cushion to quell the flames but he still managed to exceed his earlier speed of 45.65 mph. Minoia in another Bugatti could not get above 47.3 mph when establishing a new lap-record for this unique course. The Rome Grand Prix fell to Varzi's Alfa Romeo but Williams retaliated for Bugatti by winning the French Grand Prix at 82.66 mph. The fast Cremona Prize contest went to Brilli-Peri and Alfa Romeo. The pace rose to 114.41 mph, with Maserati in a car of his own manufacture making best lap (a record) at 124.4 mph. Held at Reims in the Champagne country, Phi-Phi Etancelin won the Marne GP for Bugatti at 85½ mph and the great Chiron, waving to the crowd, even managed a Bugatti victory at the German Grand Prix, around the Nürburgring, averaging

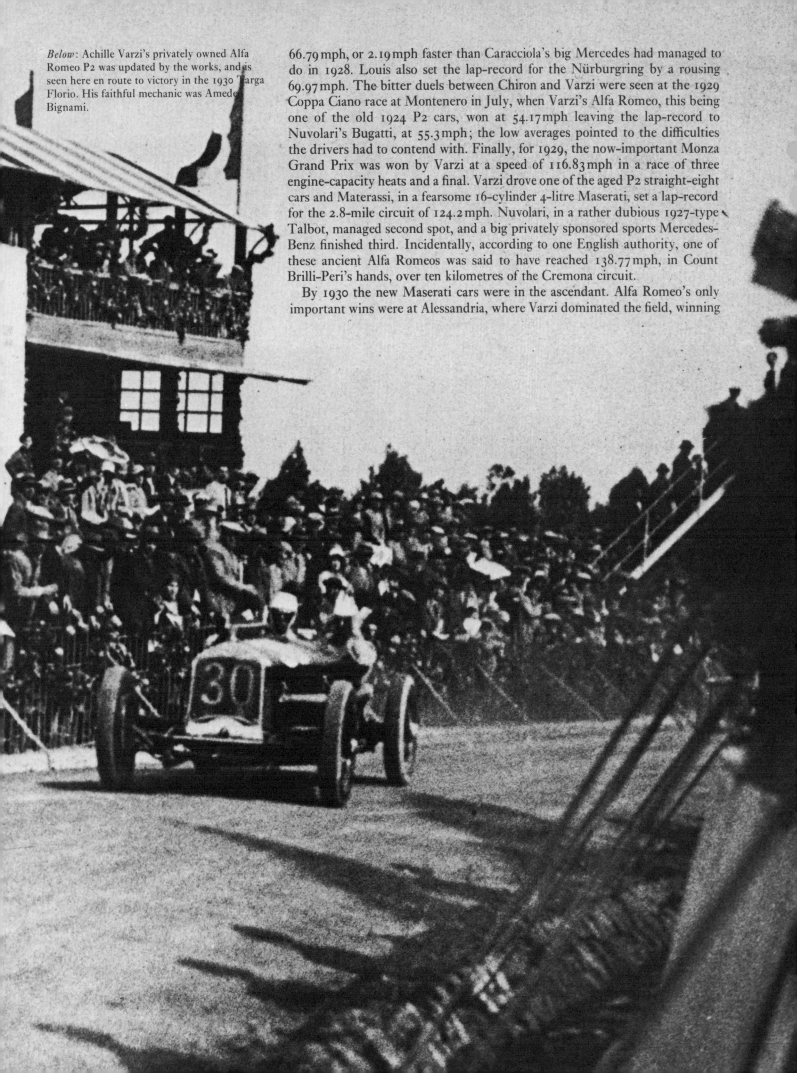

Below: Achille Varzi's privately owned Alfa Romeo P2 was updated by the works, and is seen here en route to victory in the 1930 Targa Florio. His faithful mechanic was Amedeo Bignami.

66.79 mph, or 2.19 mph faster than Caracciola's big Mercedes had managed to do in 1928. Louis also set the lap-record for the Nürburgring by a rousing 69.97 mph. The bitter duels between Chiron and Varzi were seen at the 1929 Coppa Ciano race at Montenero in July, when Varzi's Alfa Romeo, this being one of the old 1924 P2 cars, won at 54.17 mph leaving the lap-record to Nuvolari's Bugatti, at 55.3 mph; the low averages pointed to the difficulties the drivers had to contend with. Finally, for 1929, the now-important Monza Grand Prix was won by Varzi at a speed of 116.83 mph in a race of three engine-capacity heats and a final. Varzi drove one of the aged P2 straight-eight cars and Materassi, in a fearsome 16-cylinder 4-litre Maserati, set a lap-record for the 2.8-mile circuit of 124.2 mph. Nuvolari, in a rather dubious 1927-type Talbot, managed second spot, and a big privately sponsored sports Mercedes-Benz finished third. Incidentally, according to one English authority, one of these ancient Alfa Romeos was said to have reached 138.77 mph, in Count Brilli-Peri's hands, over ten kilometres of the Cremona circuit.

By 1930 the new Maserati cars were in the ascendant. Alfa Romeo's only important wins were at Alessandria, where Varzi dominated the field, winning the Bordino Prize race at 67.7 mph after he had lapped at the record speed of 70.7 mph and in the Targa Florio, which he won at 48.48 mph, again making a record lap speed of 49.1 mph. Once more, this was a staggering demonstration of the endurance of the old P2 Alfa Romeo, even though they had been modified for 1930 conditions and challenges. The Type 35 2.3-litre Bugattis were in the next two places. A private owner, René Dreyfus, had scored in the 1930 Monaco Grand Prix in his Bugatti, a Type 35C, at 64.63 mph, which was a very fine speed for this winding course. The new straight-eight 2½-litre Maserati had quickly come into its own, taking Arcangeli to victory at Rome, when Chiron's Bugatti failed right at the end, and Maserati cars gave wins to Fagioli in the Coppa Ciano and to Varzi at San Sebastian. Not only that; at Monza, Varzi drove a magnificent race to win the Monza GP in a 2½-litre car of this new make, having passed both Arcangeli, who was leading in a Maserati of the same type, and Maserati's own V16-engined model. Etancelin took the French GP for Bugatti, at Pau, with Birkin behind him in a stripped blower 4½ Bentley sports-car. Clearly, Alfa Romeo needed the new Monza and monoposto cars, for the aged P2 chassis could no longer stand up to the tuned engines

which were used in them. With the advent of Maserati, a new star had arisen, for the drivers to steer towards.

All thoughts of a Formula to control design had gone overboard by 1931, but it was stipulated that Grand Prix races should last for ten hours. This meant that two drivers would usually be nominated for each car and gave rise not only to an increased necessity for pit-work but to a new headache for team managers in deciding whether or not to take a top-ranking driver out of a disabled car and allow him to take the place, in one of their fitter vehicles, of a slower driver. It was an interesting though not enthralling period of racing; one of the highlights was the intensifying of the Bugatti–Alfa Romeo duel.

The 1931 season opened with the Targa Florio race, over a new and longer circuit adopted because a land slide had obliterated much of the former course. Chiron had already won the Monaco Grand Prix for Bugatti, who now had his new twin-cam, 160 bhp engine in the excellent and beautiful Type 35 cars. This updated version was designated the Type 51. Alfa Romeo replied with the Monza model and in the Targa Florio, over the Long Madonie course, Nuvolari, driving one of these new cars from Milan, gradually wore down the

Above: the 1931 Italian Grand Prix, at Monza, was won by Nuvolari and Campari in the new 2.3-litre 'Monza' Alfa Romeo, No. 26

Above left: Philippe 'Phi Phi' Etancelin began his racing career in French hill-climbs in 1926 with a Bugatti. His first win was at Reims in 1927, and he went on to achieve very many successes with Alfa Romeo, Maserati, including Le Mans. Enthusiast Etancelin drove a Talbot-Lago in post-war Grands Prix with some high placings, retiring in 1952. He was always distinguishable at the wheel by his reversed cloth cap

Left: the Bugatti of Count Czaykowski is about to be passed by Sir Henry 'Tim' Birkin's stripped-down 4½-litre blower Bentley in the 1930 French Grand Prix

lead established by Varzi's faster Bugatti, to win at 40.3 mph. The low average speed was indicative of the road and weather conditions. Front mudguards were used on Nuvolari's Monza to keep streams of rain water out of the cockpit. Varzi had some consolation in setting fastest lap at a mere 43.8 mph.

The first really big race of the season was the Italian Grand Prix at Monza where strong works teams from Alfa Romeo and Bugatti clashed in full force. Apart from the Monzas, Alfa Romeo had a remarkable new twin-six-cylinder *monoposto*, of 3½-litres, and developing some 200 bhp. This was entrusted to Tazio Nuvolari. It was not as successful as had been hoped; Nuvolari only managed to reach third position, after three out of the ten hours' racing. He then retired but in the later stages of the race he aided the veteran Campari in bringing his Monza home first, at 96.17 mph. Varzi's Type 51 Bugatti had dropped out earlier, while leading, with back axle failure, only four hours into the race. Alfa Romeo also set a new lap record at 105 mph, although this was actually only a very small improvement over the old, 1924, record for the full Monza Autodrome course. A sports Mercedes-Benz was able to take victory at Nürburgring, with Rudolf Caracciola winning at 67.67 mph and then the French Grand Prix, held at the Montlhéry road circuit, saw a resumption of the French/Italian inter-marque rivalry. This time, Bugatti were the victors, Chiron and Varzi, usually great rivals, united for once and won, at an average speed of 78.21 mph.

It had been a good race for the newcomers, Maserati & Luigi Fagioli, driving one of the 2½-litre straight-eight racers that had shown up well in 1930, established the fastest lap, at 85.6 mph, which was a record for this much-used circuit. Indeed, Fagioli had been well placed for four of the ten hours over which this historic title was defended, but he then dropped back with brake maladies. Despite the Maserati's promise, the battle in this race was still very much between the Alfa Romeo and Bugatti cars and a Monza Alfa driven by Campari and Borzacchini finished in second place. Their Monza ran 27 fewer miles in the ten hours of the race than did the winning Bugatti, but then the victorious French car had lost only 10½ minutes at its depot, during just five stops, while the Alfa Romeo spent 24 minutes refuelling and being generally resuscitated.

After this, Bugatti more or less dominated the 1931 season, with victories at Reims, Spa and in Czechoslovakia, the winning drivers being, respectively, Lehoux, Williams, with Count Conelli, and Chiron. At the Nürburgring for the German Grand Prix of 1931, Caracciola in a big, even when stripped, 7-litre Mercedes-Benz sports-car triumphed over all the smaller racing cars, averaging 67.4 mph. Campari's Alfa Romeo won the Coppa Acerbo at 81.68 mph, the lap-record going to Nuvolari, also driving for Alfa Romeo, at 83.4 mph.

The heavy metal got going with a vengeance at Monza for the non-Formula Italian Grand Prix. Run over an abbreviated, 4.3-mile, course, the 14-lap event was a walk-over for the Maseratis which had been enlarged to 3.8-litres for the occasion and finished with Fagioli first and Dreyfus second. The unlimited-capacity contest saw such great cars as the twin-eight, sixteen-cylinder Maserati and the 4.9-litre Type 54 Bugatti locked in combat. The big, 152 mph, Maserati was totally unsuitable for this kind of race and it was Varzi who won bravely with a 4.9-litre Bugatti, at 98.5 mph. Nuvolari set a short-course lap-record of 101¼ mph in a twelve-cylinder Alfa Romeo. From within a field of some of these road-racing giants, the final showed up the superiority of the smaller 2.8-litre Maserati and Fagioli took the honours with victory at 96.6 mph, including the time for a pit-stop to change tyres. Borzacchini was second in a Monza Alfa Romeo, while Nuvolari had to be content with third place in the twelve-cylinder Alfa Romeo. Achille Varzi gave of his best in the dangerous, Type 54 Bugatti but was hampered by bursting tyres.

Whether ten hour Grand Prix races were enjoyable to drivers and spectators is best left to the imagination; one can only wonder for example how Robert Sénéchal felt after bringing one of the old, 1½-litre, eight-cylinder Delage cars home fifth in the French Grand Prix, for he drove the entire ten hour duration himself. He is remembered as the enthusiast who, when the Delage team was in dire trouble with roasted drivers in 1926, leapt onto the track to take over, clad in a gent's natty suit and presumably with no experience of this particular hot-seat.

Fortunes changed in 1932 and Bugatti was out of the running, except for the Czechoslovakian GP which Chiron won at 67.67 mph. Otherwise, it was the season of the P3 *monoposto* Alfa Romeo ably supported by the older model. Honours were divided between Nuvolari and Caracciola, a new addition to the Alfa ranks. Nuvolari won at Monaco at 55.81 mph in the Targa Florio at 49.27 mph, at Monza (for the Italian GP) at 104.13 mph and in the French GP at Reims at 92.26 mph. He also won the Coppa Ciano and Coppa Acerbo races. Caracciola soon settled down in the team and the German driver scored at the Eifel races at Nürburgring, at 70.2 mph, in the German GP over the same demanding circuit at 74.13 mph, and again in the Monza Grand Prix, averaging 110.8 mph. Nuvolari set fastest lap in the latter race at 113.7 mph, which was another record for the Monza course.

The following year, 1933, was one of economic recession, with the German Grand Prix cancelled as a result and Maserati and Bugatti once again racing their Type 51 and 2.9-litre cars, respectively. Moreover, Alfa Romeo retired from racing and their former successes were only slowly retrieved by the Scuderia Ferrari, which, at first, entered modified Monza cars. The race distance demanded by the regulations was reduced to 500 kilometres and the major races of 1933 were the Monaco, French, Belgium, Italian, and the revived Spanish Grands Prix.

Monaco displayed the full drama of the times, with the antagonists, Nuvolari and Varzi engaging in a ferocious battle round and round the town, until Nuvolari's Monza broke a vital oil-pipe and caught fire on the final rush down to the finish. Nuvolari jumped out of the cockpit and sought to push his flaming car over the line but it was Varzi's Type 51 Bugatti that received the victor's laurels, his winning speed being 57.04 mph. Umberto Borzacchini brought a Monza Alfa into second place. It is interesting that, at the insistance of Charles Faroux, the great French motoring journalist, the start at Monaco had been based on a grid assembled on practice times, predating the modern system by many years. It was felt that on this narrow and tortuous circuit it would be unfair to draw the positions out of a hat, as was the usual method. The system made Varzi's victory entirely convincing, but did not come into general use in Europe until 1935.

Bugatti did not manage a win in the French Grand Prix, because his new 3.8-litre racers were not ready. Instead, a host of privately-entered cars of this famous make ran, but they were no match for Campari's 2.9-litre Maserati, which commanded the race and won at 81.52 mph and also set a new lap record for the Montlhéry road-cum-track circuit of 86.6 mph. Out of a dozen Monza Alfa Romeos that started, those of Philippe Etancelin and George Eyston took second and third places, while Nuvolari was so upset over the preparation of his Ferrari-sponsored car that he afterwards changed his alligiance to Maserati. This paid off for the little maestro, because he won the Belgian Grand Prix at the fine Spa road circuit, at 89.23 mph, after breaking the lap record, at 92.33 mph. Varzi was some three minutes behind Nuvolari, in a Bugatti, a close finish for those days, with another Bugatti, handled by Dreyfus third. So the bitter battle between Nuvolari and Varzi continued unabated.

Alfa Romeo managed to win the Targa Florio (Brivio, at 47.56 mph), but at the Coppa Ciano race Maserati was again in the ascendant over the aged Monzas. The same thing might well have happened in the Coppa Acerbo race had not the Scuderia Ferrari been permitted by the Alfa Romeo company to have the use of the new P3 single-seaters. Even so, Nvuolari proved able to out-race them in the Maserati, but he was obliged to come into the pits. Then Campari's P3 Alfa, which had been tailing Nuvolari, retired, so that by virtue of a non-stop run, Fagioli, in his Alfa, was the first past the finish, at an average speed of 88.03 mph, although Nuvolari had broken the old lap record, at 90.4 mph.

This was all a good augury for the remaining important Grand Prix contests. At the Italian event, run over a full fifty laps of the complete Monza Park

Above: Bugatti and Alfa Romeo maintained a fierce duel from 1931 to 1933, and here one of the greatest battles is shown, between Achille Varzi in his type 51 Bugatti (No 10) and Tazio Nuvolari in his Alfa Romeo Monza. This is the start of the 1933 Monaco Grand Prix, in which the tussle continued until Nuvolari's car caught fire just before the finish; he made an attempt to push the Alfa across the line before Varzi caught him, but did not succeed

Right: Tazio Nuvolari, after giving the Alfa Romeo type B 2.6-litre car its first win in the 1932 Italian Grand Prix

circuit, Nuvolari's 2.9-litre Maserati met formidable foes, in Louis Chiron and the wily Luigi Fagioli, both driving P3 Alfas. Nuvolari put up his expected terrific performance, but a burst tyre slowed him down and allowed Fagioli to win, at 108.58 mph. Towards the end, Fagioli lapped at the record pace of 115.82 mph, but Nuvolari the master still finished second, only 0.63 mph slower.

In the afternoon of the same day, the Monza Grand Prix was run, using the short Monza circuit. It was a tragic race, in which oil on a corner cost the lives of Count Czaykowski (Type 54 Bugatti), Guiseppe Campari (Alfa Romeo P3) and Umberto Borzacchini (Maserati 8C). The winner proved to be Lehoux's Bugatti, at 108.99 mph, with a posthumous lap-record, to the credit of the Count at no less than 116.81 mph.

Still to come in 1933 was the Spanish Grand Prix and in this race Ettore Bugatti campaigned his new 2.8-litre cars. The design for these cars led directly to that for the next season's fine 3.3-litre models, but on this initial occasion there was no way that they could equal the performance of the P3 Alfa Romeos, one of which, Chiron's, won at 83.32 mph. However this victory was possible only after Nuvolari, comfortably in the lead for Maserati, had gone off the road into a tree.

During the last two seasons, it had become evident that political factors were creeping into motor racing, which initially had been a contest between nations (the Gordon Bennett races) and later, with quite lucrative money to be earned by the top drivers, had become a means of gaining publicity and improving design for the automobile manufacturers (the French Grands Prix etc). Mussolini was apt to send the Alfa Romeo drivers—and those of other Italian-made motor cars—telegrams before a race, saying in effect, 'Win for Italy'. He had also been known to try to smooth out the rough passage between Nuvolari and Varzi, in the hope of securing further Italian-based successes. Now, with Herr Hitler planning to annex the non-German constituents of Europe, racing took an even more obviously political turn: henceforth Mercedes-Benz and Auto Union were expected to dominate all the major motor races for the prestige of the Nazi régime and Hitler somehow saw to it that enough finance was made available to each of these racing teams for them to conquer all before them (or, more correctly, alongside them).

This they eventually did, with fabulous cars, the like of which, in speed, sight, sound and smell, no-one outside German had previously seen, as they stormed the bastions of European motor-racing circles.

It took time, of course. The first of the new 3.3-litre, independently sprung Mercedes-Benz racing cars and the highly unconventional Auto Union rear-engined projectiles arrived on the scene in 1934, but for the 1934 Monaco race they were not ready. It was pipe-smoking Count Trossi who lapped at record speed for Alfa Romeo, at 59.7 mph, and Guy Moll who won for the same Italian racing stable, in the P3, now of 2.9-litres capacity, averaging 55.86 mph.

Below: Rudi Caracciola, arguably the greatest pre-war racing driver of all, screams past the Montlhéry stand in Mercedes-Benz's first offering for the 750 kg formula in 1934. The Nazi-sponsored W25, with its swing axles and unlimited budget, did not shine in France, however, as the Scuderia Ferrari Alfas stormed to a 1-2-3 victory

The much-feared German onslaught commenced with the Avus race on that fast course near Berlin in May 1934, but after lapping in training at 143 mph Mercedes-Benz decided that their cars were unready and required more work to be done on them. The Auto Unions remained to fight and although two of them retired, leaving Moll to win for Alfa Romeo in a special Scuderia Ferrari car, with faired body and 3.2-litre engine, at an average of 127.56 mph, the inexperienced Momberger came in third for Germany, behind Varzi's Alfa Romeo. Auto Union had lapped fastest, at 140.33 mph.

At the Nürburgring, the writing on the wall received its signature, for in the Eifel races Manfred von Brauchitsch, in one of the new Mercedes-Benz cars, led throughout, followed by the Italian Fagioli in another of the German cars. Fagioli had the edge on Brauchitsch and wanted to lead but he was signalled to let the German driver stay in front. Not liking Nazi orders he stopped, got out of the Mercedes-Benz, and walked away. This let the Auto Union of Hans Stuck, the hill-climb ace, into second place, and the best Chiron could manage for Alfa Romeo was third place, even though the two German cars had needed to stop for fuel and the Alfa Romeos had run non-stop.

Following a walkover for Alfa Romeo in the Penya Rhin GP, the German cars returned to challenge them at Montlhéry for the French Grand Prix in July. However, both Mercedes-Benz and Auto Union ran into countless troubles and left the race to the Italian cars, Chiron, Varzi and Moll carrying out a 1-2-3 drubbing with their Alfas and the new 3.3 Bugattis being completely out-classed. Louis Chiron was the hero of France, having trounced the terrible German opposition, winning at 85.5 mph.

Alfa Romeo then pulled off the Marne GP at Reims at 90.71 mph, Chiron winning and Varzi setting best lap, at 97.65 mph. The great run of success for the P3 Alfa Romeo drivers was on the wane, however. From now on, apart from isolated Bugatti joy at Spa, where Dreyfus won at nearly 87 mph and Brivio, likewise Bugatti-mounted, put the circuit lap record to 96.38 mph, it was German domination all the way. The Bugatti victory was carried out without opposition from either of the German teams after Chrion had overturned his Alfa Romeo and Varzi had broken a piston trying to prove that not only Nuvolari could take lap records. After that, there were only the Bugattis left in the hunt.

Apart from this, the rest of the season made dull reading for any but the German Nazi Party, with Hans Stuck taking the Auto Union first past the flag at the Nürburgring to win the German Grand Prix at 75.14 mph. He set the best lap at a record 79.29 mph in the process. Fagioli made up for his show of nationalistic temperament at Spa, by winning for Mercedes-Benz at Pescara (80.26 mph average) after Moll's Alfa Romeo had increased the lap record to 90.5 mph and then crashed with fatal results. In this race Nuvolari was second in a Maserati and Brivio's Bugatti managed to finish third. Stuck won the Swiss Grand Prix at 87.21 mph for Auto Union, Momberger also showing form by putting the lap record for the course up to 94.42 mph, Brivio's Bugatti was again well up until it needed water. The Italian Grand Prix over the short Monza course was a victory for the Mercédès-Benz of Caracciola and Fagioli at 65.37 mph, with Stuck, troubled by brake weakness, second and an Alfa Romeo third. The German domination was not yet complete, however, for in the Spanish Grand Prix it was Mercedes-Benz drivers Fagioli and Caracciola first and second, but Nuvolari was third for Ettore Bugatti. In the Czech Grand Prix, the final race of this astonishing 1934 season, while Stuck's Auto Union

Below left : a grid-full of Alfa Romeos, Bugattis, Maseratis *et al* line up for a pre-war French road race, the Grand Prix de la Marne at Reims. In the right foreground, by Alfa No. 14, is Tazio Nuvolari who won the 1932 Grand Prix de l'ACF at this circuit – also in an Alfa. It is interesting to note the proximity of the crowd to the track, typical of the period

Below right : Achille Varzi's Alfa Romeo seen at the 1934 German GP at the Nürburgring. In Nuvolari's short absence from the team, he won seven races with this car

trounced Fagioli's Mercedes-Benz, the resolute Tazio Nuvolari, now driving a Maserati, again came home in third position. The winning averages for these two races were 97.13 and 79.21 mph, respectively. Clearly, motor racing was becoming faster and far more exacting and although Germany intended to win, how wise was Hitler to ensure that she had two rival teams in the field!

The remainder of the 1934–36 period is quickly told, for German domination had now been achieved. In 1936 Auto Union played while Mercedes-Benz mainly fiddled with mechanical troubles, but 1935 had been a Mercedes-Benz year. For example, they won at Monaco (Fagioli), the Eifel (Caracciola), Penya Rhin (Fagioli), Montlhéry for the French GP (Caracciola), at Spa (Caracciola), at Berne for the Swiss GP (Caracciola), and at San Sebastian for the Spanish GP (Caracciola), leaving only the Tunis GP (Varzi), the Coppa Acerbo (Varzi), the Italian GP at Monza (Stuck) and the Czech GP at Brno (Rosemeyer) to Auto Union. Yet in the German Grand Prix, played on their home ground at the Nürburgring, it was the talented Nuvolari who vanquished the entire might of Germany, before all those German spectators, driving an aged P3 Alfa Romeo. He achieved this great victory after an infuriating fuel stop when the refuelling pump broke down and cans has to be substituted, so that the P3 was stationary for over 2 minutes, compared to the Germans' pit-stop of well under one minute!

Nuvolari was also the winner in the Coppa Ciano for Alfa Romeo, and he made fastest lap in the Italian GP in one of these cars. Otherwise, apart from a win for Dreyfus' Alfa Romeo at the Marne GP, it was Germany all the way.

As has been said, Auto Union were in the ascendant in 1936. With the formerly important Belgian, Marne and French Grands Prix relegated to sports car status and the Czech and Spanish Grands Prix abandoned, it was victory after victory for the odd rear-engined cars. Mercedes-Benz pulled off a solitary win at the Tunis GP at Carthage (Caracciola), and at Monaco (Caracciola) and there

Left: like some of the Italians, Bugatti were no too happy with being GP 'also rans' so the French introduced a sports-car formula. Here, Jean-Pierre Winmille in his 3.3-litre Bugatti wii the 1936 French GP at Montlhéry

Left: Bernd Rosemeyer, the only man successfully to get to grips with the odd-handling Auto Unions (mainly because they were the first cars he drove and he did not know any different!) came to grief at the Tunis GP at Carthage in 1936. Here, is the wreck of his C-Type after it caught fire. However, 1936 was a brilliant year for the German who escaped this particular incident

was lingering Alfa Romeo success when Nuvolari took the Penya Rhin, Hungarian, Milan and Coppa Ciano races for Italy. Otherwise 1936 was Auto Union's year, with victories over Mercedes at Tripoli with Varzi first and Stuck second, the Eifelrennen (Rosemeyer), in the German GP (Rosemeyer first, Stuck second), the Coppa Acerbo (in the order of Rosemeyer, von Delius, Varzi), in the Swiss GP (Rosemeyer beating Varzi and Stuck), and in the Italian GP, which Rosemeyer won from Nuvolari's Alfa Romeo with von Delius third. Auto Union were very fortunate to have secured the services of the young Bernd Rosemeyer, a former motor cycle racer, and it was an enormous loss to them when he was later killed attempting to break high-speed records for them when a savage cross wind upset his car. In the Eifel Grand Prix of 1936 he had to drive in heavy rain which turned to mist, but he won all the same, at an average speed of 72.71 mph as well as lapping faster than the old-timers of greater experience, at a speed of 74.46 mph. It is noticeable that although Germany would have preferred to have used entirely German drivers for their two winning teams, so fast and difficult to handle were these cars, particularly the over-steering Auto Unions, that French and Italian drivers had to be called in, and Nuvolari, and Dick Seaman from Britain were to follow.

Under political influence, racing had become more exciting in respect of speed and spectacle, and more intense as the well organised and capably engineered German teams came to show the rest of the world their superiority. In 1937, the FIA in Paris had intended to curb speeds by introducing a maximum weight limit of 750 kg, but the advances in metallurgy, readily available to the government-financed Mercedes-Benz and Auto Union teams, opened the door to enormous power from ultra-lightweight motor-cars. But the new use of softer and increased-travel suspension systems was not yet fully understood, so that the high speed and very quick acceleration of the new racing cars put a great strain on their drivers as well as making Grand Prix contests a fine sport to watch. The Titans were in action!

Right: always a hazard in motor racing is oil dropped by an ailing car. The Monaco GP is thrown into confusion after Tadini's Alfa Romeo has dropped its engine lubricant at the chicane

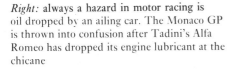

The 1937 season opened in Rio de Janeiro, for Grand Prix racing was increasing in popularity and new countries sought Grand Prix status. Here the winding course allowed Carlo Pintacuda to bring the 400 bhp, all-independently-sprung, 4-litre, V12 Alfa Romeo in first, at 51.5 mph, ahead of Stuck's Auto Union, four seconds in arrears. Also, in the Milan Grand Prix Nuvolari got his Alfa Romeo in front of Hasse's Auto Union, winning at 64.4 mph and setting the lap record to 67.8 mph. But Formula racing as such did not start until the Eifel races in June and now superior German speed and preparation prevailed, Rosemeyer winning for Auto Union at 82.56 mph from the Mercedes-Benz of Caracciola and von Brauchitsch, these latter cars having been troubled by fuel-

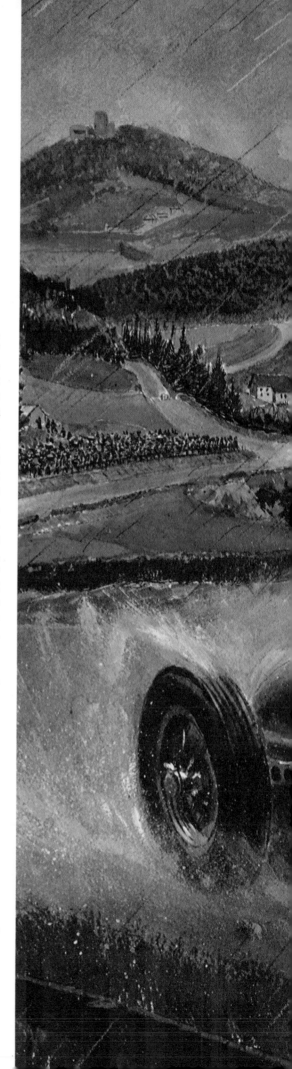

Right : hard at work earning his nickname, 'the Ringmaster' Caracciola in his 3-litre Mercedes in Germany in 1938

Inset : things did not always go so smoothly for the crack German Mercedes team. Manfred von Brauchitsch, the *Pechvögel* (unlucky bird), has some bad luck here in 1938 in Germany. While leading, he came in to the pits for a routine refuelling stop, only to have the car catch fire. Neubauer, team manager, rushes to the car, here. In an attempt to get back into the hunt after the flames were extinguished, von Brauchitsch's car ran off the road. However, Dick Seaman played a good number two and won for Mercedes instead

feed problems. Nuvolari could only manage fifth. Playing far away from home, the German and Italian teams then went to the Roosevelt Speedway in New York State for the Vanderbilt Trophy and found rather unexpected conditions. Even so the American cars could do no better than seventh, although Rex Mays, driving a 3.8-litre Alfa Romeo with a centrifugal blower, was a threat to the German cars. As it was, Rosemeyer sailed away into an easy lead to win for Auto Union at 82.95 mph, with Seaman second in a Mercedes-Benz.

Back in 1937 it was not possible to get the teams back over the Atlantic soon enough to compete in the Belgian Grand Prix at Spa, but Mercedes-Benz and Auto Union had cars and drivers in reserve. Their might was evident when Lang's Mercedes was timed over the flying-kilometre at 193 mph and the old lap record was pulverised again and again. But in the race these very quick Mercedes cars ran into various troubles, leaving Hasse's Auto Union to win at the very high pace of 104.87 mph, after Caracciola had left the Spa lap record at 108.8 mph. From then on it was Mercedes dominance all the way, with victories at Nürburgring in the German Grand Prix (Carracciola, 82.77 mph), at Monaco (von Brauchitsch, 63.25 mph) in the Swiss Grand Prix at Berne (Caracciola, 97.42 mph), in the Italian Grand Prix at Leghorn (Caracciola, 81.59 mph), and at Brno (Caracciola, 85.97 mph), with many new lap records *en route*. Behind these statistics lies some of the most exciting and worthy motor racing of all time. The brilliant Rosemeyer brought Auto Union some consolation with wins at the Coppa Acerbo at 87.61 mph and a new lap record of 92 mph, and in the Donington Grand Prix, at 82.86 mph, where he shared the lap record with Caracciola's Mercedes at an impressive 85.62 mph.

By 1938 the 3-litre Grand Prix cars were the vogue, with highly-supercharged, short-stroke engines, not much slower than the bigger cars that had preceded them, but not quite so dangerous to handle, for the new-style springing was now beginning to be understood by racing-car engineers. Alfa Romeo came up with their new Tipo 308 but were entirely outclassed, and Auto Union, who lost Bernd Rosemeyer at the beginning of the 1938 season, had hardly better luck, although Nuvolari managed to give them a win in the Donington Grand Prix. In this event many of the other ace-drivers had been eliminated because of oil dropped on the course. The crowds were again of immense proportions for a race meeting in Great Britain and the roads leading to the Leicestershire circuit were jammed with traffic. With good reason, too, for the German teams with their supporting fleets of vehicles and armies of mechanics plus the legendary Herr Neubauer controlling the Mercedes-Benz racing, were worth going far to see. The occasion was all the more dramatic because of the threat of imminent war and Nuvolari won at 80.49 mph and made a fastest lap of 83.71 mph. During the year, Auto Union netted only one more win, at Monza, and all the other races were Mercedes-Benz victories. At Pau, however, René Dreyfus took first place for Delahaye, by a whole lap, as Mercedes grappled with heavy fuel consumption, calling for pit stops in under ninety miles, and

gear-shift troubles. Nuvolari did not start, having suffered burns when his Alfa Romeo caught fire in practice. The remaining Auto Union victory at Monza was less spectacular because the race organisers had toned down the great pace of the 1938 racers by building chicanes on the course. Tazio Nuvolari drove the winning car at 96.7 mph but Lang had set fastest lap in his Mercedes–Benz at a record 101.38 mph.

Otherwise, 1938 and the shortened 1939 3-litre seasons were full of Mercedes successes. In 1938 Caracciola took the honours at the Coppa Acerbo at an average speed of 83.69 mph but, surprisingly, Villoresi's Maserati did fastest lap, at 87.79 mph. He also won the Swiss Grand Prix at 89.44 mph, while Manfred von Brauchitsch scored at the French Grand Prix at Reims averaging 101.3 mph. Britain's hero, Richard Seaman, won a memorable German Grand Prix at the Nürburgring at 80.75 mph, also setting fastest lap at 83.76 mph (and being noticeably shy on the victor's rostrum of returning a full Nazi salute). Very soon after, he was tragically killed at Spa, skidding into a tree in the wet and being dragged from his blazing Mercedes–Benz to die in hospital. Lang, a former racing mechanic, won the Coppa Ciano at 85.94 mph, sharing the record lap of 89.17 mph with his team-mate von Brauchitsch, and it was Lang who showed us a lap of 101.38 mph at England's first Grand Prix road racing circuit, Donington Park.

With the outbreak of war in September 1939, that season came to a premature close, but not before several races had been contested. Mercedes–Benz took all but the French Grand Prix and the Yugoslav Grand Prix; the latter event was actually held after war had broken out and marked an even greater spread of political international motor-racing. This, the last European race for many years, was won by Nuvolari's Auto Union at 81.21 mph, after he and von Brauchitsch (who was a nephew of the German Field Marshal), had roused Belgrade with a joint lap record of 83.9 mph. Otherwise, the season was dominated by the cars from Stuttgart. Caracciola was victorious in the German

Left : proving that it was an awful lot of car to move, four mechanics struggle to push start the 1939 W163 Mercedes-Benz of von Brauchitsch at the French GP at Reims

Below : still on the British club circuits, Raymond Mays takes the chequered flag at London's Crystal Palace in 1939 . . . again with his famous ERA fitted with twin rear wheels

Grand Prix at the Nürburgring. The classic circuit was built with previously unemployed labourers after World War I. Caracciola averaged 75.12 mph, and lapped at 81.66 mph in the last pre-war race. Lang took the Swiss Grand Prix at Berne at 96.02 mph but team-leader Rudi Caracciola set a very fast new lap record, at 104.32 mph. The last pre-war French Grand Prix at Reims had been even quicker, and Lang lapped at a record 114.87 mph. Even so, Muller's Auto Union won at 105.25 mph, after a smoking Mercedes announced that Lang was in dire mechanical trouble. Lang was certainly in the ascendancy however, having won at Pau and in the Eifel races.

Thus the 1939 season ended with German cars supreme, in the world's most exacting sport, if 'sport' it still was. Motor racing had come a long way since that first proper motor race over French roads from Paris to Bordeaux 44 years earlier.

Naturally, the war put paid to international motor racing, although the Tripoli Grand Prix was held in 1940, and won by Farina's Alfa Romeo at 128.22 mph from the Alfas of Biondetti and the veteran Count Trossi. It was to be some years before racing found its feet again, however.

CHAPTER 3

THE RACER
COMES OF AGE

THE CARS: 1939-60

Below and right: the French Talbot concern had to resort to adapting its big sports cars for use in the Grands Prix of the immediate post-war years; they were very heavy, but this disadvantage was offset to a certain extent by the cars' ability to carry more fuel and therefore pit fewer times then their purpose-built rivals. The car shown here was built in 1950, with a 4½-litre Talbot-Lago engine, and was one of three used by the works team at Le Mans, before being driven by Froilan Gonzales in the French Grand Prix (Totnes Motor Museum, England)

Wars may disrupt and eventually quell motor racing but they have never spelt the end of its continuity. So it was in 1914–18 and again in 1939–45. World War II may have changed the whole way of European life as had the conflict of a quarter of a century earlier and it certainly left Europe in a shattered condition: her motor car manufacturing plants were either destroyed or converted for the production of aircraft and munitions. All through the dark years of this tremendous struggle for power, with bombs raining down on towns and factories, the enthusiasm for motor competitions never wained.

Racing was revived by the French in the Bois de Boulogne in September 1945, and international Grand Prix racing was resumed in 1947. The Germans, who had carried all before them before the outbreak of war with their phenomenal Mercedes-Benz and Auto Union racing teams, were not exactly popular at this time. British and American bombers had dealt with their production facilities, and they were in no way able, or allowed, immediately to resume the conflict even with racing cars over the great road circuits.

If Germany was still *hors de combat* in 1947, France was eager to resume motor racing and Italy was well prepared for it. What kind of cars these nations used would depend on the rules and regulations announced in Paris by the governing body of the sport, which was soon revived and operational again. The new Grand Prix Formula was announced as early as February 1946 and it had been carefully planned to provide for the prevailing post-war situation.

Before the war, the Grand Prix racing car had reached a high degree of efficiency, both in the power developed from its small supercharged engines and in its road-holding qualities, which had been enhanced by soft non-leaf-spring suspension systems of an all-independent action, or by the employment of De Dion rear suspension. Such racing cars were so very fast and accelerative that they called for highly skilled drivers to conduct them and they were a very exciting sort of vehicle to watch when on 'full-song' and engaged in a tense battle with others of the same ilk. However, they had been possible in their final costly pre-war form only because first Mussolini and then Hitler had seen a valuable means of fostering national prestige by racing cars of Italian and German manufacture (but not always driven by nationals) in world-wide international contests. This had made available to Alfa Romeo and Ferrari and, especially, to Mercedes-Benz and Auto Union, the enormous sums of money needed to research, build, develop and operate such fabulous racing cars.

By 1947, the picture was very different. Europe was impoverished and the motor industry, in war-damaged factories big and small, was attempting to salvage something from the aftermath and to get ordinary motor cars back into production. Those who sought to go racing, whether because they thought it good publicity for their customer products, an important laboratory for automotive research, or just because they enjoyed it, had to tread warily. This was if they were to afford the luxury of participation by convincing their mostly impoverished shareholders that it was worthwhile, or even profitable.

With these inescapable factors in mind, the new controlling body, known as the FIA, sensibly came up with a Grand Prix Formula which provided for two very different types of racing car to compete together. It was for cars of not more than $1\frac{1}{2}$ litres engine capacity supercharged, and of not over $4\frac{1}{2}$ litres capacity without a compressor or supercharger. As a matter of fact, this Formula was the one which the former AIACR had been intending to introduce in 1940, had the war not intervened. However, it was a Grand Prix stipulation well suited to post-war conditions. It meant that the expensive, small, high revving superchaged engine (two or multi-stage supercharged if the designer so wished) would be pitted against the more easy to render reliable, lazy-revving and big-capacity power unit, providing the latter used normal carburettors. It was a Formula that was of immediate interest to Great Britain, France and Italy. Britain had been concentrating on *voiturette* racing from 1934 onwards, with its top capacity figure of $1\frac{1}{2}$ litres, and Raymond Mays' green supercharged ERAs (English Racing Automobiles) had done very well in this field. France was more inclined, in the terrible plight in which the

nation found itself after the end of the war, to hope that big, reliable and enduring sports cars, stripped of their road-going wear, such as windscreens mudguards, hoods, starter motors, lighting equipment, would serve as Grand Prix cars; the non-supercharged 4½-litre engine-capacity limit looked after them very nicely. The Italians were in the strongest position in 1947 however, because Alfa Romeo raced the very beautiful and effective little 'blown' 1½-litre Tipo 158 cars, the Alfettas, before the war and Maserati, a small company devoting themselves to racing-car production, brought out the 6C and then the 4C sixteen-valve, twin-overhead-camshaft, four-cylinder *voiturette* racing models before hostilities broke out. They were ideally suited to the conditions and rules of the day.

That was the state of technical play as the post-war teams lined up on the grids of circuits that had been abandoned, but certainly not forgotten, during the past eight or nine years, to try their prowess at the resuscitated game of international Grand Prix motor racing.

Apart from her economic and productive 'non condition', Germany would not have been allowed by the FIA to return to international motor racing in 1947. Italy was, as has been said, in a fortunate position to resume, but even she had to be content to develop pre-war designs. Profiting, perhaps, from pre-war German technology, the Alfa Romeo engineers put two-stage super-charging on the Tipo 158 engine, which raised its power output to 265bhp at 7500rpm, the blowers being paired in line along one side of the beautifully constructed, straight-eight 1½-litre engine. This was compared to the 254bhp at the same crankshaft speed which these engines had been producing back in 1939. Maserati, too, began to experiment with two-stage supercharging and also designed a new chassis, using tubular construction. ERA had brought out the very handsome E-type car of advanced conception, but it was never a success, in spite of having a highly developed version of the well known ERA six-cylinder engine that had itself been developed from the hemispherical head, dual-high-set-camshaft Riley Six engine, as raced by Raymond Mays. The idea of feeding this 63mm × 80mm power unit from a vast Zoller vane-type compressor, and using Porsche trailing-arm front suspension and a De Dion tube at the back, should have paid high dividends but led instead to frustration.

France had but her big sports cars to adapt to post-war Grand Prix racing, in the guise of the heavy Talbots and Delahayes, which did not look very promising, but which might not need to pause at the pits quite as frequently as the highly boosted fuel-consuming 1½-litre racers. In addition, the French Government, belatedly striving to gain prestige from motor racing, got the Centre d'Etudes Technique de l'Automobile et du Cycle to prepare a world-beating proper 1½-litre Grand Prix car. This showed enormous promise (on paper) as had its talented designer, M. Lory, who created the great 2-litre V12 and 1½-litre straight-eight Delage Grand Prix cars of 1924–27. Called the CTA-Arsenal, as it was to be built at the Government Munitions Factory, the car was a 90 degree V8, 60mm × 65.6mm, with a conventional, two-valves and two-plugs-per-cylinder-head layout, the valves being prodded by two overhead camshafts. However it had all the trimmings including two-stage blowing, of up to 30lb per sq in, from twin Roots instruments driven from the front of the engine. The aim was to achieve 300bhp from this engine which, on the test-bench, did show around 270 at 8000rpm. A chassis with all-round independent suspension was prepared for the CTA-Arsenal but, alas for French hopes, nothing more was heard of it.

It was the Tipo 158 Alfa Romeo that was the truly significant Grand Prix car of the period 1947 to 1950. By adopting the sensible attitude of continued advancement of their existing design, instead of messing around with ingenious but untried new cars, Alfa Romeo of Milan managed to outpace (on paper, at least) the impressive Type W165 Mercedes-Benz V8 of 1939. Their now very highly supercharged straight-eight engine produced 310bhp. Its chassis, too, underwent very little modification, although naturally the braking system had to be adapted to the increased performance by fitting stiffer brake drums and getting more heat away from them, thus cutting down the considerable brake fade.

Apart from the big Talbots and Delahayes and the wonderful contribution of Alfa Romeo, there were numerous offshoots of lesser designs during this period of motor-racing revival, such as the Maserati-based OSCA, the Veritas and Meteor, which were really sports cars using pre-war Type 328 BMW six-cylinder engines. There was also the 2-litre V12 Ferrari sports car that competed in stripped form as a racing car. The Maserati now appeared under Omar Orsi's direction as the two-stage-blown, tubular-chassis 4CLT model thus reinforcing their chances of success in motor racing.

In Britain, Alta were busy with a new Grand Prix car. The pre-war four-cylinder twin-cam engine now had the cylinder dimensions of 78mm × 78mm, and was thus of truly 'square' conception, and still with roller-chain-drive to its overhead camshaft. It was used in a brand-new frame with tubular side members and an ingenious method of suspension was by double wishbones. This gave all-independent action when used with rubber blocks as the damping medium, pressed on by bell cranks formed at the lower wishbones. Unfortunately, for the hopes of Geoffrey Taylor and his little factory at Tolworth, off the Kingston by-pass, near London, this Grand Prix Alta was not a

Right : seen here in the Siamese national racing colours, carried by Prince Bira, with considerable success, is the OSCA, built by the Maserati brothers after their split with the firm of the same name and based on the Maserati 4CLT. The 4½-litre V12 engine produced 300 bhp in its unsupercharged form
(Donington Collection, England)

Below : the Ferrari 125 appeared first in 1948, powered by a supercharged version of the 1½-litre V12 sports-car engine. After several modifications, this car reappeared in 1951, equipped with wishbone front suspension and swing-axle rear and driven by its owner Peter Whitehead. This example may have been built in 1949, and fitted with a twin-cam, two-stage-blown engine, but Whitehead raced it successfully with the more conventional single-cam engine
(Donington Collection, England)

wildly successful racing car and the marque gradually faded away.

After two years or so of the new régime, Ferrari came up with his Colombo-designed 2-litre racer, which owed much to his satisfactory sports car of that engine capacity. The new GP Ferrari was something of a sensation, because of its very compact size and therefore light weight, into which chassis Ferrari had put a supercharged V12 power pack producing 230bhp. This engine was of 55mm × 52.5mm bore and stroke, so now there was an 'over-square' engine, the first since that of Mercedes-Benz which had trampled on the Italians at Tripoli in 1939. Like its Alfa Romeo rival, this Ferrari ran at 7500rpm but was content with one Roots supercharger, and a single overhead camshaft operating valves inclined at 60 degrees. It was fitted with a five-speed gearbox, but the handling was not particularly good, the swing-axle rear suspension no doubt responsible for the high degree of oversteer produced on corners. Double wishbones were used at the front, and transverse leaf-springs were employed both front and rear. This, the first of the post-war Ferraris, fell between the winning form of the Tipo 158 Alfa Romeo and the lesser capabilities of the 4CLT/48 Maseratis.

Below: the 1948 Maserati 4CLT/48 was the ultimate development of the 4C, introduced in 1938 as a supercharged Voiturette racer. Following a debut win in the hands of Ascari and Villoresi, at San Remo, the model was immortalised as the 'San Remo' Maserati. It enjoyed a position of near-dominance between 1948 and 1950, with Ascari, Bira, Fangio and Parnell among an illustrious list of drivers, before a rapid decline of fortunes brought its famous career to a sad close. The car shown is the ex-Parnell example (Donington Collection, England)

At quite the opposite extreme were the big Lago-Talbots, which Anthony Lago of Paris hoped might have their racing chance when the very highly boosted 1½-litre cars had to go into their pits to refuel. Lago had built a single-seater version of what were otherwise purely sports cars in 1939, and he now introduced what seemed a rather unconvincing answer to the fast and furious small supercharged machines. It had a long-stroke engine, with six cylinders measuring 93 × 110 mm bore and stroke, respectively, so the capacity was actually 4.48 litres. The valve gear consisted of inclined valves in the cylinder heads, opened and closed by means of short, light, pushrods moved by a couple of camshafts located high up in the crankcase as on a Riley engine. A sort of 'refined lorry engine', some said. The drive went through a Wilson pre-selector gearbox, which had been used from 1934 to 1939 by ERA, and which enabled the driver to pre-select the required gear before a corner, and then to make a lightning change by merely pressing a pedal. This arrangement had the dis-advantages of being very weighty and also of having fairly wide gear ratios. The 4½-litre Lago-Talbot did have an off-set prop-shaft which enabled the driver to sit low in the car, and to some degree overcome the drag of such a

large and heavy motor car. The rigid back axle was again a retrograde feature, judged by the number of independent suspension systems in use at the time, and it was suspended on half-elliptic leaf springs. Front suspension was independent, by a simple system of a transverse leaf spring and lower wishbones. The power output of 250 bhp, and the car's weight, were not a happy combination, but these rather appealing 'heavy-metal' Lago-Talbots scored in those races where the lighter and far more powerful cars either ran into mechanical troubles or forfeited their superior speed in stops to take on more fuel or change their tyres. The interest in atmospheric-induction 4½-litre Grand Prix cars was very limited however.

As the scene moved closer to the pre-Hitler concept of road racing, the cost of participating began to move upwards again and the game became mainly one between wealthy manufacturers. To encourage participation at a lesser level, the FIA contrived Formula Two, for supercharged cars of up to 500 cc, and non-supercharged cars of up to 2-litres. No-one seemed able to cope with a blown half-litre beast, so this racing was at first a 2-litre Ferrari benefit.

The 1949 season was disappointing if you were an Alfa enthusiast, because the great Milanese firm decided to drop out of racing while the Tipo 158 cars were at the top of their exceptional form. True, they had ready a remarkable 52×52 mm flat-twelve-cylinder racer dating back to 1940, but this was never raced. Nor was the very sensational Dr Ferry Porsche-designed, space-frame, flat-twelve-cylinder Cisitalia, which was intended to run at 10,000 to 12,000 rpm, anticipating a power output of 500 bhp. This car had two superchargers, a five-speed gearbox, cylinder dimensions of 56×51 mm and, most notably, a centrally mounted engine driving all four wheels. A clutch enabled the driver to disconnect the drive to the front wheels at his discretion. Built at the Cisitalia works in Turin, the car was tested in South America and, although Nuvolari expressed interest in driving it, its sponsors went bankrupt and the project folded up.

The British BRM (British Racing Motor) was another dubious racing car of intended Grand Prix calibre, which made its debut during 1949. It was inspired by racing driver Raymond Mays, of ERA fame, and he persuaded the British motor and accessory companies to contribute in cash and in kind to the building of this highly advanced V16-cylinder 1½-litre, supercharged, all-British racing car, to the design of his friend Peter Berthon. It was, unfortunately, a disaster from the word go, except in lesser races, and then only after an enormous amount of mostly fruitless development.

The BRM design sought to use the 1½-litre supercharged part of the prevailing Formula to the fullest advantage. The engine had sixteen cylinders, in blocks of four, in a 135° Vee. Between each pair of blocks rose the drive for the twin overhead camshafts, which operated two valves per cylinder. The camshaft drive was by means of a gear train, from which the final drive was taken, and then via a short shaft to the clutch. The dimensions of this

ambitious V16 racing power unit were microscopic, being 49.53 × 48.26mm, a swept-volume of 1.48-litres. Such small pistons and light moving parts were intended to enable a maximum crankshaft speed as high as 10,000 to 12,000 rpm to be reached, and a power output in the region of 400bhp was visualised. Very lofty supercharge pressures, of up to 70lb/sq in were obtained by twin centrifugal blowers mounted on the front of the engine, drawing from two horizontal carburettors. To save weight, ignition was of the coil-and-distributor type. This BRM was a very courageous attempt to put paid to Alfa Romeo and any other opposition on the circuits to British prestige, but it was to prove far too complex and the unusual system of centrifugal supercharging meant that the immense power came in over a very limited rev-band. This made the car extremely difficult for even top Grand Prix drivers to control or use to its full effect.

The V16 BRM had a chassis that had borrowed a great deal from the pre-war Mercedes and Auto Unions, and the front trailing-arm independent suspension was very like that of the 1937 C-type and 1939 E-type ERAs. The difference here was that the torsion bars had been deleted, in favour of Lockheed oleo-pneumatic struts, which relied on air under compression for suspension and oil for damping, operated from an extension of the upper suspension arm. More complication! At the rear of the BRM there was de Dion semi-independent suspension, with the same kind of Lockheed suspension struts as at the front. The transmission incorporated a five-speed gearbox and the open propeller shaft ran at an angle, so that the driver's seat could be positioned low down beside it. This was mostly a crib from the pre-war 1½-litre, and 3-litre Mercedes racers. The chassis frame consisted of two side members, united by tubular cross members, and the special fuel was carried in a saddle tank over the luckless driver's legs, with an additional fuel tank in the tail. This unfortunate BRM was announced with much aplomb, but apart from missing the 1949 racing season, it was uncompetitive for the reasons given, and initially suffered from embarrassing starting-line breakdowns.

Ferrari must take the credit for a more sensible approach to racing in those days. By increasing the length of his 1½-litre chassis and adopting twin overhead camshafts and two-stage supercharging for the V12 engine, Ferrari ensured a decent increase in performance and obtained better roadholding by altering the rear suspension. This car was still the work of engineer Colombo, but at the end of 1949 Enzo Ferrari decided on a complete change of policy. Employing Aurelio Lampredi as the development engineer and designer, Ferrari switched from the blown 1½-litre to the opposite non-supercharged 4½-litre format. His reasons were two-fold: in the first place he wished to avoid the very high cost of maintaining between races his delicate supercharged engines, and in the second place Ferrari had much experience of normally aspirated power units from his successful 2-litre V12 sports-cars and he now realised that a bigger version could almost equal the power outputs

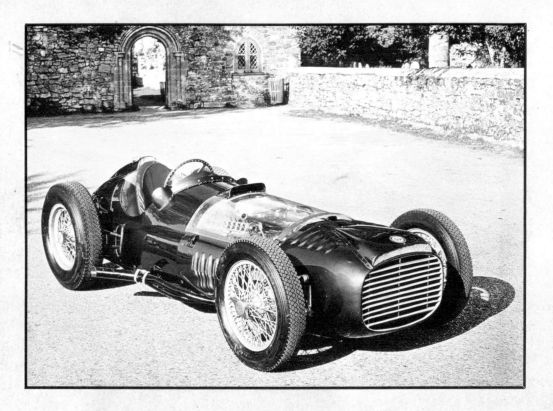

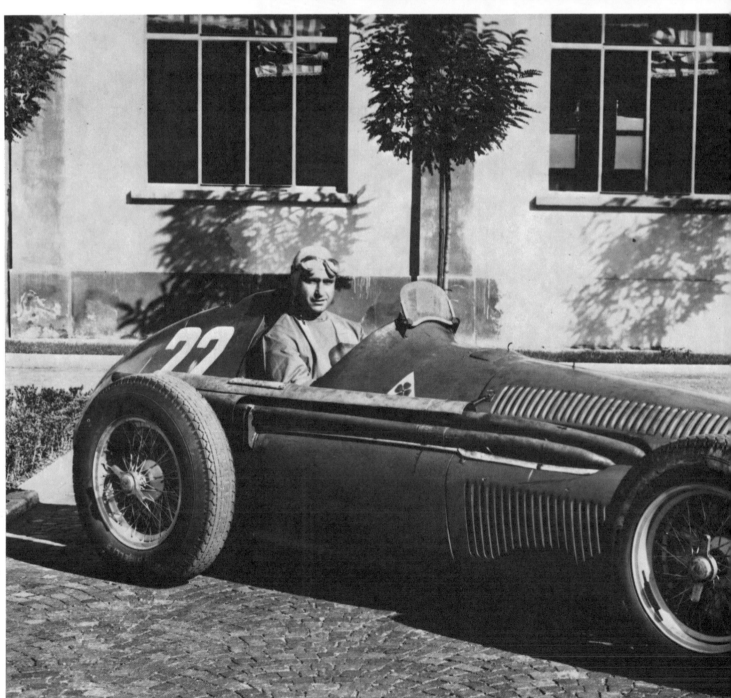

Left: proving that the war did not slow down their progress at all, Mercedes-Benz produced the W196; this is the streamlined version

Below and below right: the Alfettas, although thirsty, were remarkable racing cars. Their final race, the 1951 Spanish GP at Barcelona, gave them a win: a fitting time for the company to withdraw from the sport

which were being squeezed from little high-revving blown motors, and more reliably too. He may also have preferred a closer link with the sort of cars he was selling to his customers.

However, the Grand Prix scene was immediately rendered more interesting when Alfa Romeo announced that they intended to stage a come-back in 1950. Now would be witnessed a battle-royal between the two great Italian makes of Ferrari and Alfa Romeo, using diametrically opposite kinds of racing car: the former large and heavy, but reliable and fuel-thrifty, the latter small, compact and beautiful. Would these little racers last the distances, or have sufficient performance over the Ferraris to balance-out the time that they would presumably lose during refuelling pit-stops? One of the most interesting periods of Grand Prix racing was about to begin, and the race-by-race aspect will be looked at in the next chapter.

From the foregoing it will be realised that what Alfa Romeo of Milan intended to do was to return with their already very convincing little Alfettas, developed into what were to become known as the Tipo 159 cars. They were compact, with a wheelbase of 8 ft 2 in, and capable of 180 mph.

The revived 1951 Alfettas were at first credited with having increased their maximum revs from 7500 to 8500 rpm, enabling the power output to reach 350 bhp. It was also said that these effective straight-eight engines, at the end of their useful run, had shown a little over 400 bhp at 9000 rpm on the test rig. It seems more likely that, as raced during the 1951 season, they were delivering some 385 bhp at the former top limit of 7500 rpm. To achieve such outputs it was essential to use fuel of the alcohol 'dope' variety that would go far towards cooling the tortured engine internals, and it is certain that as a consequence of this, the Tipo 159s had the very heavy fuel consumption of only 1½ miles per gallon. To carry as much fuel in the tail tanks of the cars as possible, without affecting the roadholding characteristics was a problem; it will be appreciated that as the fuel level drops in the course of a race, a car's weight distribution is altered, often very drastically. The Alfa Romeo engineers used de Dion instead of swing-axle rear suspension for the 159s, but they retained the transverse leaf springs of the 158 design. The axle was located by means of radius arms and an ingenious A-bracket. Wider brake drums were fitted to the Tipo 159 cars and to try to reduce the refuelling problem, a tankage of 65 gallons was contrived about the cockpit. In the engine department the original bore and stroke dimensions were retained, *ie* 58 × 70 mm, and the increase in power was obtained from subtle improvements to supercharger boost, valve timing, exhaust system and porting.

The 4½-litre Ferrari which was soon to fight it out against these much smaller Alfa Romeos had a very similar chassis to the previous cars, except that Lampredi preferred a de Dion rear end. It was used in Formula Two as well as in Formula One races with the old 2-litre unsupercharged engine until the bigger F1 power unit was ready for it. Weight was saved in the de Dion assembly by having side radius arms to locate it, thus eliminating the need for a rotating joint. Strength for the chassis frame was gained from a spaceframe structure that at first merely formed the scuttle of the body. The big engine had a single overhead camshaft, driven by chain, over each cylinder bank of the 60 degree vee engine with 24 inclined valves. The engine started life as a 72 mm × 68 mm, 3.3-litre unit, but was soon expanded to 4.1 litres by opening out the cylinder bore to 80 mm and then, finally, to 4490 cc, by keeping the bigger bore in conjunction with an increase in piston stroke to 74.5 mm. It is significant, especially as most modern Grand Prix engines are non super-charged, that this 4½-litre Ferrari engine was producing a claimed 380 bhp at 7500 rpm by the end of the 1950 season, which made the car only slightly slower than the Tipo 159 Alfa Romeos on the straights, a deficit which could often be wiped out by the Ferrari's fewer pit stops for petrol. For 1951, the 4½-litre Ferrari was further improved by altering the combustion-chamber shape and using two spark plugs per cylinder. This pushed the horsepower to rather more than the previous 380 and that this engine had plenty of development left in it is shown by a special which produced no less than 430 bhp.

Right: the racing cars of the 50s demanded not only courage and skill of their drivers, but also great physical strength. Froilan Gonzalez, 'The Pampas Bull', is seen here at the wheel of a 1951 Ferrari 375. The car was powered by a 4½-litre V12 engine, notable for its remarkably large piston area; at 93.6 square inches, it was larger than all but the C-type Auto Union and some ancient behemoths

Below: surely the most magnificent failure in motor racing: the V16 BRM had tiny cylinders and a Rolls-Royce-designed supercharger running at an astonishing 39,000 rpm. Although the engine never reached its projected 600 bhp output, 525 bhp was seen in the workshop. The engine was unfortunately better known for its exquisite sound than for its longevity

Left: the Ferrari 500 with which Alberto Ascari won two consecutive World Championships in 1952 and 1953. The original engine was a 1980 cc, twin-overhead-camshaft, four-cylinder unit of Formula Two derivation. It developed 170 bhp at 7000 rpm. The engine shown here is a 3-litre unit, also with four cylinders, installed many years ago by a former owner for the 1954 Tasman racing series in Australia and New Zealand. This chassis is possibly the most successful in Grand Prix history
(Donington Collection, England)

The BRM was proving an embarrassment to poor Raymond Mays and the 'big but unblown' theme of Ferrari, Talbot and Delahaye was followed by OSCA, who brought out a V12-cylinder engine of 78 mm × 78 mm, 4.47 litres, to be accommodated in a 4CLT Maserati chassis. This is how racing recovered from the war years and proved so very interesting. However, when it was announced that the 1½ litres blown/4½ litres unblown Formula was to hold good until a new Formula was announced from Paris to take effect in 1954, Alfa Romeo again withdrew from the scene, not wishing to build the necessary new cars for only two more seasons of the then current Formula. Mercedes-Benz had hinted excitingly that they intended to return to motor racing, but not until the new Formula came into use. So, F1 tended to take on a subdued aspect, in 1952, with only Ferrari ready to race his 4½-litre cars. For this reason, many organisers took a look at the situation, with the V16 BRM still giving much trouble, and then decided to hold only Formula Two races, which attracted big and varied fields. Lampredi had brought out one new F1 car for Ferrari, as he found that the big 4½-litre model lacked the torque desirable for certain kinds of race circuits. This was a four-cylinder unit of 90 mm × 78 mm, 1.98 litres, which was installed in the Formula Two frame, with de Dion rear suspension. Using twin spark plugs per cylinder and a dual-choke Weber carburettor for each pair of cylinders, it was an effective tool. The attention bestowed on ordinary, as opposed to supercharged, power units in the 1950–54 period was responsible for the introduction of ram pipes for the carburettor air intakes, tuned in conjunction with the valve timing and the exhaust system of an engine to give a mild boost without resorting to mechanical complications. It is thought, however, that J. G. Parry Thomas had played with the idea of ramming a little extra air into the engine of his racing Leyland-Thomas at Brooklands back in 1925.

Before we leave the declining Formula One years leading up to 1953, it must be mentioned that in Britain the courageous performances of the ERA *voiturettes* were followed by an attempt on the part of HWM to break into full-time racing. Their car was an Alta-engined single seater, using a wishbone and coil-spring front suspension system and a de Dion rear-end, in which quarter-elliptic springs both located and sprung the de Dion tube. The 1952 season may have been less than stimulating in respect of new cars, but it did witness more different makes of cars competing in important races than ever; Colombo left Ferrari to collaborate with Bellantani and Massimino in creating a new Formula Two Maserati with a tubular chassis, a twin-cam six-cylinder engine, two exhaust pipes, and the now-fashionable carburettor ram-pipes; Gordini evolved his successful racing version of the French Simca into a difficult-to-drive, 75 × 75 mm bore and stroke, six-cylinder car, employing the former 1½-litre-type chassis, and HWM went over to the use of torsion bars for their de Dion axle and adopted inboard brakes at the rear.

Two very significant developments took place at that time. The first was

Below: leading up to their own Vanwall Grand Prix racing car, Vandervells experimented with a modified Ferrari, the *Thinwall Special*. The name came from the thin-walled bearings used in the engine

the installation of a 2-litre Bristol engine into the sort of chassis that Cooper of Surbiton had evolved for their 500 cc, rear-engined, Formula Three racers, and in which Stirling Moss had his racing baptism. The larger car had its six-cylinder, triple-carburettor, BMW valve-geared engine mounted at the front, under a conventional bonnet. The second development was a very strong bid for British motor racing victories by Rodney Clark and Mike Oliver with the Connaught, a car financed by McAlpine and built in Surrey. The power unit of the latter was at first a modified Lea-Francis engine. It must also be mentioned that this period of racing-car development saw British engineers refining the disc brake, which BRM now fitted, as did Vandervell, who were using a 4½-litre Formula One Ferrari the *Thin Wall Special* for their early experiments. These experiments were to lead to Mr Tony Vandervell realising his life's ambition, which was to win Grand Prix races with a British car – his 2½-litre Vanwall. At this time his team's successes were still some way in the future.

In what remained of F1 racing under the existing regulations, Ferrari was persuading 400 bhp from the unblown 4½-litre motor and was seeking better

Below and below left: the Maserati 250F epitomised the racing car of the 1950s, with the tyres now looking fatter, the body smoother and finer contoured and the engine ever more efficient. The overhead camshaft 2460 cc engine of this car, which was driven by Perdisa, Mieres and Collins, produced about 250 hp in 1955 when it was built. Of course, it was with one of these cars that Fangio continued to create his own niche in motor-racing legend (Donington Collection, England)

cooling and greater rigidity from the drum brakes. Meanwhile, both Ferrari and Gordini had been trying out 2½-litre versions of their 2-litre, Formula Two power units, so as to be fully prepared for the coming new Grand Prix Formula.

So to 1954 and the new 2½-litre Formula. It had been introduced not to kill the speed of current Grand Prix cars, as had once been the aim behind restrictive rulings, but to encourage research into non-supercharged engines, which were rightly thought of as being of more value to production-car engineers than the highly supercharged power units which the preceding Formula had encouraged. This was sensible thinking, because in a road-going auto the expense, noise, and fuel-thirst of supercharged engines was unpalatable and in any case the normally aspirated type was now known to give 100 bhp per litre in Formula Two racing cars. All the Grand Prix contenders went for these 2½-litre, carburetted, motors. There was a general move towards chassis frames constructed of small-gauge tubes, de Dion rear suspension, and a concentration of weight in the centre of the car to make it controllable on corners, where a dumb-bell effect of weight at each end was detrimental.

Ferrari came up with an engine of 94mm × 90mm bore and stroke, the Type 625, for installation in the Type 500 car, and then produced the 2.49-litre, 100 × 79.5mm, engine with big valve areas and two sparking plugs in each cylinder. This was used in the bulbous 'Squalo' model, with fuel carried in side tanks, as a sop to the aforesaid low polar moment of inertia or dumb-bell effect. Maserati raced a six-cylinder car, developed from their old Formula Two machine, which incorporated a compact gearbox on the back end of the car, turned 90 degrees from normal, spur gears taking the drive to the differential, from which jointed-shafts took the drive out to the wheels. This was the Maserati that was to become justly famous – the great 250F, which is still raced in suitable historic car races to this day. In 1954 guise

it had the 84×75 mm six-cylinder engine using twin overhead camshafts, triple, double-choke, Weber carburettors, and an exhaust system of three pairs of outlet pipes; ignition was by magneto to twelve sparking plugs. Connaught were trying hard, on a slender budget, with the $93\frac{1}{2} \times 90$ mm, four-cylinder Alta engine, on which they used fuel injection into the inlet ports. The gearbox used in these British-green racers was an Armstrong Siddeley-type pre-selector and the company even made a fully streamlined Connaught for the faster circuits. It all paid off, when one of these cars won a Grand Prix for Britain for the first time since Sunbeam had done so in 1924.

It was now that Vandervell set out on what was to be an even more successful effort for Britain. The Vanwall used a $2\frac{1}{2}$-litre, four-cylinder engine with a cylinder-head design based on that of the single-cylinder Norton motor-cycle engine, the engine of the bike on which millionaire Tony Vandervell had started his racing career. Hairpin valve springs were fitted to the twin-overhead-camshaft, four-cylinder engine. There was much trouble with throttle connections at first. Vanwall had previously bought one of the big, $4\frac{1}{2}$-litre Ferrari cars and from this many valuable lessons had been gleaned.

The 2½-litre Vanwall used a similar kind of four-speed gearbox, incorporated in its back axle, and the Goodyear disc brakes they had fitted to this bigger Ferrari were adopted for the exciting new car. BRM had fortunately been persuaded away from contesting the 1954–57 Formula with a blown 750 cc engine and were about to embark on restoring their very tarnished reputation, with a new 2½-litre, four-cylinder car.

Most exciting news of all was that Mercedes-Benz were returning to Grand Prix participation. The great German company, which had heard it all before, had done most of it, and knew, from painstakingly documented experience and experimentation, how to wring the best from any Formula, saw the new challenge as best met with 76 × 68.8 mm straight-eight-cylinder engines. This new W196 design used twin overhead camshafts, driven from a train of gears rising from the centre of the crankshaft in the middle of the paired cylinder blocks. The combustion chambers were conventionally hemispherical and the gear-drive to the overhead camshafts was as on the BRM and pre-war Alfa Romeos, but the inlet ports were arranged to run vertically into the cylinders, as on pre-war 328 BMW sports-car engines. Where this new Grand Prix

Below: the magnificent W196 Mercedes-Benz was brilliantly engineered in every detail. The chassis was a true spaceframe and the engine was a delightful straight-eight unit with overhead camshafts and desmodromic valve gear. With these cars, Fangio and Moss were seldom beaten

Mercedes-Benz was so very advanced was in the use of desmodromic, or positive, valve opening and closing and the employment of fuel injection directly into the cylinders. Cams closed and opened the overhead valves without the aid of springs. Moreover, this advanced engine had the full roller-bearing treatment, for big-end and main bearings, with a built-up crankshaft and one-piece connecting rods, and the traditional Mercedes-Benz method of welding steel water jackets round the cylinders was again made use of. This fine power producer was planned in unison with the entire W196 car, so that it was tilted over in the space frame to reduce height and therefore wind drag. The chassis was a stressed tubular affair of one-inch diameter tubing, with double wishbone and torsion-bar front springing, and a return at the rear of the chassis to swing-axle suspension, but on a new low-pivot system, in conjunction with torsion-bars. The drive was taken from the centre of the engine's crankshaft, passing through a five-speed gearbox, mounted at the back, behind the differential assembly. All the wheels were retarded by means of inboard drum brakes of enormous size, cooled by turbine-type finning, and thus having no effect on unsprung weight. These

great Grand Prix cars were the work of Rudolf Uhlenhaut and Dr Nallinger. They were at first given all-enveloping streamlined bodywork, enclosing the road wheels. This proved to be a mistake on normal road and semi-road circuits, even the great Fangio hitting the markers at Silverstone as vision was badly impaired. Ordinary bodies were soon substituted.

It is significant that, at this period of racing, these non-supercharged engines were able to develop at least 100 bhp per litre, and soon 300 bhp was to be released, while the power was transmitted to the road through tyres of rival makes, Mercedes-Benz using those made by Continental, other racing-car constructors relying on the products of Dunlop, Pirelli and Englebert. The day of the wet/dry tyre compound, which has been such a vital aspect of modern motor racing, was still far distant. Weights were down to around $13\frac{1}{2}$ cwt, Mercedes-Benz, for example, using bodywork made of Electron sheeting only 0.028 inches thick. Speeds varied from about 165 to 170 mph with the Vanwalls nudging 180 mph. In 1954 Lancia joined in, with their new D50 cars. Here was seen yet another step forward, as the Lancia's ninety-degree V8 engine was used to stiffen the chassis frame and the front suspension was attached to it, as is done with the rear suspension of today's lightweight Grand Prix cars. Lancia used the popular multi-tubular frame, composed of small-diameter tubing, and the also popular transaxle at the back for the de Dion suspension and they also located the clutch at the end of this transmission line, operating it hydraulically. The engine was of conventional twin-cam formation, breathing through Solex instead of the customary Weber carburettors, and was said to produce 260 bhp. Pannier fuel tanks on the Lancia D50 were a distinguishing feature, the idea being to gain some reduction in air turbulence between the road wheels, as on some of the pre-war Land Speed Record cars. This also kept the weight of the fuel within the compact wheelbase, so that the emptying of the tanks would not adversely affect cornering powers and road-clinging, as would have been the case with a tank in the car's tail.

The other rather stubby car was the Ferrari Squalo, or Type 555, which emerged for the 1955 season with several improvements to the unchanged basic design. The former multi-tube frame was abandoned for one with longitudinal tubes of large size and the fuel load was now accommodated in the centre of the car, thus giving the fattened appearance that caused this Ferrari to become known as the 'Supersqualo'. Ferrari also persevered with the older Type 625 cars, and for 1955 gave them coil-spring front suspension and a five-speed gearbox. Maserati went on racing the effective Type 250F cars but had evolved a revised cylinder head for them, with enlarged valves, and triple Weber 45DCO carburettors, flexibly mounted to keep a stable fuel-level in the float chambers. Fuel injection had been tried on the Maserati which Stirling Moss was driving but a reversion was made to Weber carburettors; disc brakes too were useful to Moss in enabling him to brake later than his rivals into corners.

Top and above: the Jano-designed Lancia D50 brought only the second completely new design to the grids of 1954. The very stiff 90° V8 engine was utilised as an integral part of the chassis and incorporated the mounting points for the front suspension. The clutch, gearbox and final drive were all mounted at the tail of the car. The distinctive pannier fuel tanks not only stabilised the centre of gravity within the wheelbase but also contributed to reducing aerodynamic turbulence between the wheels (Lancia collection, Italy)

Above: BRM's P25, 2½-litre car made its debut
in August 1955 and continued to be raced, albeit
in modified form, during 1956, 1957, 1958 and
1959. The four-cylinder engine was very much
oversquare and produced 272 bhp on an AvGas.
This particular car was built up from the remains
of car number 2510, which was crashed in
spectacular fashion at Avus in 1959, when Hans
Herrmann suffered brake failure on Berlin's
highspeed banked track
(Donington Collection, England)

From this it will be appreciated that chassis design was beginning to have as important an effect on the speed of a racing car round a circuit as engine power. In these exciting mid-nineteen-fifties years of Fangio/Moss domination, the modern art of 'setting-up' a racing car, and tuning its suspension characteristics to suit a given circuit, had not emerged. The reliability of the racing engine was much improved and it is a startling thought, or was to all those who had been in charge of the temperamental racing power units of the pre-war decades, that although sparking plugs could still oil-up, or cut-out from other causes, in the W196 Mercedes-Benz, with its deeply canted-over engine, it was necessary to remove one of the front wheels before a plug could be changed on the eight-cylinder unit. The aforesaid effect of chassis design and layout on lap speeds was portrayed when Mercedes-Benz, whose substantial financial resources enabled them to field a large number of variants of the W196, found that appreciable advantage was derived from having three different lengths of wheelbase; although these differed by only 2½ inches in the case of the short and medium-length chassis, the lap speeds set by Moss and Fangio at the Nürburgring improved by 5½ seconds when they drove the 7 ft 1 in wheelbase Mercedes. However, there was a difficulty! The short-wheelbase car was so difficult to drive that it was the medium-length Mercedes that was used for road racing – which is a nice illustration of the sophisticated state of the game at that period.

It was not entirely to the big battalions that racing successes were going. At Syracuse the Connaught of Tony Brooks won, from the Maserati of Musso, a car that the Connaught was capable of out-accelerating, although possibly not of out-braking, even with disc brakes. The Alta engine had had the fuel-injection system by SU removed from it and it was now getting its fuel via two twin-choke Webers. The Connaught may not have been delivering more than a mediocre 240 bhp but it had been deliberately planned to give power over a wide range of engine speed and good torque from low speeds, achieved by the timing of its valves and the shape of its inlet and exhaust piping. It would run to 7000 rpm but was not usually extended beyond 6500 rpm, whereas both of the current Ferrari racing engines would peak at 7500 rpm.

As 1956 dawned, the 2½-litre BRM was seen to continue its conservative design, which conformed to the prevailing formulae, except for the fact that oil-damped Lockheed suspension struts were fitted, borrowed, as it were, from the disastrous V16, 1½-litre, BRM. The Vanwall had been suspect in handling and during the winter Colin Chapman, later of Lotus fame, had been engaged as a technical consultant. This one-time civil engineer had designed for the wealthy Mr Vandervell a very impressive, scientifically stressed, full spaceframe chassis. Nor was this all. The Vanwall now appeared with sleek aerodynamic coachwork, devised by Frank Costin, Chapman's aircraft-expert friend, and the 2½-litre, four-cylinder engine with its Norton-type cylinder heads, hairpin valve springs on exposed valve stems, and its high-pressure

Bosch fuel injection was continually being developed. There were inboard rear brakes, air-cooled, of Goodyear make.

Maserati went on with the Type 250F cars, both in five-speed and four-speed forms, and with some experimentation with a fuel injection system of their own devising. Gordini were still in the hunt, with their ladder-frame, eight-cylinder, petrol-burning cars, the engine being based on that of their Le Mans sports-car, and the chassis having all-round independent suspension.

Historians would never forgive us if we omitted to refer to the return of the Bugatti Company to Grand Prix racing. This was done with the Type 251; of highly original design, its straight-eight twin-cam engine was placed transversely behind the cockpit, which was itself in the centre of the box-section, spaceframe, chassis. To the latter was attached a de Dion rear system of springing, employing an ingenious crank-and-rod connection to coil springs. From the centre of the transverse crankshaft came the spur-gear drive, to a five-speed gearbox of the Porsche synchromesh kind and at the front of the car, Bugatti tradition had been firmly upheld by the fitting of a beam axle! Although everyone, the writer included, wished the new Bugatti well – two

Left and below left: Maurice Trintignant gives the Bugatti 251 its only race, at the French GP at Reims in 1956. Bugatti's reappearance was not a success, and many thought the 251 to be too radical. Its spaceframe chassis, mid-mounted engine and telescopic dampers were a forecast of what was to come. Even the structures in front of the wheels were to be copied by Ferrari in the 1970s in an effort to aid air flow over their balloon tyres. Unfortunately, no more was seen of the Bugatti, a car which could have been a Grand Prix winner given development and a bit more enthusiasm

Far left: the factory Ferraris at Monza in 1958. Car no. 14 has disc brakes and was the first racer from Maranello to feature them after Enzo himself refused to follow the trend of other racers

Below: the Ferrari Dino of 1957 seen at Goodwood. This car was the basis for the successful mid-engined cars of the early 1960s

had been built – the Type 251 appeared only in the French Grand Prix at Reims and was hardly a success. However, for the record, let us mention that it was of 75×68.8 mm bore and stroke and ran up to 9000 rpm. Moreover, as one writer of note has pointed out, its telescopic shock absorbers were a glimpse into the future and this Bugatti's engine and gearbox arrangements gave a foretaste of the Lamborghini Miura, a roadgoing sports car of over a decade later. The 250F Masers had reverted to the well known twin exhaust tail pipes and Vanwall was, in employing a body in which the driver was enclosed up to his shoulders, very gently leading us towards the present-day conception of a Grand Prix car which is seen, but in which the driver is all but out of sight.

The next important GP racing car was a V12 Maserati with twin overhead camshafts to each bank of cylinders, 24 coils to attend to the firing of its two sparking plugs in each cylinder, and six Weber 35IDM downdraught carburettors. It was, however, not raced. 1957 saw the significant introduction by Ferrari of a V6-cylinder, $1\frac{1}{2}$-litre, Formula Two car, rumoured to develop no less than 190 bhp, on petrol, at 9200 rpm. It was a pointer to future Ferrari F1 plans.

Then there came the most radical departure of all, the move to put the engine behind the driver, as is so in all modern GP cars. This happened when Rob Walker entered Jack Brabham in a Cooper, with the sting in its tail represented by a Coventry Climax engine enlarged from its customary Formula Two size. This far-reaching trend was continued first when the Cooper Car Company itself installed a 1.9-litre Coventry Climax power pack into the back of such a car, with disc brakes, and subsequently when Bob Gerard contrived a six-port, 69×100 mm, Bristol engine of 2250 cc for the back end of his Cooper chassis.

The 1954–57 Formula went out on some technically interesting and important notes. Ferrari had introduced the famous Dino Ferrari, its type name being that of Enzo Ferrari's son; the car's Formula Two V6-cylinder power unit was gradually enlarged, the first stage taking it to 1860 cc, with megaphone exhausts. Maserati had more power than anyone else in the field, their $2\frac{1}{2}$-litre, $68\frac{1}{2} \times 66$ mm, engine giving over $4\frac{1}{2}$ bhp for every square inch of its piston-area, which measured an aggregate of 67 square inches, while the gallant Vanwalls were now giving 310 bhp and were safe up to a top crankshaft speed of 10,000 rpm. In due course the Dino Ferrari unit was opened out to the full $2\frac{1}{2}$ litres, or more precisely, two versions were run in 1957, one having a capacity of 2417 cc and the other being of 2200 cc.

Although the Formula governing GP racing was much the same to the end of 1960 as it had been for the preceeding four years, the FIA now stipulated that the racing engines must function on petrol, at once dispensing with the artificial cooling effect of alcohol fuels. The mixtures used had provided engine reliability for those who were prepared to put large quantities of fuel of this 'forgiving' nature in the tanks of their cars before the start of a race and at the refuelling stops. Ferrari had the happy advantage of their Formula Two engines already being petrol burners, and now enlarged them into proper Grand Prix Formula cars. Maserati, however, withdrew from racing as a consequence of the changed ruling, even though the definition of petrol was stretched to mean 'AvGas' aviation spirit, of 130 octane rating. Vanwall and BRM were also very hard hit by the change. The Vanwall had relied on extreme nitromethane mixtures to produce its claimed 290 bhp, as installed in the car, and this engine would lose nearly 30 bhp if run on petrol; their fuel-injection system had to be drastically retuned for straight petrol fuels to release even that much horsepower. The four-cylinder BRM engine, with its stroke/bore ratio of $0.73:1$, while giving an effective piston-area figure and very high rates of rotation, was very dependent on cooling from alcohol for its internals. Particularly prone to overheating were its valves, of which the inlet valves were much larger than normal and the exhaust valves were of more usual size.

The Ferrari, now called the Type Dino 246, its 65-degree, V6-cylinder, engine being of 85×71 mm (2417 cc), was good for 9400 rpm according to some authorities and probably gave 280 bhp in its 1958 guise.

Lotus now came onto the scene, with Formula Two-type cars, powered by the 'stretched' Coventry Climax engine. At first of only 2-litre and 2.2-litre capacity, these new Lotus cars were not only extremely light but they had suspension refinements that were the first of the great Colin Chapman innovations that have become the hallmark of the Lotus stable down the years. The BRMs were heavier but had been developed into effective racing cars with good torque characteristics, liked by most drivers. The rear-engined Coopers were on the way to absolute success and by 1959 had double wishbone independent suspension at the back, still in conjunction with a transverse leaf spring. Although tyre sizes were generally increasing, BRM changed from 16 in to 15 in diameter covers. Dunlop were rapidly ousting all opposition as leaders on racing-tyre techniques, with the new R5 racing tyre, which was finding favour with several teams.

Aston Martin entered F1 racing with the too heavy DBR4/250, developed from the better known Type DBR/300 sports-car, but of old-fashioned chassis conception, for all its close resemblance to a Maserati 250F. Maserati, in fact, had been in the ascendant up to their retirement from racing, having carried Fangio to his fourth successive World Championship. This was a triumph, really, for the conventional, well constructed, sensibly developed product of a factory well versed in racing, and employing the top drivers. Although there was far more to winning a 1959 motor race than absolute power, it must be remembered that whereas the Dino V6 Ferrari was pushing out a useful 290 bhp at this time, the Coventry Climax, although its fire-pump power unit background had been transcended, was only good for about 240 bhp, at the most. Yet by the close of the 1959 racing season the rear-engined genre had made it, very definitely, over the front-engined cars, whose now superseded layout had dated back to the Panhard-Levassor conception of 1895.

All manner of things had emerged during this 1958–1960 Formula. Vanwall had gone back to normal racing bodywork, but Connaught had come up with their semi-faired-in creation, nicknamed the 'toothpaste tube', and Porsche had brought out a single-seater RSK. To their credit, BRM had an early attempt at building a rear-engined car, although at the beginning of the 1960 season their old front-engined models were the ones which they raced. Lotus had been defeated in 1959 by poor roadholding qualities, so Colin Chapman started again, with a clean sheet of drawing paper. The result was the Lotus 18, which had the notably light weight of 980 lb (empty) and also boasted an impressively low frontal area. Behind the driver, in an almost genuine space-frame of multi-tubular type, there lived the Coventry Climax FPF engine, while fuel, oil and water were accommodated in the nose of the Lotus, which was of a mere 9 square feet frontal area. Low roll centre rear springing was a very deliberate aspect of the new car, but Chapman retained the magnesium-alloy disc wheels, of the shape that had distinguished his Type 16 Lotus from other contemporary racing cars.

Left: the first GP contender from Lotus was the 1958 Lotus 16, with lines reminiscent of the Vanwall; both cars' bodywork was designed by Frank Costin. The design was aimed at reducing frontal area and had the engine both inclined and angled to the car's axis to run the drive line alongside the low-seated driver. The Chapman-strut rear suspension was so efficient that the car was plagued with persistent understeer and it was never very successful

Right: the six-cylinder, 2493 cc engine of the 1959 Aston Martin DBR4/250 produced 280 bhp at 8250 rpm

Below: the DBR4/250 had de Dion rear suspension and disc brakes, but by the time it was introduced the writing was on the wall for front-engined cars

The lesson was that by putting the engine behind the driver it was possible, in a short, compact car, to save weight and reduce frontal area, and therefore wind drag. Chapman had only 240 bhp to play with, but from an engine weighing but 290 lb, which can be compared to the 450 lb of earlier GP engines. In this context, the rear-engined BRM was 100 lb below the avoirdupois of its earlier front-engined ancestors and also had nearly two square feet less body-work area exposed to frontal drag. So Cooper with the benefit of experience were on a very good wicket, especially after they had introduced coil-spring rear suspension and gone over to five-speed gearboxes. Ferrari had also turned to the use of a Dino 246 motor, behind the driver, in his factory cars. It was the Scarab, sponsored by the American Lance Reventlow, which was now looking old-fashioned, although just introduced to the European Grand Prix scene; the car had a front-located engine, a Chevrolet gearbox, and was of heavy conception, with a very upright driving position. Its saving grace was that it made up in beautiful finish what it lacked technically.

So the 2½-litre years ran out, characterised by the emergence of the new theory that the engine should be placed behind the driver to gain a compact body form. The BRMs of this kind were steadily improving, and the day of the Lotus was obviously soon to dawn, being held back for the moment by obscure carburation maladies that for some peculiar reason did not trouble the Coopers. Both the latter makes, Lotus and Cooper, if one can use 'make' in this context, were of less weight and could therefore out-strip the BRM on acceleration. This led to a new version of BRM with some 60 lb in weight lopped off it and with double-wishbone rear springing, which Vanwall had also adopted. Although the so-called European Grand Prix of 1960, run at Monza, was won by a front-engined Ferrari, the day of the conventional racing car in this sphere was over.

Thus came the beginnings of the change that was to render a road-racing motor car, the highest form the racing automobile could take, something quite different from the cars used for business and pleasure by the ordinary citizen. As the years advanced, the gulf widened. There was also the fact that much importance was being placed on the new Drivers' World Championship, which drew public interest more to the drivers than to the technical quality and performance of the racing cars. This was the commencement of the 'circus' aspect which has engulfed modern Grand Prix motor racing.

By 1960, the Driver's World Championship had run for a decade. It had seen Farina, Fangio (five times), Ascari (twice), Hawthorn and Jack Brabham (twice) in the seat of honour, these aces relying on Alfa Romeo (twice), Ferrari (three times), Mercedes and Maserati, Mercedes alone, Maserati alone, Lancia-Ferrari and Cooper (twice). It is significant that it was Brabham who took the crown in the last two years of the 2½-litre Formula, with Cooper cars, and that it was he who had pioneered the rear-engined conception of Grand Prix racing car, which was soon to dominate the sport.

Top and above: Cooper were the progenitors of the modern rear-engined layout for GP cars, although several manufacturers had used the configuration earlier. Before they went into the F1 arena, Cooper were already well known for their 500 cc F3 cars and machines such as this 1957 F2 car. This model is powered by a 1½-litre Coventry Climax four cylinder engine, producing 106 bhp. After a successful career in F2 it was campaigned by Patsy Burt in hill-climbs, gaining over 160 awards (National Motor Museum, England)

Above: the first post-war motor race meeting was held in the Bois de Boulogne, Paris on 9 September 1945. This is the start of the Coupe Robert Benoist for 1500cc cars, which was won by Henri Louveau, seen on the right of the first three cars. Left is Deho (Maserati) and in the centre is Bonnard's unusual special single seater, composed of an MG R-type chassis and an eight-cylinder supercharged engine

THE RACES: 1939-60

Racing was somewhat slow to resume after the war had ended, although the delay was not the result of any lack of enthusiasm; all through the dark years of the fighting, bombing, and food and petrol rationing, plenty of enthusiasts made it clear that they wanted to witness racing cars in action just as soon as possible after the foes had been defeated. When hostilities ceased, it was lack of resources which proved the major stumbling block to an immediate resumption of full-scale motor racing. There was also the inescapable fact that the 1936–39 era of racing would be a difficult one for the post-war sport to live up to.

When racing began again it did so on a modest scale. The scene was Nice, where they contrived to hold a Grand Prix race in 1946; the race was won by the greying Luigi Villoresi – he has been called the man who *was* motor-racing – at the wheel of a 1½-litre Maserati. Only three weeks later a similar joyous occasion unfolded at Marseille, with something of the pre-war sounds, sights and scents to thrill the onlookers. It was Raymond Sommer who won this time, also in a 1½-litre Maserati; Tazio Nuvolari, a wiry little man, and ailing now, but perhaps still the very greatest of them all, set fastest lap speed and then went on to win at Albi. Nuvolari accomplished this with a Maserati, being followed home by Louveau and Raph in the same make of car. In spite of Maserati's early success, the sport had to wait only as long as the return of the Alfa Romeo 'Alfettas' to see a walk-over for the Milanese manufacturer.

Below: the Isle of Man circuit could have been Britain's Nürburgring; here are the Maseratis of Bob Ansell and Reg Parnell in the 1948 Empire Trophy

Ten years after making their racing debut, the splendid Tipo 158s ran away with the 1946 Grand Prix des Nations, which was staged, ambitiously, at Geneva. The winner was Dr Farina, and he was followed home by Count Trossi and Jean-Pierre Wimille, pre-war aces again in action; Wimille made fastest lap at 68.76 mph and the race average, set by Farina, was 64.1 mph. Two more races of this calibre were staged during 1946. There was the Circuit of Turin, longest of the revived races, at 174 miles, which saw Achille Varzi, another pre-war *pilote*, take the honours from Wimille, at 64.62 mph, both in the victorious Alfa Romeos, with third place filled by Sommer's Maserati. Once again fastest lap went to Wimille, at 73.58 mph – things were warming up. The year 1946 concluded with the shortest of these resuscitated Grands Prix, the Circuit of Milan, over 52 miles; the race was dominated by the Alfa Romeo team, with Trossi winning, from Varzi and works test driver Sanesi, the winning average being 55.59 mph. The Alfa driven by Varzi, but taken over by Farina, set fastest lap, at 56.7 mph.

Motor racing had well and truly started again and all looked forward to 1947, especially those who had watched Varzi beat Wimille by a mere half-second in that race at Turin. Five races to the prevailing Grand Prix status

Right: Raymond Sommer

Below: Alfa Romeo 158s in full cry at the 1946 GP des Nations, at Geneva

were organised. There were about twenty lesser events in which the independents, including a number of British drivers, like Reg Parnell and bespectacled Bob Gerard, had a chance of success, but it was the professionals who claimed the limelight. In the Swiss and Belgium Grands Prix the Alfa Romeos continued to make the pace, the order in both races being Wimille, Varzi, Trossi; the average speed of the former race, over 137 miles, was 95.42 mph, and at Spa, where the distance was 310 miles, the average was 95.28 mph. In the first of these 1947 contests Maserati had the honour, such as it was, of making fastest lap, when Sommer motored round at 97.03 mph, but at Spa the best time was done by the winning Wimille, at a speed of 101.94 mph.

Varzi and Sanesi, in that order, held off the Maserati of Grieco at Bari, the winning Alfa averaging 65.15 mph for the 165½-mile race, and at the Italian Grand Prix, back to almost former glory, the expected Alfa Romeo grand-slam was seen once again, with Trossi, Varzi and Sanesi in the order of finishing, and the winning speed was 70.29 mph. The terrors of Milan were absent from the 314 mile French Grand Prix, giving the unsupercharged cars their chance; popular (and pre-war) veteran Louis Chiron pulled off victory in a Talbot, at 78.09 mph, from the Maserati of Louveau.

Left: the cars line up for the eighteenth Italian GP, at Monza in 1947, with the grid dominated by works Alfa Romeos and Maseratis. Trossi, Varzi and Sanesi led an Alfa grand slam

Right: the start of the 1946 Turin GP, again with Alfa Romeo and Maserati to the fore. The race, which was won by Varzi's Alfa, decided the result of a 20 million lire national lottery

Below: the Alfetta of Dr Giuseppe Farina at the shortest of the 1946 Grands Prix, the Circuit of Milan. Alfa Romeo again scored a 1-2-3 victory in the event, with Trossi winning

Below: Jean Pierre Wimille in 1948. The action picture shows Wimille on his way to victory in the 1948 French GP, at Reims, with an Alfa Romeo 158. Had there been a World Championship in that year, Wimille would have won it, but he was killed in Argentina the following year before the championship was instituted

Right: the only real opposition to Alfa in 1948 came from Maserati. This is Louis Chiron racing in Jersey

It wasn't GP racing, but in the great Mille Miglia sports-car contest Nuvolari made a memorable swan-song; although he was by now a very ill person, he defied adversity and heavy rain, to bring a 1100 cc Cisitalia home in second place, only a quarter of an hour behind the winning 3-litre Alfa-Romeo, driven by Biondetti.

The new Formula began to take hold for the 1948 racing season. In the European GP, held at Berne, Switzerland, it was the compact, highly-supercharged, Alfa Romeos that dominated, driven into first and second places by the experienced, pipe-smoking Trossi, and Wimille, the former averaging 90.81 mph from start to finishing-flag, and the latter setting up the fastest lap of the Swiss circuit, at 95.05 mph. Third place was secured by Villoresi in a Maserati. These Alfa Romeos continued to be the racing sensation of the age, for in training for the French Grand Prix of 1948 at Reims, Wimille lapped at 112.2 mph and although in the event he was not able to do better than 108.14 mph, this gave him victory, at 102.1 mph; Wimille's team-mate Sanesi was second and the rising star, Alberto Ascari (son of the Antonio Ascari

Left: Luigi Villoresi in a 4CLT/48 Maserati won the 1948 British GP at Silverstone, from Alberto Ascari in a similar car. The race was a revival of an event last held at Brooklands in 1927

Right: Achille Varzi, a few months before his death at Berne in 1948

Below: Raymond Sommer having a hard time in the wet with his Ferrari 125 at the Italian GP in Turin. Villoresi, seen here following in his Maserati 4CLT, beat Sommer for second place, behind Wimille's victorious Alfa Romeo

who had been killed at Lyon in this very race, before the war) third, also in an Alfa Romeo. In the Italian GP Wimille won again, after the other Alfas had met with trouble, from Villoresi's 4CLT Maserati and Sommer's Ferrari, at 70.38 mph. The *marque* from Milan had been placed 1-2-3 in the Monza GP, in the sequence Wimille, Trossi, Sanesi. The race-average was a remarkable 109.98 mph and Sanesi lapped at 116.95 mph, with one of these 1500 cc cars. Achille Varzi had been killed while practising at Berne, when his Alfa Romeo overturned, Wimille was the victim of a fatal accident in South America, at the wheel of a Simca *voiturette*, and during 1948 Trossi died from cancer.

At the difficult round-the-houses Monaco Grand Prix Maserati returned to the forefront, when Farina won at 59.61 mph from Chiron's Talbot, with de Graffenreid, the keen Swiss driver, third in another Maserati. The winner lapped the Monaco course at 62.32 mph. The British Grand Prix was run over the new aerodrome circuit at Silverstone and was a victory for Villoresi, who averaged 72.28 mph and also set fastest lap, at 76.82 mph. His new Maserati team mate, Ascari, backed him up with second place, and third place went to Bob Gerard's ERA.

Perhaps it was the loss of some of their best drivers that persuaded Alfa Romeo to drop out of racing in 1949. The Tipo 159 racers, which were then scattered unceremoniously about the factory, or tucked into odd corners gathering dust, had started in 19 races since 1938, of which they had won 16, finishing 1, 2, 3 on no fewer than ten occasions. They suffered defeat only at the hands of Maserati (twice) and the W165 Mercedes-Benz of Hermann Lang. It was an impressive record.

With Alfa Romeo out of contention, and the strong, level-headed, enormously talented Juan Manuel Fangio now occupying the driving seat of a Maserati, this Italian make dominated the 1949 races: Fangio won at San Remo (62.78 mph for 178 miles) and at Pau (52.7 mph for 87 miles), being followed in by the Maseratis of B. Bira and Baron de Graffenreid in the former race, and by Gerard's ERA and Rosier's big Talbot in the latter. Bira, the diminutive Siamese Royal driver who had been sponsored and managed by his cousin Prince Chula before the war, was still on form, for he made fastest lap at San Remo, at 64.66 mph, and repeated his show of speed at Silverstone in the British Grand Prix. This race was a victory for E. de Graffenreid in a Maserati, with the irrepressible ERA second, and Louis Rosier's Talbot placed third, an interesting mixed outcome, the winner averaging 77.31 mph. In the Belgian Grand Prix Rosier came into his own, winning with a Talbot at 96.95 mph, outclassing both Villoresi and Ascari in their Maseratis. Dr Farina also in a Maserati, since Alfa Romeo's withdrawal from racing, made fastest lap at over 101 mph.

The scene then shifted to the Swiss GP and here Alberto Ascari was in the ascendant, coming first past the finish; Farina's Maserati averaged a fraction more than 95 mph to establish the fastest lap speed, and the winner himself averaged 90.76 mph for this 181-mile contest. This year the Italian GP at Monza took on the mantle of the European GP and it was another victory for the chubby, Roman-nosed Ascari. He was now in a Ferrari, and averaged over 105 mph, though in practice he had lapped even faster, at 112.72 mph. Phi-Phi Etancelin was second in a Talbot and Prince Bira third in his Maserati. The GP de France had previously been won by Chiron's Talbot from Bira's Maserati, and Britain's Peter Whitehead had taken third place in a Ferrari. Whitehead was later to go on to victory in that years Czechoslovak Grand Prix at Brno. At the converted Silverstone airfield circuit, the newly formed British Automobile Racing Club had revived, under its new colours, the pre-war Junior Car Club's International Trophy Race, this being won in 1949 by Ascari, at 89.58 mph, after he had lapped triumphantly at 93.35 mph – Silverstone was already a fast course. Ascari was followed home by his team-mate, Villoresi, but only in third place, for Farina had forced his Maserati between the two Ferraris.

So it was that motor racing started up again in the post-war years. It was well established by the time the 1950 season opened.

Far left: French Champion from 1949 to 1952, Louis Rosier raced Lago-Talbots to victory in the Belgian, Dutch and Albi Grands Prix. The Clermont-Ferrand garage proprietor won Le Mans with his son in 1950, and raced his own Ferraris and Maseratis in Formulae 1 and 2 and sports car events. Rosier, normally a safe driver, was killed at Montlhéry in 1956 aged 51. Jean Behra, *centre left*, instantly recognisable in his chequered helmet, was France's greatest driver of the 1950s

Left: the Maserati 4CLT/48 of Swiss Baron Emanuel de Graffenried, on his way to victory in the 1949 British Grand Prix at Silverstone

Below: the 1949 French Grand Prix was a sports car event, but Louis Chiron won the country's premier Formula 1 event at Reims in the ageing unsupercharged 4½-litre Talbot

The remarkable aspect of the 1950 season was the return of Alfa Romeo to the fray, with the revised Tipo 159 cars, which, once again, swept all before them. Indeed, they won all ten races in which they started, in spite of some notable setbacks. It is not always a good thing when one make of car dominates racing, except for the manufacturer and the drivers of that make, of course, but no-one could challenge Alfa's superiority. After Farina had been involved in an accident, Alfa Romeo used the services of the great Fangio at San Remo and the lone Alfa won, in wet weather, from Villoresi's two stage supercharged Ferrari, while Ascari spun and crashed his Ferrari. Next, it was to England, where for once the sun shone, and the Royal Family, led by HM King George VI, were present at Silverstone to watch the racing. This event, which was the British Grand Prix with the added status of the title of the European Grand Prix, was another entirely convincing triumph for the 'Alfettas', which would have arrived at the end of the race in 1-2-3-4, order, Briton Reg Parnell having been invited to drive one of them, had not Fangio's car developed valve trouble eight laps from the finish. So the result was first Farina, second Fagioli and third a very happy Parnell.

Below: the handsome Italian Doctor of Political Science, Giuseppe Farina racing at a very wet Silverstone in 1950. He took his Alfa Romeo 158 to victory twice at Silverstone that year, winning the British Grand Prix, the very first World Championship event, and the rain-soaked *Daily Express* International Trophy race

Above: the first lap fracas at Monaco during the 1950 Grand Prix, caused when race-leader Farina spun at the Tabac corner, wet with sea-water. Several other cars were involved, but Fangio managed to squeeze his Alfa Romeo through the gap and motor on to victory. In the photograph a Talbot and a Maserati thread their way through the carnage; this kind of accident is always a possibility at Monaco, where there are no run-off areas and few legitimate passing places

At the Monaco Grand Prix, with Prince Rainier in attendance, there was a historic pile-up on the very first lap, when the usually wily Farina skidded on the harbour front and half the entry was, so early, unfortunately eliminated. Fangio proved his skill in getting through the *melée* and, although both the other Alfa Romeos were out of the hunt, Fangio just motored on, to win with no-one challenging him. It is worth comparing his times with those of the mighty pre-war Mercedes-Benz, over this round-the-town course. Fangio had lapped at 64.56 mph. In the race he managed 64.09 mph and his winning average speed was 61.33 mph. Caracciola's fastest lap in the last pre-war running of the event had been 66.79 mph, a record which was to stand for eighteen years. Behind the Master came Ascari and Chiron. At Berne the race was rather dull after the Ferrari challenge to the 'Alfettas' had ended with both retiring early. The stage was then all set for another Fangio walk-over, but his car dropped a valve nine laps from the finish and it was Farina who took first place, his fellow Alfa Romeo *pilote* Fagioli being but 0.4 of a second behind him and Rosier coming in next, in one of the big Talbots. Sommer was the hero of Spa in 1950, in a Talbot, but even his inspired driving and the pit-stops for fuel necessary to the Alfa Romeos could not stop Fangio, who won from Fagioli. Sommer's early pace probably resulted in the loss of oil pressure which sidelined Farina before Sommer himself dropped out of the race with engine failure after 20 of the 35 laps; Rosier was third.

The French Grand Prix had returned to its full glory by 1950 and it remained to be seen whether the flying Fangio could equal the sort of performance put in at the fast Reims circuit by the pre-war monsters. He was timed over a lap at 116.2 mph in practice, against the actual pre-war lap record of 117.5 mph. In the race he went round the course that winds through the fields of the champagne country at 112.35 mph and won at 104.83 mph. Fagioli was second but Farina had been delayed by fuel feed problems after nine laps. These Alfa Romeos victories were becoming monotonous! Suffice to say that Farina and Fangio contested Bari, and Fangio and Fagioli Pescara, with Fangio the victor in both races, although Fagioli suffered a broken road spring on the last lap of what was intended to be his race at Pescara. Rosier had been actually pressing Fangio and the latter was obliged to rush over the line to prevent a disaster, instead of allowing Fagioli to limp to victory.

There was a confrontation between the big, unblown Ferraris and the super-charged Alfa Romeos at Geneva and the challenge was strongly apparent, in spite of Ascari, driving for Ferrari, retiring six laps from the end with water pouring out of his car's exhaust system, allowing the race to go to Fangio, with his new team-mates, de Graffenreid and Taruffi, second and third. Villoresi had also been pressing the smaller cars but crashed, taking Farina with him. The challenge of the big Ferraris came to a head in the Italian Grand Prix, when five Alfas met two Ferraris, Serafini replacing the injured Villoresi. The smaller cars would stop twice for fuel, the non-blown Ferraris only once.

Alfa Romeo, on the day, did some intelligent swopping about of their drivers and Farina won, from Ascari and Fagioli. Fangio had two cars blow up on him, but lapped at 117.445 mph, which was a race lap record. The forthcoming Barcelona race promised to be a most exciting return round, but Alfa Romeo stood down, leaving the interesting sight of two V16 BRMs running in a continental race for the first time, with Walker and Parnell nominated to drive them. That debut evaporated when Parnell's car succumbed to a sheared drive to the notorious centrifugal blower and Walker retired with a lack of power, a grave disappointment for the English onlookers, after Parnell's car had been timed to do 186 mph over a kilometre in practise. The result was a Ferrari 1-2-3, in the order Ascari, Serafini and Taruffi, the last named having lost a couple of laps after spinning off.

This Alfa/Ferrari battle continued into the 1951 season. Villoresi won at Syracuse and at Pau, while Ascari took the honours at San Remo in a full 4½-litre Ferrari. At Silverstone the rain was so heavy that the *Daily Express* International Trophy Race had to be stopped after a mere six laps. It was a race run in heats, however, so some racing was seen beforehand. In the Final

Right: a freak storm brought chaos to Silverstone's 1951 International Trophy meeting, with hailstones and nine inches of rain falling in half an hour. Here, Baron de Graffenried's Maserati struggles blindly through the impossible conditions, which caused the race to be stopped after six laps. Reg Parnell's Thinwall Special was leading at the time, and was awarded the Trophy

Below: Juan Manuel Fangio in an Alfa Romeo 159 at the European Grand Prix of 1951. This turned out to be a race-long duel between Fangio and Ascari, enacted at the ultra-fast Reims circuit. Such was the pace that both drivers used up their own cars and had to borrow from their slower team-mates, the Fangio/Fagioli Alfa beating the Ascari/Gonzales Ferrari by one minute

three English drivers held off the ace Italians during the thunderstorm, and Parnell's Thinwall Ferrari, forerunner of the latterly invincible Vanwalls, was actually placed first, Duncan Hamilton's big Talbot second, and Fangio third, after Fangio had taken one heat and Farina the other, for Alfa Romeo, both at over 90 mph. At Berne the Ferraris were in trouble and it was Fangio who gave a masterly performance in very wet conditions. He led all the way, except when in the pits for fuel. After Ascari had developed trouble and Villoresi had hit the markers, it was Sanesi who harried the Alfas, actually coming in second, between Fangio and Farina. Spa provided excitement of a different sort, apart from the sheer speed. Fangio lapped at over 120.5 mph and while in the lead, on the 15th lap, he stopped to refuel and for a change of wheels. A wheel jammed on its spline and lost the swarthy Argentinian all chance of World Championship points – yet he remained ice-calm throughout. The race was won by Farina, followed by Ascari and Villoresi, the Alfa Romeo the victor by a narrow margin, at 114.32 mph. Alfa Romeo won again at Reims in the French/European GP, with a car shared by Fangio and Fagioli, and at last, in practice, Fangio bettered Lang's 1939 Mercedes-Benz lap record with

a speed of 119.99 mph (against 117.5 mph). There could now be no looking back. Moreover, Neubauer and Lang were among the spectators! In the race Ascari's car threw a rod but, after the Alfa Romeo had won at 110.97 mph, the Ferrari, jointly handled by Gonzales – the 'Pampas Bull' – and Ascari, was second and Villoresi's Ferrari third, a nice balance of technical perfection against the might of 4½ litres.

In the British GP it finally happened: Ferrari defeated Alfa Romeo. It was a terrific battle between Gonzales, in his furious style of sliding his corners and Fangio holding a classic line through them in his Alfa Romeo. Fangio went ahead, but to yells from the crowd, the podgy 'Pampas Bull' took the lead again on lap 39, after being in arrears to his Argentinian friend by as much as six seconds. From that moment on, it was Gonzalez' race. He even refuelled without losing the lead. He won at 96.11 mph, from Fangio, with Villoresi's Ferrari third. Farina, after lapping within an ace of 100 mph, retired while in 3rd place, with his engine on fire, and Ascari had gearbox trouble.

The BRM position was only slightly improved in this 1951 British Grand Prix for, although both cars finished the course in fifth and seventh places,

Left: the colourful and talented Jose Froilan Gonzales. His aggressive driving style and bulky frame caused him to be called the 'Pampas Bull', and he was particularly successful in 1951, winning the British Grand Prix for Ferrari and being well placed in the other Grands Prix

Below: a somewhat unconventional situation for an Alfa Romeo, caused when German driver Paul Pietsch lost control at the Nürburgring's North Curve during the 1951 German Grand Prix. His one-off drive ended when the Alfa disappeared over the banking and destroyed itself on a road outside the circuit. Pietsch emerged unscathed

drivers Reg Parnell and Peter Walker suffered great physical exhaustion, due to the heat and fumes, and the effort of keeping the ill-handling cars in the right gear. The limelight of the Grand Prix circus had now settled on Fangio and Gonzalez, both of whom showed their great prowess by quickly mastering the difficult Nürburgring circuit in readiness for the 1951 German Grand Prix. Another pre-war German driver was now to be found racing again, for Alfa Romeo had contracted Paul Pietsch for the occasion. It was the Alfa/Ferrari battle all over again, except that this time the Alfettas ran into a series of troubles. Farina went out with over-heating and no oil-pressure, Bonetto had supercharger failure, and Pietsch damaged the car after charging over a bank. This time it was Ascari who brought his unblown Ferrari home first, and, even with an unexpected stop for fresh rear tyres, he finished half-a-minute ahead of Fangio's Alfa and Gonzalez in another big Ferrari. At Pescara the Alfa challenge was absent, but Gonzalez' Ferrari was the only one to shine. He finished first some 7½-minutes ahead of the nearest Talbot, Rosier's 4½-litre car with Etancelin's Talbot third. At Bari Fangio had a fine victory, finishing over a minute ahead of the redoubtable Gonzalez, who had driven well after a

poor start. Much mechanical trouble befell the others – Ascari's engine caught fire, Farina's Alfa suffered a burnt-out piston, and a shunt caused Villoresi's Ferrari to lose its oil-pressure. Meanwhile, Taruffi brought a 2-litre Ferrari home third. So it can be seen that the blown/unblown conflict was still wide open. In the Italian Grand Prix four Alfas with de Dion suspension and new air-intakes were to meet four big Ferraris, which had bigger fuel tanks and other minor improvements. Both BRMs were withdrawn before the start due to gearbox lubrication problems. After a race of much fluctuating fortune, the reliability of Ascari's Ferrari won the day at a speed of 115.45 mph, from Gonzalez' Ferrari and Farina who had lapped at a rousing 120.97 mph but had been delayed by slow Alfa pit-work and a leaking fuel tank. Next came the Ferraris of Villoresi and Taruffi.

In Italy, Fangio had retired with a blown-up engine, nevertheless he led the World Championship by two points from Ascari, a very satisfactory outcome of the Alfa/Ferrari duel. So it was in far away Barcelona that the 1951 World Championship would be settled. Tyre troubles marred the Ferrari attack and Fangio finished at a canter, his Alfa Romeo averaging 98.76 mph. Gonzalez was second for Ferrari, Farina third for Alfa, and Ascari fourth. Fangio, when in a hurry, had lapped at over 105 mph. Before we leave this interesting 1951 season it is worth mentioning that Dr Giuseppe Farina came to Dunrod with the Alfa Romeo for the Ulster Trophy Race, and to Goodwood. He beat Reg Parnell in the Vandervell-Thinwall-Ferrari on both occasions and left the Goodwood lap record at a stirring 97.36 mph. It is also of interest that Mercedes-Benz carefully unwrapped their 1939 3-litre Grand Prix cars and took them to two formula libre races at Buenos Aires. On both occasions they experienced a similar problem to that which beset them before the war, poor carburation, and both times a 2-litre two-stage supercharged Ferrari sufficed to vanquish them, but its driver was the great Froilan Gonzalez.

The 1952 season was not a particularly notable one for Alfa Romeo had again dropped out of racing and the Grand Prix organisers chose to run the races for Formula Two cars. Therefore neither the BRM nor the out-dated Talbots were eligible, and opposition to the Formula 2 Ferraris came from Gordini, Cooper-Bristol, Maserati and Connaught. Ascari won all seven World Championship qualifying rounds, and he was well on his way to a good season when he won the first three races of the year, at Syracuse, Pau, and Marseilles. His chief rival, Fangio, was out of racing for most of the year following a crash at Monza. The works Ferraris were not at Silverstone for the *Daily Express* Meeting. After Hawthorn in a Cooper Bristol and Manzon in a Gordini had won the heats, Lance Macklin and Tony Rolt went on to finish first and second for HWM. Ferrari was back in the Swiss Grand Prix with three 'works' cars for Farina, Taruffi, and Simon, the former Alfa-Romeo drivers having found new employment, and it was Taruffi the perfectionist who won.

At Spa-Francorchamps it was Ascari and Farina from Manzon's Gordini and Hawthorne's Cooper-Bristol. Much the same picture emerged at the three-hour race against the clock at Rouen-les-Essarts, but the new names of Maurice Trintignant on Gordini and Peter Collins on HWM figured on the results sheet in fifth and sixth. From the British point of view the results looked better at Silverstone, with Hawthorn's Cooper-Bristol third and the Connaughts of Dennis Poore (later to mastermind the Norton-Villiers motor cycle concern) and Thompson fourth and fifth, albeit three laps in arrears.

The great Jean Behra placed his Gordini fifth at the Nürburgring, breaking the monotony of a run of Ferraris. Ascari's tutor, Luigi Villoresi, finished third in his Ferrari at Zandvoort and at the final race at Monza, whilst Gonzalez placed his Maserati second at the latter. Gonzalez had more success in non-championship events in 1952, winning the Easter Goodwood meeting with the Thinwall Special and also leading the BRM 1-2-3 in an end-of-season meeting there.

It is interesting to note that points scored in the Indianapolis 500 could also be counted towards the World Championship, a provision only abolished in 1960. Ascari won from Villoresi, with Gonzalez third and Hawthorn fourth. The Dutch Grand Prix was to much the same pattern, with Ascari winning,

Right : Alberto Ascari won sixteen Grands Prix in 1952 and 1953 and, not surprisingly took the world championship title in both years. In 1955, while recovering from an accident in Monaco, Ascari crashed fatally testing a Ferrari sports car at Monza

Far right: the Villoresi brothers, Emilio and Luigi, were quite successful in motor racing, although Luigi lived long enough completely to overshadow his brother's achievements before the war in an Alfetta; 'Gigi' is seen here winning the 1951 Marseilles Grand Prix in a Ferrari 166

Below: in 1952, Frenchman Jean Behra was just beginning to show signs that he was soon to become a force to be reckoned with on the circuits. Here at that year's Pau GP, however, he finds things difficult with his Gordini after spinning on oil dropped by Villoresi's car

and Farina's Ferrari, finishing second. Gonzalez climbed into Bonetto's Maserati after the final drive had gone on his own ASS6G, and brought the car in third, ahead of Hawthorn's Ferrari. It was all drama at Spa during the 1953 Belgian Grand Prix. Gonzalez opened with his customary fire, building up a useful lead over Fangio and Ascari, until his accelerator-pedal snapped right off! That gave Fangio the lead for three laps. Then his Maserati engine

Far left and left: Mike Hawthorn and Juan Manuel Fangio who are seen again *below* dicing for the lead on the last straight, at the 1953 French Grand Prix, held on the fast Reims circuit. The race-long duel came out in the favour of the Englishman from Farnham, Surrey. He was a mere one second ahead of the Argentinian at the finish line, after averaging 113.65 mph.

Right: Italian *marques* in battle on their home ground in 1953, Monza. Here, the Ferraris of Farina and Ascari head the Maseratis of Fangio and Marimon. On the last lap, Ascari spun when passing a slower car and took with him Farina and Marimon. Fangio, however, scraped by to win

blew up, so the *maestro* leapt into Johnny Claes' Maserati, got back up to third place, then slid on some oil and crashed. So it was his young team-mate Marimon who took third spot, behind the Ferraris of Ascari and Villoresi. The French Grand Prix, held in the sweltering heat of the Reims countryside, was a sensation. Hawthorn in the Ferrari and Fangio in the Maserati ran side by side along the final straight, after a race-long battle. Hawthorn thought that Fangio had lost bottom gear and staked all on a last-second spurt out of Thillois hairpin to win by one second. Mike then collapsed with emotion and exhaustion, his name made from that day on. Gonzalez, never to be entirely outdone, had closed to within a tenth of a second of Fangio, so the finish of this race had all the appearances of a sprint event. Ascari finished fourth.

In the British Grand Prix at Silverstone, Ascari returned to his unbeatable form, and nothing Fangio could do would stop him from winning, while Farina was third and Gonzalez was fourth, turning a convenient blind-eye to the

black flag held out for him, as his car was thought to be dropping oil. At the Nürburgring there was drama again, as Ascari lost a wheel when leading. Unhurt, he jumped into Villoresi's car to pursue Farina, but the Ferrari's engine blew up. Clearly here was a man keen to collect World Championship points. So it was Farina, Fangio and Hawthorn. Stirling Moss, new to Grand Prix racing, was sixth in a Cooper-Alta. Monza, the final Championship round, was almost unbearable – an all-time classic! Four cars of Ascari, Farina, Fangio and Marimon raced within a second of one another, with continual passing and repassing. Even a long pit-pause did not stop the last-named from rejoining this fierce battle. Then Ascari spun round and round as he overtook a slower Connaught, and he was hit by Marimon. Fangio found a gap and won for Maserati. Farina came second, Villoresi third and Hawthorn fourth.

The World Championship returned for Formula One cars in 1954, and marked the revival of Mercedes-Benz in Grand Prix racing. BRM were saved from oblivion when Alfred Owen stepped in to re-finance the British team and build new cars. Lancia took on Vittorio Jano's new ideas and had Ascari and Villoresi to drive their D50s. Millionaire Tony Vandervell was developing his Vanwalls, and the season looked decidedly promising! At the Argentine Grand Prix the new Mercedes were absent. Fangio scored the first victory for the 250F Maserati although the Ferraris were superior in the dry. When rain came Fangio stopped to change to ribbed tyres, an early example of rain-tyre, and continued, catching all the others to win. This was Fangio at his best. Ugolini had thought that more than the regulation number of mechanics had officiated at the Fangio tyre-change, so had signalled Farina to slow. His protest was not upheld, however.

Spa Francorchamps also went to Fangio and the Maserati, with Farina, injured in a sports-car race, driving pluckily in a Squalo Ferrari. The Mercedes-Benz debut came at Reims, for the French Grand Prix. With Fangio transferring to them, and backed up by Hans Hermann and Karl Kling, it was as if the pre-war story had come to life. Ascari's Maserati lasted but a lap and with others falling by the wayside it was a Mercedes benefit, the streamliners of Fangio and Kling finishing one-fifth of a second apart, and Hans Hermann set fastest lap at 117 mph before his machinery exploded. Twenty-one cars started, and only six survived. Mercedes were outclassed in the British Grand Prix because their all-enveloping bodies were ruinous to vision from the cockpits. So Gonzalez won for Ferrari, with Hawthorn's Ferrari second and Marimon's Maserati third. At the German Grand Prix Mercedes had the orthodox bodywork, and Fangio's W196 took the honours. But Hermann over-revved his engine and blew up, and Hermann Lang spun and could not restart his engine. Kling actually got past Fangio but his rear suspension broke. Hawthorn's Ferrari was second, Trintignant's Ferrari third, and Kling's Mercedes-Benz fourth. Sadly, Marimon was killed when his Maserati crashed in practice. It was not all Mercedes' year, however. Fangio led all the way at Berne, in the rain, Gonzalez being second and Hermann third. At Monza Fangio just won, with a sick car, although Moss was the moral victor, his Maserati 250F having retired with a split oil tank. The Ferraris of Hawthorn and Gonzalez were second and third. At Barcelona Hawthorn won from Luigi Musso's Maserati, with Fangio third in a Mercedes with an air-intake choked with dead leaves.

Fangio netted his third World Championship in 1955, a year dominated by Mercedes-Benz. In the second round of the Championship at Monaco, Ascari's Lancia dived over the harbour wall into the sea. Ascari swam to shore none the worse for wear, but he was killed a week later in an inexplicable crash at Monza while driving a sports Ferrari. Mercedes had the British Grand Prix at Aintree buttoned-up, Moss being permitted to lead Fangio home. Mercedes withdrew from racing in 1956 after the Le Mans tragedy of 1955 when Levegh's car disintegrated in a grandstand killing over 80 spectators. Fangio was driving for Ferrari, who had taken over the V8 Lancias, and he was again World Champion. At Monaco, Moss in a Maserati beat Fangio, with no holds barred, Fangio battering his Ferrari about to such an extent that he stopped, and resumed in Peter Collins' car. Collins won at Spa, with Paul Frère, the journalist second in another Ferrari. Stirling Moss was third, after losing a wheel, in Pedisa's Maserati. Fangio won the British and German Grands Prix and Moss just took the Italian, in spite of a worn rear tyre, from Fangio, who had taken over Luigi Musso's Ferrari.

The year 1957 was a jubilant one for Britain, because all Tony Vandervell's hard work and investment paid off. Vanwalls won three Grands Prix, although Fangio, back in a Maserati, took his fifth World Championship. At Monaco there was an enormous crash which eliminated Moss, Collins and Hawthorn. Fangio had held back and he went on to win, from Tony Brooks' Vanwall. Then, at Aintree, Moss won a memorable victory for Vanwall and the same

Below left: the two great Argentinian racing drivers of the 1950s, Froilan Gonzales and Fangio. They are standing on the rostrum after finishing first and second in the 1954 Swiss GP at Berne, with Fangio leading his compatriot home

Right and below: the Lancia-based Ferrari in action, piloted by two of the most successful British drivers of the 1950s, Peter Collins and Mike Hawthorn. Aintree is the setting in 1955, *right*, while Collins is seen at Reims busy winning the 1956 French Grand Prix

combination had a very convincing victory at Pescara. Yet before this Fangio had driven the race of his life in the German Grand Prix to catch the Ferraris of Hawthorn and Collins, after his Maserati had refuelled. He set a new lap record of 91.52 mph for the Nüburgring, smashing his own lap-time ten laps running. At Monza three green Vanwalls occupied the front row of the grid, a sight to gladden the Englishman's heart, and Moss won from Fangio's Maserati and von Trips' Ferrari, after Brooks had set fastest-lap for Vanwall, at 124.04 mph. The following year saw the Vanwalls really 'on song', so that Hawthorn was lucky to win the World Championship, driving a Ferrari, by a single point from Moss's Vanwall, but at Reims, Musso was killed and at the German Grand Prix Peter Collins lost his life, robbing Hawthorn of two close friends. Brooks won the Italian Grand Prix for Vanwall and when his car blew-up at the Moroccan event, Hawthorn was able to finish second to Moss. After Vanwall had retired from racing, the rear-engined cars came into their own, the lightweight Coopers being a match for the Ferrari and the 1959 World

Championship being won by the steady Australian, Jack Brabham. Thus did this new era of racing establish itself, with the rear-engined Cooper-Climax cars winning five Grands Prix in a row during the 1960 season, and bringing 'Black' Jack Brabham his second World title. The BRMs were now doing better, with Graham Hill and the American driver Dan Gurney in their cockpits, and the Lotus team was out in force, with Jim Clark, Alan Stacey, John Surtees and Innes Ireland in the team. Outside sponsorship had arrived, too, the Yeo-man Credit Team, for instance, having Tony Brooks, young Bristow and Henry Taylor, together with Oliver Gendebien, as its drivers. Enthusiast Rob Walker had a rear-engined Lotus for Moss to drive, as an independent, and

Inset far left: a smiling Tony Brooks is seen before the start of the 1958 Italian GP at Monza; he had a lot to smile about for he and his Vanwall won the race, as seen *inset above*

Right: Hawthorn and Collins snatch the lead at the start of the 1957 German GP at the Nürburgring. Fangio, on the far left, made an unscheduled pit stop, but still went on to win. In doing so he broke the lap record ten times and clinched his fifth World Championship

Inset right: leader of the rear-engined revolution, three times World Champion Jack Brabham

Inset far right: Phil Hill's Ferrari Dino 246 at Reims during the 1960 French Grand Prix. The car's transmission broke just after half-distance

Moss used this to very good effect at Monaco, driving a memorable race in the rain. But mostly it was Brabham's year, and he even held off the Ferraris of Phil Hill and 'Taffy' von Trips in the French Grand Prix at Reims. It was a measure of the effectiveness of the new type of rear-engined racing car that Brabham there averaged 131.8 mph, this speed beating the previous lap record, which Jack lifted to a sensational 135.05 mph. In the British Grand Prix Graham Hill, after a bad start in his BRM, stormed through to catch Brabham, but with victory in sight Hill spun, stalled again, and so it was Brabham's race, in the Cooper. Moss had an appalling accident at Spa, when his Lotus shed a wheel, but he was back before the year was out.

CHAPTER 4

THE AGE OF REASON

THE CARS: 1960-83

The decade and a half from 1960 to the mid 1970s saw drastic changes in many aspects of motor racing; the new wave of thinking that began to emerge at the end of the 1950s gathered impetus as the commercial rewards for motor racing snowballed. The old order was rapidly changing: from being a sport, with a playboy image, motor racing was growing into a brash, commercialised and utterly professional business. For all the purists' scorn of the path of modern racing huge financial rewards have bred more intense competition than ever before, spawned innumerable racing car manufacturers and technologists, pushed the state of the art to new frontiers and brought the sport a bigger following than at any time in its history. The revolution can be traced through the cars.

1961 saw the birth of a new formula for Grand Prix cars of a mere 1½ litres, with a ban on supercharging, a minimum dry weight of 450 kg and with commercially available petrol as the obligatory fuel.

The remarkable success of the rear-engined Coopers towards the close of the 2½-litre formula had made a profound impression on the sport, and to even the most conservative observer it was apparent that the days of the front-engined racing car were at an end. The adoption of the 1½-litre formula, and the attendant advantages inherent in its compact mechanical elements, hammered the final nail into the coffin. Already the move to the 'kit-car' had begun, when a competitive engine, in the guise of the Coventry Climax FPF, became freely available. No longer did the building of a Grand Prix car have to begin with the enormous technical and financial resources necessary to

Below: the Lotus 18 was designed as a multi-formula car and was raced in events as diverse as the one-litre Formula Junior and the Grands Prix of the 2.5-litre formula. It had a spaceframe chassis and was clad in aluminium and glassfibre panels. Front suspension was independent by wishbones and coil-spring damper units, and the rear suspension was also independent, by coil springs, transverse links and radius arms. The car illustrated is Rob Walker's Grand Prix 18 which Stirling Moss drove to victory in the 1961 Monaco Grand Prix

design and build engine and transmission. The way was open for more constructors to emerge and for chassis development to benefit from the attention that had so long been absorbed in the search for power.

The successes of Vanwall and Cooper had lifted British motor racing from the doldrums in which it had so long languished. Cooper were joined in the revolution by BRM, Lola and Lotus and British Racing Green became a colour to be feared rather than ridiculed. Simplification came to be the path to pursue and the work of designers like Colin Chapman of Lotus brought a new elegance to racing engineering. Although Cooper were the progenitors of the modern rear-engined layout, it was Chapman who realised its greater implications and began the gradual refinement which still continues.

The Lotus 18 made its first appearances in $2\frac{1}{2}$-litre form, under the previous formula, and when the formula changed in 1961 the car was given a $1\frac{1}{2}$-litre, four-cylinder Coventry Climax engine and thrown back into the fray by Rob Walker's private team. It was typical of the position in which the British teams found themselves. When the $1\frac{1}{2}$-litre formula was announced, the British constructors dug in their heels and clung steadfastly to the notion that, by boycotting the new formula, the days of the $2\frac{1}{2}$-litre cars could be extended. The FIA dug in with even more verve and, although they conceded a reduction in the weight limit, from the originally agreed 500 kg to 450 kg, the $1\frac{1}{2}$-litre limit stood. While Lotus, BRM Cooper and, particularly, Coventry Climax procrastinated, Ferrari had forged quietly ahead under the guidance of designer Chiti. Their new Formula One car was built around a massive tubular chassis, like that of the Cooper, with the sting in the tail coming from a 65 degree V6 engine, the Dino 156. In its earliest form this engine gave almost 180 bhp at 9000 rpm, an advantage of some 30 bhp over the ageing Climax four. At Monaco, the wire-wheeled, shark-nostrilled Ferraris appeared with a 120 degree V6, giving another 5 bhp, and only an inspired performance by Moss in a Lotus 18 robbed the new car of victory. While the 18 was showing that it could, in the right hands, still perform miracles, Chapman, with his works cars, was pursuing his quest for lightness, compactness and simplicity. His offering for 1961 was the Lotus 21, which aroused great interest at its debut in Monaco, in the hands of Jim Clark.

In his attempts at further reducing the frontal area – equatable with increasing usable power – Chapman had laid his drivers even lower in the multi-tubular chassis, inclined the engine 18 degrees and moved the front springing inboard of the bodywork, where it was operated by a cantilevered upper wishbone of streamlined section. The rear suspension featured transverse links to relieve the drive shafts of suspension duties and enable rubber doughnut couplings to be utilised at their inboard ends.

While the aerodynamic advantages were of little consequence at Monaco, the car soon proved its worth on the faster circuits, scoring Lotus's first ever Grand Prix victory at Watkins Glen. It was clear that when Coventry Climax's new V8 engine appeared, the Lotus would be a force to be reckoned with. The V8 did appear briefly in 1961, being used by both Moss and Brabham, but it was plagued by overheating problems.

Like the FPF it had a stroke to bore ratio of 0.95 with twin, chain-driven, overhead camshafts on each bank. The 90 degree engine had a two-plane crankshaft, which necessitated the use of a crossover exhaust system; this was the only system which could fully utilise the pressure pulses associated with such an engine. Its accommodation was to give chassis designers some severe headaches.

The new BRM V8 unit was also revealed that year, at Monza. For once BRM seemed to be on the right track. This engine was a 90 degree V8, with gear drive to the twin overhead camshafts. A stroke to bore ratio of 0.74 and consequently large piston area promised adequate rewards. The engine had Lucas fuel injection, transistorised ignition and, in spite of its two-plane crank, separate exhaust banks.

For the time being, the challengers to Maranello's superiority had to plod gamely along with outdated designs and the only serious competition came from Moss in the Lotus 18 – more a reflection of his talent than of the car's prowess. Ferrari, of course, won the Championship by a handsome margin.

The second season of the new formula dawned with more promise: Ferrari were now faced with real opposition. Coventry Climax had supplied their new engine to Cooper, the new Brabham team, Lotus, Bowmaker-Lola and Rob Walker. Porsche too had developed an eight-cylinder engine, of flat, air-cooled

Below: Porsche's contribution to the 1½-litre formula was the 804. It featured an air-cooled flat-eight engine of 1498 cc which produced 185 bhp at 9200 rpm. Even though the car won several Grands Prix, its driver likened its performance and handling to that of a roadgoing Volkswagen Beetle

configuration, and BRM had the V8 that was to win them the Championship, in a cliff-hanging finale.

Ferrari themselves had changed the 156 but little, perhaps a sign that the lack of competition had inspired too much confidence. Significantly, the poor showing of the experimental, front-engined, four-wheel-drive Ferguson car in 1961 had not encouraged others to pursue that course. The major bombshell came again from Chapman's fertile brain, in the form of the sensational Lotus 25. This car, which made its debut at Zandvoort, was a milestone; gone was the multi-tubular chassis and in its stead was a tremendously light and rigid aluminium 'monocoque' or, more accurately, stressed-skin chassis with transverse bulkheads. Its success was to sound the death knell of the traditional tubular designs and, if any one car can be so described, the 25 was surely the father of all subsequent Grand Prix cars.

With the exceptional improvement in torsional stiffness that this chassis, with its rigidly mounted engine, offered, Chapman was able to treat the suspension in isolation from the vagaries of the rest of the car. Although little more than half its weight, the 'monocoque' was three times stiffer than the 21's 'spaceframe'. With the driver even more reclined and inboard suspension at the front, the frontal area was down to eight square feet. The rear suspension was by wishbones, radius arms, transverse links and coil spring/damper units.

After a season-long battle with Hill's BRM, Clark needed to take the final race, in South Africa, to win the title. He was beaten by an engine oil leak and BRM were at last on top of the world. Their Championship winner was, in comparison, very conventional. It had a light, compact, multi-tubular chassis with outboard wishbone suspension. Its only distinctive feature was the use of eight individual, upswept exhaust pipes, which earned this P56 the nickname

of the 'Stack-pipe BRM'. By Spa even these individual pipes, which had a tendency to fall off, had been replaced by an integrated system.

Cooper's T60 was memorable more for its looks than its performance and, although McLaren scored a victory for the team at Monaco, their days in the vanguard were over. Porsche too were among the winners in 1962, Gurney won at Rouen and Solitude with the torsion-bar suspended, flat-eight car.

A famous name appeared in the constructors' ranks that year when Jack Brabham introduced the Ron Tauranac designed Brabham BT3 at the Nürburgring. The car was 'British Standard F1', a tubular chassis pushed along by a Climax V8. The only other significant car of the season was Eric Broadley's first F1 Lola, built for Reg Parnell's Bowmaker Finance team. With John Surtees at the wheel it scored two seconds and several lesser placings, but it was to be the last F1 Lola until 1974.

1963 was the year of Jim Clark and the Lotus 25, the much modified car helping Clark to seven victories from ten Grands Prix. It was Lotus's first constructor's title and Clark's first Drivers' Championship. No one had expected that things could have been different. The Coventry Climax engine had been redesigned with a single-plane crankshaft, allowing the use of a much simpler exhaust system, and a stroke to bore ratio of 0.76 – improvements which netted 195 bhp at 9500 rpm. Its only opposition came from Hill's BRM P56, which won in Monaco and the USA, and from the latest Ferrari. The 156B still had a tubular frame, but with a new body, suspension and – at last – alloy wheels. The 120 degree V6 boasted Bosch fuel injection and four valves per cylinder. Surtees rewarded Ferrari with victory at the Nürburgring. The company also revealed a new car with a monocoque chassis and V8 engine. This was the car in which Surtees was to capture the 1964 World Championship. Although Ferrari were to rely on the V8 for the following year, too, 1964 also saw them reveal the flat-twelve-engined type 512. The engine in this latter car used the engine as an integral part of the chassis, a practice which was later to become universal.

The Coventry Climax was now producing marginally over 200 bhp with a further reduction of stroke to bore ratio to 0.63; the addition of four-valve cylinder heads took the output to 210 bhp for 1965. Either Lotus or BRM could have taken the 1964 championship in the final round, Lotus with the latest version of the 33 or BRM with their monocoque type 261. The 61 had been introduced in 1963 and was notable for its use of a full monocoque, which extended over the drivers legs and behind his shoulders, in contrast to most other manufacturers' linked-pontoon types. For 1964, the 261 monocoque extended right back around the engine, but on some four-valve cars this had to be cut away to accommodate the exhaust system! Also in 1964 a young BRM engineer, Mike Pilbeam, had experimented with a four-wheel-drive car, based on a P56 chassis and designated P67, but four-wheel drive was again rejected as a failure.

Above: the engine of the 1961 World Championship winning Ferrari was designed for the new 1½-litre formula by Carlo Chiti. The cars started the season with a 65 degree V6 unit, the Dino 156, running on carburettors and producing 180 bhp at 9000 rpm. This was soon replaced by a 120 degree V6, a fuel injected version of which is shown here. It is also interesting to note the massive tubular chassis and Ferrari's continued use of wire wheels.

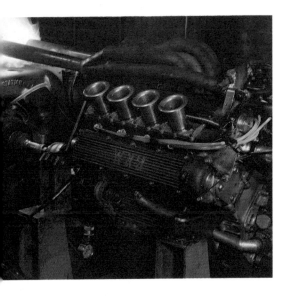

1965, the final year of the 1½-litre formula, saw Lotus dominant again, with the latest 33 winning six races for Clark. BRM relied once again on updated P261s, which often proved to be the fastest cars of all. With the induction tracts between the camshafts, the V8 was now able to better 210 bhp.

The swansong of the formula was to have been a flat-16 engine from Coventry Climax, for Lotus, Brabham and Cooper only. This FWMW had a crankshaft compounded of two separate single-plane units, phased at 90 degrees to each other and joined by a central, spur gear, driving the eight cams and all ancillaries. This effectively divided the engine into four banks and demanded four separate cylinder heads. Although the engine showed 220 bhp at 12,000 rpm on test, it never raced, as the company withdrew from the sport, for financial reasons.

While Climax tested the FWMW, the final race was being won by possibly the most powerful and imaginative car of the formula, the Honda V12. The Japanese motor cycle company had revealed their car at the Nürburgring in 1964. Extensive use of needle roller bearings, common to motor cycle practice, allowed up to 13,000 rpm, and large piston area and four valves per cylinder

Top: BRM's 1.5-litre V8 on the testbed. This was the company's final shot at the one-and-a-half litre formula which ended in 1965. The engine used fuel injection and produced 200 bhp at over 11,000 rpm

Above: everything finally clicked for BRM in 1962 when Graham Hill captured the World Championship in this Type 56. Powered by a 1498 cc V8 engine, this car marked the beginning of a four-year run of success for the marque

coaxed from it a reputed 230 bhp, on Keihin carburettors and coil ignition. This engine and a six-speed gearbox were mounted transversely in the monocoque chassis, which featured inboard front suspension. The beautifully prepared car's undoubted speed silenced most sceptics.

Far from being dull and underpowered, the cars of the 1½-litre formula had provided fast, close and technically fascinating racing. In five brief years, Grand Prix design particularly of chassis, tyres and suspension, had made huge strides. No less than 22 ostensibly separate makes had attempted to qualify for World Championship races in the period, and a handful of them will long be remembered.

It remains a matter for conjecture what stirring contests might have ensued between the V12 Honda, flat-12 Ferraris and the Climax flat-16 Lotuses *et al* had the formula not changed again for 1966.

The new rules were heralded as 'The return of power'. Engine capacity had

been doubled, to a maximum of 3 litres, while a category for supercharged engines (of $1\frac{1}{2}$-litres) made a return. The minimum weight limit was raised by only 50 kg – to the 500 kg limit which was originally envisaged for the $1\frac{1}{2}$-litre formula – and the requirements for use of pump petrol and open wheels remained. One might have been forgiven for thinking that after the fiasco of the start of the previous regulations perhaps this occasion would have found the teams in a better state of readiness. It was not so. Although the new formula had been announced in 1963, the withdrawal of Coventry Climax had left most of the 'kit car' teams in a sorry predicament, and once again they were faced with a situation of compromise. Ferrari, of course, were more ready than most. Their new car was based on a scaled up $1\frac{1}{2}$-litre-type chassis, carrying a V12 of a full 3 litres. The engine used two valves per cylinder and fuel injection in the centre of the Vee. The chassis was a semi-monocoque, with stressed panelling on a tubular structure. The 312 initially looked as though it might follow the path of the 156 of five years earlier, but reliability proved not to be its strong suit.

Full 3-litre cars were few and far between in the first season but the ones that were around were technically interesting. Following in the path of fellow Antipodean Brabham as a constructor, Bruce McLaren entered the arena with a very interesting machine. The chassis of the first McLaren was usual in that it was of monocoque configuration, but rather than the traditional riveted and bonded aluminium panelling, this car employed an aviation-type material called Mallite. This consisted of two much thinner aluminium skins sandwiching a core of balsa wood, with the grains running from face to face, the whole being bonded together into an enormously light and stiff sheet. The very advanced chassis which was thus built up was unfortunately let down by the lack of power from the de-stroked Indianapolis Ford engine which propelled it. While losing 1.2 litres from its original 4.2, the engine unfortunately lost much of its specific output and very little of its excess weight.

The season was to belong to the man in whose footsteps McLaren was following, Black Jack Brabham himself. In slightly opportunist vein, Brabham and Tauranac penned the BT20, a simple spaceframe chassis with even simpler outboard springing all round and of the smallest dimensions possible. Into this they fitted their master stroke, a cheap, light and unusually simple V8 engine built by the Australian Repco organisation around the bones of a mass-production Oldsmobile V8. The engine had all the right basic ingredients, with a very short stroke and single-plane crankshaft; the addition of single-overhead-camshaft cylinder heads, with two valves per cylinder, netted an initial 285 bhp at 8000 rpm. That in itself was far from spectacular, but in such a mild state of tune the engine had a wide spread of usable power, lots of torque and a miserly thirst for fuel. Capitalising on this simplicity the two Australians made the car by far the lightest on the grids and one of the most reliable. The car took the Championship with consummate ease.

Left : the 36-valve V12 engined Ferraris of Ludovico Scarfiotti and Mike Parkes at Monza before their first and second place triumph in the 1966 Italian Grand Prix. Scarfiotti was the first Italian to win his home Grand Prix since Ascari in 1952

Below : the screaming 3-litre Honda RA273 made its debut at the 1966 Italian Grand Prix. Its engine was a large, 60° V12 four-cam unit with four valves per cylinder. Drive was taken from the centre of the crankshaft to negate whip, and this heavy engine produced 430 bhp at 11,000 rpm. Richie Ginther was lucky to escape unhurt when the car crashed at high speed during the race. Its best showing was at Mexico City when Ginther finished fourth and set fastest lap.

Left : the combination of Lotus 49 and Cosworth-Ford double-four-valve engine proved unbeatable at the outset, with Graham Hill and Jim Clark dominating the 1967 Dutch Grand Prix

Right: the Cosworth-Ford DFV V8 marked the start of a new era in motor racing, being a reliable, high-performance engine which was available to all-comers.

Far right: the Aubrey Woods/Harry Weslake designed Weslake V12 engine which powered Dan Gurney's Formula 1 Eagles in 1966 and 1967. This 3-litre unit developed 380 bhp

Below : Jackie Stewart's BRM P83 in the pits at Monza, 1966. The BRM 3-litre H16 engine was based on the cylinder blocks of the old 1½-litre engine, and its only success was when it was fitted to Jim Clark's Lotus 43 for the 1966 United States Grand Prix

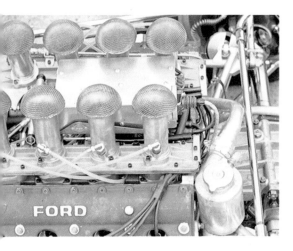

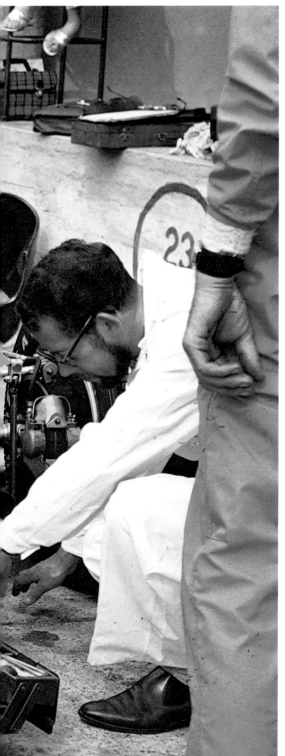

Of the others, Lotus initially relied on yet another development of the 33, whose superior handling could not compensate for the paucity of power of its 2-litre Climax or BRM engines. BRM themselves started the season with 2.1-litre versions of the P261, using a 2070 cc, 270 bhp engine, developed for the Tasman series. It was enough to give Stewart victory in the opening race but thereafter every race was won by a 3-litre car. BRM's own 3-litre was another 16-cylinder concoction, with a reputation akin to that of their first example. Aero-engine thinking had been cribbed to make a 16-cylinder unit short enough for rear mounting; two flat-eight units were mounted one atop the other, with their two crankshafts coupled to a common output. Use of major components from the successful V8 should have ensured both power and reliability but, owing to severe vibrational problems, neither was forthcoming. The most power ever seen from the unit was 420 bhp – far short of target – and its most memorable characteristic was sudden and violent self destruction. BRM used the engine as a stressed, suspension-carrying unit in the monocoque P83 car but the H16's only success came in a Lotus 43 chassis, at Watkins Glen, with Clark driving.

Three other full 3-litre cars appeared in 1966. Having started the season with a Coventry Climax 2.7-litre four, Dan Gurney's All American Racers' Eagle appeared at Monza with an all new V12 engine, designed by Harry Weslake and Aubrey Woods. Both car and 380 bhp engine were beautifully made and very purposeful.

Cooper began the season with 3-litre engines in their T81s, by courtesy of Maserati. Unfortunately, the sports-car-derived V12s were massive and thirsty and gave only 320 bhp to propel the equally bulky 'bathtub' monocoque chassis. The car was developed to some extent during the season and won the final race in Mexico. The Cooper may have been heavy but the latest Honda was even more so. To compensate, their V12 engine was again the most powerful of all. It was of 90 degree, four-camshaft configuration, with induction between the cams and a tangle of exhaust pipes emerging from between the cylinder heads. Honda claimed 420 bhp and, again, none argued, but the power was wasted on the grossly overweight chassis.

Some of the cars of 1966 were effective but there was little sophistication; the real technical advances came from the tyre industry. After several years of near monopoly, with their R5, 6 and 7 designs, Dunlop suddenly had competition, from the radical ideas of American manufacturers Firestone and Goodyear. The wide, concave-moulded, low-profile tyres which then emerged were the forerunners of the huge slicks of the mid seventies.

1967 was the most significant year in recent racing history: it marked the genesis of the Ford-financed Cosworth DFV V8 engine which filled the void left by Climax's departure. The engine was to dominate F1 racing for many seasons to come.

Again it fell to Chapman to set the trend: for 1967, the DFV was available exclusively to Lotus. The Lotus-Ford 49 made its bow in Holland, and a spectacular bow it was. The car itself was a logical development of previous

Left: the complexity of the 1968 Matra MS11's V12 engine made it a difficult car to develop. With the original six-pipe exhaust system the V12 was a good match for early DFVs in terms of power but not tractability: with this later, four-pipe, system flexibility improved but maximum power suffered as a consequence

Below: McLaren were among the first to join the Ford-Cosworth DFV users after the engine became generally available in 1968. This M7A, taking shape at the McLaren works, shows the use of the DFV as a stressed unit on the monocoque

Lotuses, with refinements aimed at better handling and brake cooling; the
engine, which was suspension bearing and fully stressed, bolted directly onto
the vertical back of the abbreviated monocoque. It was straightforward and
beautifully conceived; individually, car and engine were interesting, together
they were sensational. At Zandvoort Hill took pole position and Clark won
the race. The writing was on the wall.

Although the 49 was dominant throughout 1967, reliability cost it the
results that it promised, and it was the Repco Brabham that emerged again as
champion. The Eagle won in Belgium and the Honda, now with a Lola-
inspired chassis and Surtees driving, won in Italy. Everthing else was shared
between Lotus and Brabham.

For 1968, the DFV was available to all-comers and, at last, the constructors
had access to an engine which was a match for any other. Examples were
quickly snapped up by McLaren for their M7A, and by Matra, to be used
pending completion of their own V12. The only intruder into a Ford grand
slam was Jacky Ickx, with the latest Ferrari 312, with a four-valve V12. This
car won at Rouen, where the Honda was second. Honda also produced an air-

cooled, V8-engined car at that race but Jo Schlesser crashed it, with fatal results, after the engine cut out on the fast downhill sweeps. No further cars were built.

BRM abandoned the H16 in favour of the ubiquitous V12, which also found its way into the Cooper T86B. That car and the Alfa Romeo-engined T86C were the last of the Coopers. Honda's ambitions in F1 seemed to die with Schlesser and the Eagles returned to their USAC eyrie in 1968. After Clark's tragic death at Hockenheim, Hill's capture of the world title was a much needed morale booster for Lotus. The 1968 car was the 49B, a long wheelbase development of the 49.

Technically, 1968 was most significant for the proliferation of fins, spoilers and, ultimately, huge, moveable, suspension-mounted aerofoils, on both ends of many cars. Several near tragedies, directly attributable to these devices, led to their size and location being strictly limited by new regulations. While rules on wings had been tightened up, limits on advertising on cars were relaxed and racing took on a colourful new face.

1969 saw a clean sweep by Ford-powered cars, the DFV being used by everyone except BRM, Ferrari and the Matra prototype. Stewart took the Championship for the Ken Tyrrell run Matra-Ford team. Lotus, Brabham (with the BT26A) and McLaren (with the M7A) all won rounds; in spite of the new wing and safety regulations – which demanded fire extinguisher systems and leak proof fuel tanks, and increased the minimum weight limit to allow for them – lap speeds were generally quicker.

Interesting from a technical standpoint was the appearance of four-wheel-drive cars from Matra, McLaren, Lotus and Cosworth. Again, the system was not the sought for panacea. The McLaren M9 made only one race appearance and the Matra MS84 was overshadowed by the conventional car. The Robin Herd designed Cosworth was a strange looking device which never reached fruition. The possible advantages of four-wheel drive could now be reproduced by much simpler, and cheaper, aerodynamic means – without the penalties of extra weight, power losses and unpredictable handling. Even Chapman's four-wheel-drive venture was short lived. The Lotus 63 owed much of its design to the 1968, turbine-powered, Indianapolis car and was a stop gap, pending the introduction of a similarly powered Grand Prix car. The Matra MS84 and the Brabham BT26 were the last tubular-framed cars to appear in Grand Prix racing.

Having taken a back seat in 1969, Chapman yet again rocked the establishment in 1970 with his type 72. By relocating the radiators at the sides of the cockpit, Chapman was able to give the car a distinctive wedge shaped profile, with low polar moment of inertia and tremendous aerodynamic efficiency. The rest of the car was equally novel; suspension and brakes were both inboard and the suspension medium was torsion bars. Few people could have foreseen the extraordinarily long competitive life that lay ahead of the 72.

Left: the Tyrrell 001 as it appeared at its auspicious debut in 1970 when Jackie Stewart set fastest lap in the non-championship Oulton Park Gold Cup, before retiring. In 1971, Stewart won six Grands Prix in this car and took the World Championship. The hammerhead shaped nose-cone, which still housed the radiator, was intended to reduce the drag imposed by the ever-widening front tyres and produce down thrust

Below: the trend-setting Maurice Phillipe/Colin Chapman designed Lotus 72 as it first appeared in 1970, at the start of its five-year racing career. Featuring such attributes as a smooth ride, excellent traction through torsion bar suspension, good aerodynamics with its wedge-shaped body, and inboard mounted disc brakes, the car was driven to victory in four Grands Prix in 1970, enough to give Jochen Rindt the World Championship. Sadly, Rindt was killed at Monza whilst trying for a greater maximum speed by running the car without aerofoils

The first four races of the season went to four different marques, including Lotus, but the sequence of successes in mid season by Rindt and the 72 were enough to secure the title, even though Rindt was killed in Italy with three rounds remaining. After Rindt's death, the flat-12-engined Ferrari 312B became the car to beat. Only Fittipaldi with the Lotus 72 succeeded.

Three new marques appeared in 1970. Amid a blaze of publicity, March entered the arena with both works and privately entered cars. Most significant was Ken Tyrrell's example for World Champion Stewart. Other than its use of aerofoil section side fuel tanks, the March 701 was quite conventional. Tyrrell himself was already at work on one of the best kept secrets in racing; at the Canadian Grand Prix Tyrrell 001 started from pole position. It was an auspicious debut. Slightly less successful was the Surtees TS7, another offering from a driver turned constructor.

For 1971, designer Derek Gardner refined 001 and produced 002 and 003. The car's bulbous aluminium monocoque was designed to keep the fuel load central and the cars were distinguished by wide, shovel noses, designed to give maximum downthrust. The final form of the nose also improved top

Right : the March 711 chassis was designed by
Robin Herd, with bodywork influenced by Frank
Costin. The car handled well but the engine
cooling was not particularly efficient and the
car was usually raced in 1971 without the engine
cover and radiator ducting

Below: the Ralph Bellamy designed McLaren
M19B with its rising-rate front suspension took
first place in the 1972 South African Grand Prix,
giving Denny Hulme and the McLaren team
their first Grand Prix win since 1969

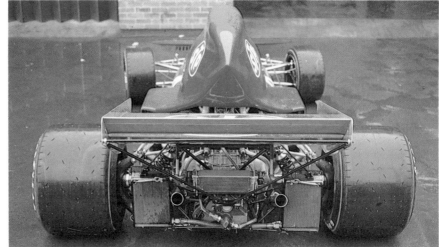

speed and stability. Others were quick to copy but the originators reaped the rewards, with Stewart taking his second championship. One of the tweaks tried on the cars during the season was an ingenious double-disc-brake system, with floating calipers, but its advantages were dubious.

March's 711 caused quite a stir, with its aerodynamic, Frank Costin-designed, body. Although the design was very effective in wind tunnel testing, it suffered badly in the turbulent company of other cars.

1971 saw a revival for BRM, with two mid-season victories for their P160, V12-engined cars. The only other winner was the Ferrari 312B2, whose ever improving flat-12 engine was now giving around 460 bhp. The car briefly featured troublesome inboard rear suspension. The Matra MS120B was very quick on occasion but driver Amon's luck was as bad as ever. Brabham's 'lobster claw' BT34, with split front radiators introduced an interesting new shape but had little success.

Probably the most interesting car which will be seen under the 3-litre formula was the Lotus 56B of 1971. This, the world's first gas-turbine-powered Grand Prix car, was a direct descendant of the Type 56 Indianopolis car, which came within an ace of winning the 500 in 1968. The 56B used a Pratt and Whitney STN6/76 turbine to a 3-litre equivalency, determined principally on intake area. Power was transmitted to the four-wheel-drive system through a 2-inch wide Morse chain and two pedal control was all that was required. The chassis was a complex monocoque wedge with brakes and suspension inboard all round. The car's main drawback was one of controllability, or lack of it. The 450 bhp turbine suffered a lag in throttle response, committing the driver to making all his judgements in advance. More important, it offered no engine braking, putting the onus on the car's massive ventilated disc brakes. With the Lotus 72 far from outclassed, the 56B was quietly shelved.

1972 was a hard fought season from which Chapman emerged with his biennial championship, the 72D taking five victories to Tyrrell's four. The interlopers in the Lotus/Tyrrell show were Ferrari, McLaren – with the M19A, featuring rising rate suspension – and BRM. BRM's victory was more a result of Beltoise's brilliance in the wet at Monaco than of the car's competitiveness.

March had an innovative but dismally unsuccessful season. Their search for a low polar moment of inertia car led to the 721X, on which Herd mounted the gearbox between the engine and the final drive. Enforced use of Alfa Romeo mechanicals prevented a direct comparison with its competitors. This 721X was superseded by the 721G, based on the firm's successful F2 design. Also on the scene in 1972 with varying levels of success were the Matra MS120C, with a very wide and flat chassis and a magnificent engine note, but no luck, and the Tecno, whose flat-12 engine drew obvious comparisons with its Italian compatriot.

Stewart and Tyrrell were back in the ascendancy in 1973; Gardner's 006

Left: the Tyrrell 006 that Jackie Stewart drove to win the 1973 World Championship. Unlike their counterparts of earlier days, who sat almost on top of their machines, Grand Prix drivers were by this time strapped very securely into their cars. With cornering forces, even in the early 1970s, amounting to upwards of 2*g*, these men would have collapsed from sheer exhaustion had they been obliged to hold themselves in position within the cockpit rather than being physically restrained. Note that the effort of driving was reduced as much as possible to give every racer the best chance of concentrating on winning the race in hand: the gear lever was as close as practically possible to the steering wheel rim and the gauges were positioned so that 'normal' readings – or the rev counter red line – were placed eye-catchingly at the top of the dials. Much of this still applied in the turbocharged era of the '80s, but race-winning still required one vital ingredient: a driver of exceptional talent

design took five victories, in a season dominated by three Ford-powered makes – Tyrrell, Lotus and McLaren. 006 was a typical Tyrrell, with a wedge-shaped monocoque, side radiators and the highest of high airboxes – designed to collect cool undisturbed air from above the body-induced turbulence. It was a year of elation and tragedy for Tyrrell, the championship success being tempered by Stewart's retirement and Cevert's death in America. The remarkable Lotus 72D again provided most of the opposition but McLaren's new M23 proved to be very quick. The Gordon Coppuck designed car was very much a second generation Lotus 72, embodying the side radiator, wedge layout of that car. The latest regulations demanded wider deformable structures on the flanks of the cars and the M23 used these to good effect to achieve excellent aerodynamic penetration. The M23 was to share another feature with the Lotus 72, its long competitive life.

Involvement from America returned with the appearance of the UOP Shadow DN1, designed by former Eagle and BRM man Tony Southgate. The young Englishman Lord Alexander Hesketh entered James Hunt in a March 731, looked over by the former March designer Dr Harvey Postlethwaite; the car proved consistently faster than several works entered cars.

At the end of 1973, Hesketh announced that the team would build their own car and V12 engine for the following season. Although the engine never materialised, the Postlethwaite designed Hesketh 308, bearing a fair resemblance to the March, did.

Much driver shuffling in the closed season saw Emerson Fittipaldi in the latest McLaren M23. In a season where McLaren tried numerous variations of track, wheelbase and aerodynamics, Fittipaldi emerged as 1974 champion. It was one of the most competitive seasons ever: McLarens took only four of the season's fifteen races, the rest being shared between Brabham, Ferrari, Lotus and Tyrrell. Brabham's winner was one of the most attractive cars of the whole formula, the BT44 designed by Gordon Murray. In this car, Murray had used a monocoque with sloping sides whose angle matched that of the cam covers of the DFV engine, resulting in a beautifully neat and compact car. The Ferrari team was at last emerging from the doldrums and the performances of the 312B3s were more impressive than their results record. The car had been constantly developed around the very powerful flat-12 engine, until it had superb traction and handling to match its near 500 bhp. Lotus's wins came once again from the 72, now in 72E guise, the team having quietly abandoned the revolutionary Lotus 76. That car was introduced with an automatic clutch and split, two-footed brake pedal. These features and a two-tier wing which was on the original car were soon dropped and the team reverted to the ever faithful 72. Tyrrell's fortunes seemed to take a turn for the better with the introduction of 007, which was again a development rather than a revolution. 1974 was a year which saw many other new cars, none with much distinction and all built to virtually the same formula of simple monocoque chassis and Cosworth engine, the major differences being in the aerodynamics of the cars. One that did stand out a little way from the crowd was the BRM P201, another slope-sided monocoque, this time using a V12 engine, and flattering in its early performances only to deceive. Attempts at breaking into Grand Prix racing at the bottom end of the financial scale, by teams such as Token and the disastrous Japanese Maki, foundered rapidly. Even the reasonably wealthy, Frank Williams run, Iso team found it very hard to break into the big league. The emergence of two new American teams, Parnelli and Penske came too near to the end of the season to show much other than that the cars were totally conventional and superbly presented.

All Ferrari's earlier promise finally netted the results in 1975 and Niki Lauda took the world championship away from the Ford-powered cars for the first time since 1968, once more fuelling the longstanding pronostications that the DFV's reign was over. The introduction of the Ferrari 312T marked the beginning of a long run of successes for the Maranello *marque*. The outstanding feature of the 312T was its use of a transversely mounted gearbox, yet another variation on the low polar moment theme, but this time one that worked. One other car that looked as though it was on the road to success was the latest Shadow, the DN5; a sterling performance in Argentina, in practice, and another in the Brazilian race were highspots in an otherwise frustrating season. New cars appeared from Lola, Ensign, Frank Williams and the Brazilian Copersucar team, formed by Wilson Fittipaldi. The return of Lola to F1 was not a successful one and before the end of the season the Hill team, which was running their cars, had built their own contender. Alas the potential of the team was never fully realised as the key personnel, including Hill and the designer Andy Smallman, were killed in a flying accident in November 1975.

The Hesketh team's swansong was the 308C which made its debut in Italy. The car featured an extremely shallow monocoque tub with the fuel load carried centrally, and low line air intakes which anticipated the 1976 rules, which banned high air boxes. Alas, the Hesketh team were to be disbanded at the end of 1975 and the car was never developed to the extent it deserved.

Before the end of the 1975 season, Tyrrell dropped a bombshell when he revealed his new car – known then as Project 34 – to a disbelieving world; Project 34 had six wheels. Far from being the publicity grabber that many dubbed it, P34 was developed over the closed season and the early part of 1976 to be among the top three competitors. Gardner's thinking in providing the car with four mini-sized front wheels was to maintain – or even improve – the tyre contact area and consequently braking and steering power, with a reduction in frontal area to give a higher top speed. When early brake-cooling and setting-up problems had been overcome the car showed that its major advantage was that the narrow front track allowed the drivers to go much deeper into the corners before turning in, allowing them to brake a little later and harder. Perspex windows in the cockpit sides, to allow the drivers to see the tiny wheels, also let spectators in on the fact that the six-wheeler was something of a handful to drive. Whether P34 would have been quicker than a newly developed conventional Tyrrell is a matter for conjecture but several other teams were rumoured to be thinking along similar lines. The other departure from the wheel on each corner theme came from March whose 1977 car featured four small rear wheels, all driven. The advantage was again supposed to be aerodynamic, aimed at producing a smooth airflow underneath the rear wing, as well as above.

Even without the six-wheelers, 1976 was a year with plenty of interest on the machinery front. Ferrari brought a de Dion suspension system back into racing for the first time since the mid fifties, on the rear of their 312T cars. A de Dion front end was tried, too, but not raced. Colin Chapman's interest had turned towards building a fully adjustable car that could be changed quite dramatically in track and wheelbase to suit various circuits. The car originally had a complex front suspension system with the brake calipers in the air stream between the wheels and the body and acting as an intermediate suspension upright. During the season the car was gradually simplified and became

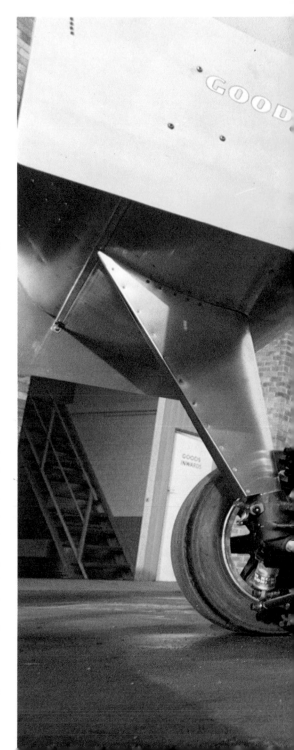

Right : Lord Hesketh, James Hunt and the 1975 Hesketh 308C; the car was very low, apart from the turret-like cockpit, and featured rubber springing. After the demise of the racing team from Easton Neston, the Frank Williams equipe took over the project

Below right : Vittorio Brambilla's March 751 of 1975. While other manufacturers were striving to build more advanced cars, March made their car as simple as possible. When it held together, it was faster than most in a straight line

Below : March in 1977 surprised many by deciding to take the six-wheel route, although they differed in having four of theirs driven. It was quickly adaptable to the more normal four-wheeled configuration, they hastened to add

competitive, winning the final race of the season to restore some faith in Lotus's flagging fortunes.

Two 'new' engines made their bow with Brabham introducing the BT45, designed around the Alfa Romeo flat-12 unit, and the Ligier team making an impressive debut with their Matra engined car. The Ligier-Matra JS5 was originally dubbed the 'Flying Teapot' because of its enormously high airbox but that soon disappeared in deference to the new regulations and the car proved extremely quick. The Alfa-engined Brabham was less successful, occasional bursts of speed being wasted by a notorious lack of reliability.

New cars abounded during the season but all the others were very ordinary offerings which were rewarded with varying degrees of success. The four-wheeled Marches were very quick and very unreliable; the new Copersucar did not reward Emerson's faith with any speed; and the new Surtees TS19 was disappointing after an extremely promising early showing. One high spot was Mo Nunn's showing with his shoestring-budgeted Ensign team who ran a very economical and simple chassis with results that often embarrassed the bigger teams. A sign of things to come may also have been seen at the final round of the championship at Mount Fuji where James Hunt clinched the title with his McLaren M23, leaving the M26 to make its real debut in 1977: among the quicker cars at Fuji were local entries – promising to be back.

Formula One now has such a crowded calendar that making real changes to the cars in mid season is a thing of the past, steady development is all that can now be undertaken. In spite of regular rumours, the day of the big manufacturer is over and the face of motor racing is very different from the earliest days.

Above: McLaren's successor to their twice world championship winning M23 was the M26, introduced in July 1976. The M26 owed much to designer Gordon Coppuck's aircraft design experience. Like the first Grand Prix McLaren, the monocoque tub of this car utilised composite materials in its construction. Unlike the Mallite, aluminium/balsa sandwich, used on the M3, the material used on the M26 was an all aluminium sheet and honeycomb sandwich. The driver protection structures used Nomex honeycomb material. The major suspension features of the M23 were retained but the new car had less frontal area and weight plus considerably more rigidity

In spite of its early introduction, protracted testing and use of aircraft inspired honeycomb chassis materials, the M26 was a late developer. Hunt put the M23 (latterly fitted with driver adjustable rear anti-roll bars) on pole three times before the M26 made its race debut in Spain. The car's main problem was in the steering, which was heavy and inclined to severe understeer. By mid-season, suspension changes and a switch to front radiators made the M26 a formidable weapon in Hunt's hands.

1977, however, was not to be dominated by any one car—at least not in terms of results—and it was the newest team of all which opened the scoring. The Wolf WR1 was designed by ex-March and Hesketh man Harvey Postlethwaite and was a thoroughly conventional Ford kit car, blessed with excellent traction and the ministrations of a dedicated team. Its debut win in Argentina probably owed more to Scheckter's fitness than to the car's outright speed, but it is significant that – aside from engine breakages – the team did not suffer a single mechanical failure all season.

After two doubles – for the Ferrari 312T-2 in Brazil and South Africa and for the remarkable Lotus 78 in Long Beach and Spain – Scheckter took the original WR1 chassis to a memorable win at Monte Carlo, marking an unsurpassed century of victories for the splendid Cosworth DFV.

In its ten year history, the DFV had powered eight World Champions and taken seven constructors' titles. It had scored more points and more fastest laps than any other engine in the history of the Championship. From around 408 bhp in 1967, its output had risen to a touch over 480 bhp a decade later. Most important of all, it had undoubtedly kept Grand Prix racing within financial reach of more than a privileged few, had shaped the whole character of the sport throughout the 'seventies and, it might be argued, saved a branch of racing otherwise doomed by spiralling costs.

Cosworth, however, were not without their problems, and their fortunes played an important role in a highly competitive season. In the face of increasing opposition from the Ferrari, Alfa and Matra twelves, Cosworth made available to Lotus, Tyrrell and McLaren a total of nine 'development' engines. These had various features, including magnesium heads and cam

Below: putting six wheels on the Tyrrell P34 was a brave departure from the norm which met with mixed fortune over two seasons of racing. In the 1976 Swedish Grand Prix the cars romped home first and second, but in 1977 they simply couldn't make the best of the latest Goodyear rubber

Bottom: the Wolf WR1 came from the pen of former March and Hesketh designer Dr Harvey Postlethwaite and was a straightforward offering with an aerodynamically efficient shape, outboard suspension, and side radiators. In deference to saving weight, the bodywork was made in Kevlar and carbon fibre – claimed to save 20lbs in comparison with the more commonly used glassfibre

Left and below: the start of the revolution. The Lotus 78 used a very narrow monocoque chassis, housing most of the fuel between the driver and the engine and flanked by the aerofoil section side structures revealed here by the removal of the side plates. The radiators were mounted in the leading edges of the 'wings' and air flow was kept under the car by flexible skirts which bridged the gap between the side plates and the ground. Chapman's 'wing car' not surprisingly soon brought a host of imitators, but by the time they had arrived on the scene Lotus had taken the idea another step forward . . .

carriers on some engines, giving a two per cent power increase and, more important, a nineteen pound weight saving. Alas, longevity was not the engines' forte and on too many occasions they cost their users valuable points as they failed.

One of the development engine users was unquestionably the car of the year. It was the Lotus 78, and, as so often before, with it Colin Chapman introduced a new concept, brilliant in its simplicity and devastating in its efficacy. The 78 brought a new term to the Grand Prix glossary: wing car. By building the chassis as narrow as possible and locating all the fuel in the centre of the car, behind the driver, Chapman was able to use the whole of the car's side pod area to good aerodynamic effect. In essence the side structures were large inverted aerofoils, carrying the cooling systems and supplemented by flexible skirts to keep the airflow over the lower, working, surface. The 78 incorporated lessons of weight distribution learned from the later developments of the 77, moving more weight (including the oil radiator) to the front to help in generating efficient front tyre temperatures. It also featured such niceties as an oil tank incorporated within the engine bellhousing, which also held an annular clutch slave cylinder, and a Salisbury-type differential which, on occasion, could be run virtually as a locked unit. Lotus's own gearbox proved troublesome however and the car relied mostly on the trusty Hewland FG400. Just as the 25 and 72 before it, the 78 was destined to spawn a host of imitators.

Also among the winners, of course, were the 312T-2 Ferraris and it was with this car that Niki Lauda was to take his second World Championship. He was also to notch up the season's second winning century, this time for Goodyear tyres who had opened their account through Ritchie Ginther way back in the 1965 Mexican Grand Prix. It was in a way ironic that a Ferrari should score Goodyear's hundredth win, for relations between the two companies were becoming very strained. Ferrari owed their success much more to the strength of the flat-twelve engine than to the cars' handling, which for most of 1977 was dreadful. Characteristically, and in this case perhaps with some justification, the Maranello company could not shoulder the blame for such inadequacies and pointed the finger at Goodyear. The root of the problem was that Lotus now dictated tyre parameters and the smooth way in which the 78 got on with the job allowed it to use a much softer – hence grippier – compound than the rest. Ferrari made no secret of his pique and was soon to be seen talking to other possible tyre suppliers – backed no doubt by the size of the potential Fiat market.

For their part, Goodyear had played a role as important in its way as that of Cosworth, creating general availability and being fundamental in most development work. The company's test and development programme was a major part of the sport by the mid 'seventies. The Vehicle Dynamics Programme, instituted in 1975, set out to lend testing more of a scientific basis.

Above: the 1977 World Champion, Niki Lauda, in the Ferrari 312 T-2. The lusty and reliable flat-twelve engine, transverse gearbox, and wide monocoque gave the car a very square configuration in plan

With the aid of applied mathematician and polymer scientist Karl Kempf, a means of interpreting and recording the cars' dynamic behaviour through on-board instrumentation was evolved.

Goodyear's development programme and their advice to circuit owners on eliminating some of the causes of punctures led to much closer racing with less of an element of chance about it. Their testing sessions and their own test facility in Luxembourg speeded chassis development for many a team.

To Goodyear's credit, the company did not abuse the monopolistic situation, but in a highly competitive sport there was a natural frustration in having no-one else to beat. Japanese Dunlop and Bridgestone tyres had made a brief incursion into the Goodyear monopoly at Fuji in 1976 but a more formidable rival arrived on the scene in 1977 when Michelin radial tyres appeared on the Renault RS01.

Aside from its tyres, the Renault was one of the most significant cars to appear for many years; it marked the return of *direct* participation by a major manufacturer (coincidentally, the one which had won the very first Grand Prix in 1906) and it marked the first time since 1954 that anyone had pursued the supercharging option. At the British Grand Prix, encouraged by the success of their Formula Two and sports car engine programmes, Renault wheeled out their turbocharged $1\frac{1}{2}$-litre challenger.

The turbocharging option was an attractive one to Renault for several reasons: first of all, the Gordini-developed engine could be used in this

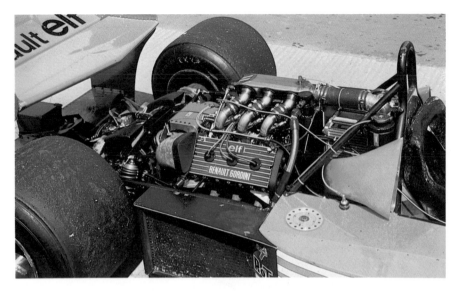

Formula One guise, turbocharged 2.1-litre form for sports car racing (it was to win at Le Mans in 1978) and as a normally aspirated 2-litre unit for Formula Two: furthermore, it bore more relation to the way Renault foresaw the passenger car engine developing than did a highly stressed, larger capacity motor. Turbocharging in itself is an attractive way of achieving good thermodynamic efficiency and hence providing ample power without incurring the penalty of an increased fuel load. The turbocharger is essentially a centrifugal supercharger (which works most efficiently at very high rotational speeds) driven by a small turbine powered by otherwise waste exhaust gases. The considerable dynamic and heat energies of the fast moving exhaust gases are therefore channeled back into the engine instead of simply being thrown away. As an engine works better on cooler, hence denser, fuel charges, the pressurised air from the Renault's turbocharger is piped forward to an intercooler placed between the driver and the engine and is then fed back to the inlet ports via short pipes each equipped with Kügelfischer fuel injection nozzles. A waste gate controls the upper limit of boost and also allows some control over the slight lag caused by the fact that the turbine must be spinning very quickly before the engine produces sufficient power. This, however, remains one of the turbocharged engine's major drawbacks.

The Renault engine itself was a relatively simple V6, with exaggeratedly oversquare bore and stroke dimensions of 86 × 42.8mm and a nominal compression ratio of just 7:1. The large bore allowed plenty of valve area, the two inlets and two exhausts being set in a very flat pent-roof arrangement, and it also gave lots of piston area to aid internal cooling. With four belt-driven overhead camshafts, a cast iron block and Marelli electronic ignition the engine was immediately good for around 510bhp at 11,000rpm, with an impressive spread of power. Unfortunately, in spite of not being *per se* a highly stressed unit, the engine did lack reliability. Early turbocharger problems prompted inlet and exhaust manifolding changes and a change to the turbine but then gave way to valve and piston problems. However, imitation is the sincerest form of flattery and Ferrari and Alfa were far from reticent about the fact that they already had their own turbo motors under development.

For the most part the rest of the year's offerings were mundane in comparison, but at least their numbers reflected the healthy state of the sport during the late 'seventies. The other race winners were the Shadow DN8 (helped along by an inspired Alan Jones in appalling conditions in Austria) and the Matra V12-powered Ligier JS7. Both teams had long been bridesmaids and both had come very close to winning in the past, so their victories were popular ones. With a claimed 520bhp delivered at 12,300rpm, the screaming Matra MS76 engine was probably the most potent and high revving engine of the current crop. It had been a long road to victory since the first Matra V12 appeared in 1968 but it was the sweeter for the waiting . . .

The car which at last looked most likely to succeed, but in the event never quite made the winner's circle, was another 'twelve'. The Alfa-powered Brabham BT45B was often capable of running near the front but all too often it was not around when the flag dropped. It too was laying claim to 520 bhp, at 12,000 rpm, and its performance gave no reason to doubt the figure. On the debit side, the engine was notably thirsty and demanded a big chassis to accommodate it, its 615 kg being surpassed only by the Tyrrell P34 at a hefty 630 kg.

In spite of the ministrations of Karl Kempf's computer analysed on-board monitoring systems, P34 had a dreadful year. Its main problem was incompatibility with the latest Goodyear compounds; during a troubled season it gained some ten inches in the front track, reverted to its old style bodywork and put on a good deal of weight, but to no avail.

The Penske PC4s became known as ATS but continued to perform like Penskes. The new Fittipaldi F5, designed by ex-Lotus and Ensign man Dave Baldwin, showed occasional pace as did the very similar Ensign N177 itself. None of the numerous March offerings or the Surtees TS19 had much success and of the remaining runners the most interesting was perhaps Dave Purley's Lec CRP1, designed by Mike Pilbeam. Alas the Lec's promising career was cut short by Purley's dreadful accident in practice for the British Grand Prix. His survival spoke volumes for the strength of the car's chassis. Of Pilbeam's earlier employer's offering, the overweight, overheating, underpowered BRM P207, the less said the better. . . .

'1978' cars began to appear before the wheels had stopped turning in '77 and there was plenty of technical interest on one of the first, Gordon Murray's elegant Brabham BT46. Retaining the ever improving Alfa engine, Murray evolved a compact triangular monocoque chassis with integral surface coolers, obviating the need for separate radiators. In theory the surface coolers would save a lot of weight and eliminate a significant amount of cooling drag. The outer skin of the chassis was formed of a double-skinned element of high strength aluminium, ribbed on its exposed surface, through which flowed the oil and coolant. Murray's innovative approach did not stop with the cooling system; digital instrumentation with information modes selected by the driver was backed by a pit-triggered lap time display, all the information appearing on a panel on the steering wheel. Borrowing from longstanding USAC practice the BT46 was also fitted with on-board pneumatic jacks with a quick action connector for a pit air bottle. Murray also gave some thought for the driver, with a built in cooling panel and immensely strong protection areas. The braking system used steel discs with a carbon fibre skin as the friction surface, and the pads were also carbon fibre based – the system owed much to Dunlop's work on Concorde.

Sadly, Murray's radical new approach met with problems from the start and, although the oil cooling systems worked, the water cooling effect was seriously inadequate and the car reverted to conventional radiators (in the front nose wings) even before the season started. The BT46 did manage to win two races during 1978, but both were in controversial circumstances. At Anderstorp, Sweden, the team arrived with a BT46 equipped (à la Chaparral) with an engine driven fan, mounted, vertically, at the rear – which turned out to be the only view most people saw. The fan sucked air from under a completely sealed engine cover which was also sealed to the ground by a perimeter of sliding skirts. Brabham pointed out that it was for cooling purposes but those who saw it disappear into the distance thought otherwise and the protests came thick and fast. It was considered to infringe the rules regarding moveable aerodynamic devices; it was feared that it might pick up track debris and hurl it at its pursuers; it was thought to corner just too fast for safety – with probably dire consequences if something caused the suction to fail in mid-corner; and it was argued that to compete with 'the fan car' everyone else would have to take the same, expensive, route. The Swedish win was allowed to stand, but the car was declared illegal and reverted to its more conventional guise. In this form it 'won' at Monza, but only after two cars which led it over the line had been penalised for jumped starts.

The car which won on the road at Monza was Chapman's own version of the 'ground effect' theme but, with another touch of genius, Chapman managed to achieve much the same ends without resorting to an extractor fan. In the Lotus 79, the flow of air over the car did the job itself, exhausting air from below the bodywork and sucking the car on to the road. The 79 was a development of the 78, true, but it took the state of the art a step further. The 78's major shortcoming had been a lack of straightline speed. With the 79, Chapman retained the narrow monocoque but tidied up the elements intruding into side airflow, tucking front and rear suspension well inboard and adopting an up and over exhaust system. The crucial part of the design, however, was the adoption of very efficient sliding skirts around the lower edge of the monocoque which effectively sealed the car to the ground; air was now exhausted from above the car and not allowed back in underneath, sucking the car down on to the road and giving the tyres all the down force they needed. The only part of the 79 which did not work was the troublesome Lotus gearbox around which the car had been designed. Had it worked it

Top: Carlos Reutemann in action in the flat-twelve Ferrari 312T-3 of 1978. The engine was reputed to develop about 510 bhp and the T-3 gave Michelin their first Grand Prix win

Above: Clay Regazzoni in the Shadow DN9 at Long Beach in 1978. The DN9, powered by the ubiquitous Cosworth DFV engine, came out on top of a High Court action with the Arrows team

Left: designer Gordon Murray's imaginative Brabham-Alfa BT46 of 1978, as originally introduced, with surface cooler radiators

Far right top: the car of 1978: this is the 'ground effect' Lotus 79 which took Mario Andretti to his world championship title

Bottom right: designed by Patrick Head, the Saudia-backed, Williams-Ford FW06 was driven to good effect by Alan Jones during 1978

would have allowed clutchless gearchanges and two pedal control – shades of the Lotus 76. Instead the team was forced to revert to the heavier Hewland box once again. In this form the 79 won six Grands Prix (seven disregarding the penalty at Monza) and with the 78 having won two more, Lotus took the Drivers' and Constructors' Championships once again.

Naturally there were many imitators of the 78 now in circulation but they were already a step behind. The next 'wing car' to appear was the Arrows FA1, designed by Tony Southgate and Dave Wass and the product of an outfit born over the winter out of the Shadow team. The next wing car was the Shadow DN9, also designed by Southgate and Wass before their departure to Arrows. The remarkable similarity of the cars led to cries of plagiarism which landed Arrows in the High Court where it was deemed that FA1 owed more to DN9 than just its parentage and FA1 was promptly banned. It was quickly followed by the new Arrows A1 which never quited lived up to the promise of the earlier car; nor, strangely, did the near identical Shadow. . . .

The only car which presented a real threat to Lotus dominance was the Ferrari 312T-3, which appeared right from the beginning of the season shod

with Michelin radials. The T-3's record was rather chequered and the Michelins ranged from faultless to fragile with no apparent reason. Michelin did have the whip hand over Goodyear in that supplying only two teams they were able to try many more compounds on each without having to carry vast stocks of covers. Goodyear for their part limited their supply of special qualifying tyres to selected teams and those who showed most potential in practice. They usually included the latest Ligier – the JS9 – and the beautifully simple and compact Williams FW06, designed by Patrick Head for Frank Williams' Saudi Arabian sponsored team. The Williams showed that it was still possible to be a front runner with a simple, well engineered lightweight car and a determined driver.

With the departure of Derek Gardner back to the motor industry, the design onus at Tyrrell passed to Maurice Phillippe who rapidly shunned what was proving to be an expensive blind alley with the six-wheeler and penned a very straightforward successor, Tyrrell 008, distinguished mostly by its very low, flat monocoque and the fact that it won at Monaco.

Wolf brought a new shape to the circuits with WR5, a 'wing car' with the radiator sitting on the front of the cockpit over the driver's legs. After such a good start in 1977 the Wolf team sadly lost much of its impetus and although Scheckter put in some stirring drives, notably in Monaco, he was obviously losing heart and looking forward to a new challenge at Ferrari.

There was little else of much import in a year in which Lotus superiority seemingly demoralised more than one team. There were new names on the grids in the form of Martini (the French Formula Two championship winners soon finding Formula One to be a much tougher proposition and quietly fading away), the Theodore TR1 from Ron Tauranac and the crude, March-based Merzario A1 for Arturo himself. ATS moved on from redubbing Marches and Penskes to building their own cars – the D1 – which showed occasional turns of speed. The latest incarnation of the Hesketh team persevered with the 308E; Surtees traded in the TS19 for the equally mediocre TS20; Emerson struggled on with Fittipaldi F5A and Ensign did likewise with the N177, which probably suffered more from a lack of finance than from a lack of technical promise; at McLaren, the M26 had an absolutely dismal season and the feelings of relief at Colnbrook when the season came to a close were doubtless mirrored in many other camps.

All thoughts of the invincibility of the Lotus 79 went out of the window as the 1979 season opened in South America; confirming its testing performances, the Ligier JS11 – now Cosworth powered, allowing it to make the

most of a beautifully engineered ground effect chassis – simply pulverised the opposition. It was a spectacular demonstration of the importance of tyre compatibility for, it seemed, the latest, slightly taller, Goodyears suited the Ligier to perfection but left the Lotus struggling for rear end grip.

For once there was much of technical interest to be seen on the grids. A completely new engine is a rare happening and so there was much interest in the new V12 Alfa Romeo unit, around which Gordon Murray had designed the spectacular Brabham BT48, taking advantage of the narrowness of the new unit to allow a proper ground effect chassis.

The new engine was a sixty degree V12, retaining the heads and some of the internals of the boxer engine. It was used, of course, as a stressed unit, and had an up and over exhaust system in deference to ground effect requirements.

Predictably, 1979 started with a good sprinkling of Lotus 79 look alikes on the grids, the most blatant of which were without doubt the Tyrrell 009, McLaren M28 and the Wolf WR7. It did not take a very gifted seer to predict the arrival of many more variations as the season progressed.

Above left: after a fairy tale season in 1977 with the WR1, great things were expected of the Harvey Postlethwaite designed Wolf WR5 in 1978. Handling problems plagued the car and driver Scheckter wanted better so left the team at the end of the year

Left: Maurice Phillippe's first car for Tyrrell was the 008 with shallow monocoque, forward pointing canard wings and Karl Kempf's on-board computer. Depailler won at Monaco through determination, but thereafter the car's weight was too much of a handicap

Above: the Ligier team honed to perfection the Lotus ground-effect principle with their JS11, and the car was by far the quickest in the early part of 1979 with drivers Laffite and Depailler

Right: with ground effect cars becoming necessity rather than luxury, Alfa forsook the centre of gravity advantage they had with their flat-twelve for the necessary lateral compactness of a V12 seen here in the 1979 Brabham BT48

There was some original thinking to be seen however. The new Fittipaldi F6, designed by Ralph Bellamy, appeared with very abbreviated side pods (through which passed the exhaust system) flanking the slimmest of monocoques, devoid (initially at least) of wings. From Mo Nunn came a new Ensign, the N179, which carried its water and oil radiators immediately ahead of the driver and over his legs. By cleaning up the side pod area the Ensign proved exceptionally quick in a straight line but its development was delayed by overheating problems, in an attempt to cure which the radiators were quickly moved back into the side pods!

Best of all was the new Ferrari, the 312T-4, disproving the widely held belief that the flat-twelve precluded the use of a ground effect chassis. The T-4 moved all its fuel into a single central tank behind the driver and swept the exhausts up through the rear of the side pods. The very slim front end was supplanted by a curiously shaped but apparently effective aerofoil section upper deck and the whole lot was wheeled out on its Michelin radials to take a convincing one-two on its maiden outing in South Africa, followed by the same result with apparently equal ease for Villeneuve and Scheckter at Long Beach. . . .

Once again, however, Colin Chapman was aiming one step ahead; on a snowy March day at Brands Hatch he unveiled the Lotus 80, with not a wing in sight. In fact there were two wings, one was a venturi section – sealed by skirts – under the elongated nose, the other was the rest of the car. Now only the front suspension intruded into the side airflow, even the drive shafts being taken through the side pods which filled all the space between the rear wheels. When the 80 began testing it soon became apparent that all was far from well, with the detail design if not with the concept. The sliding skirt system, on which the ground effect relied, proved troublesome and was redesigned, but sceptics could not entirely suppress an 'I told you so' attitude as the car donned wings during further trials. Such problems, however, are the stuff on which the Colin Chapmans of this world thrive and the Lotus, once again, was but the vanguard of a new philosophy.

The prime technology of Formula One had now moved firmly from chassis and suspension design to aerodynamics. While Chapman struggled for once, and McLaren learned that having a larger car was a poor way to generate more downforce, a new leader was emerging in the unlikely personna of the long-time underdog, Williams. At Long Beach, Williams showed off the elegantly simple FW07, designed by Patrick Head and being no more than a beautiful interpretation of current convention. Air was channeled through a venturi created by the road and a carefully shaped underbody profile. The

Above: with the 312T-4, Ferrari dispelled, by a convincing one-two victory on their maiden outing, any notion that using a flat-twelve engine precluded building an efficient ground effect chassis. By locating all the fuel load in a central tank behind the driver, adopting a very narrow centre section and taking the exhausts well upwards at the rear, the sides of the car were left relatively clear for aerodynamic appendages, supplemented by the strange 'foredeck'.

Above: after years of shoestring struggling, made possible only by exceptional dedication and sacrifice, Frank Williams, helped by Saudi finance and the design expertise of Patrick Head (*background*) finally made it to the top in 1980

Right: the combination which took Williams to the Constructor's Championship in 1980, Alan Jones, who won the Drivers' Championship and the elegantly simple FW07, seen here in the 1979 Dutch Grand Prix, which Jones won

air was kept in laminar flow along the length of the car by sliding skirts, sprung to stay in constant contact with the road throughout all suspension movement and tipped with ceramic rubbing strips to minimise wear. This controlled air flow, escaping only at the rear, effectively sucked the car onto the ground without recourse to fans or motors. Cornering speeds took another leap and as 1980 dawned, Williams, not Lotus, was the team to be copied.

It was no more than just reward for Williams that he maintained the momentum of 1979 and scored a memorable Drivers and Constructors World Championship double, with Alan Jones leading the team. They won against ever more effective opposition. Towards the end of 1979, Brabham had reverted from Alfa Romeo to Cosworth power in the BT49 and this provided the most effective opposition to the Williams, in the hands of Nelson Piquet. The emphasis placed on clean underbody airflow may be judged by the fact that Brabham experimented with specially made taller and narrower Weisman gearbox casings simply to clean up further the air exit area. Ultimately, Williams won six races (plus the unsanctioned Spanish Grand Prix) and Brabham won three. The other winners were Renault and Ligier, with three and two wins, respectively. The latest Renault, the RE20-25 series was a development of the previous car, the engine now with twin turbochargers, better intercooling and 520 bhp at 11,000 rpm, compared to the 470 plus of a good Cosworth. Sadly, although the Renault was potent it still lacked reliability, being particularly prone to valve spring failures. Cosworth engines on the other hand won no less than eleven races (plus Spain) to bring their total to 136.

Undeterred by Renault's problems and probably spurred by uncharacteristically dubious reliability with their own normally aspirated flat-12, Ferrari joined the ranks of the turbocharged engine builders after Monza. Like the Renault EF1, the Ferrari engine, designated 126C, was a V6, a configuration well suited to the narrow chassis dictates of a true ground effect car but inevitably nullified to some degree by the need to locate complex exhaust plumbing, the turbocharger itself and the vital intercooling within the airstream. The Ferrari engine was less oversquare than the Renault at 81×48.4 mm but it was also lighter and more powerful. With a compression ratio between 6.5 and 7.5:1 the 126C claimed 540 bhp at 12,000 rpm. The turbos suffered a further disadvantage in their compatibility with ground effects in that their more pronounced thirst (typically 15 to 20 per cent more than a Cosworth) demanded a bulkier and heavier fuel load.

Little else was new in 1980, virtually all the remaining cars being developments of previous chassis with largely speculative aerodynamic revisions.

Left: although Gilles Villeneuve looks pleased during early tests of the early 126CK turbo-engined Ferrari, the car never really fulfilled its potential. The KKK turbocharged engine was powerful but reliable only to a point and the power was wasted on a chassis which was years behind the despised 'kit-car' front runners in terms of modern thinking and materials

Below: another team which introduced turbo power in 1981 was former European Formula Two Champions Toleman whose 1494 cc four-cylinder unit, developed by Brian Hart again squandered its obvious power on a chassis possibly even worse than that of the Ferrari

Lotus derived the 79X from a mixture of 79 and 80 ideas but neither that nor the subsequent 81 produced any results. Ensign, Shadow and Arrows produced new designs, the N180, DN11 and A3 respectively and although all three showed promise on odd occasions they were never more than 'best of the rest'. The increasingly frustrated Fittipaldi team took over the assets of the disbanded Walter Wolf Racing and produced some very conventional and mediocre hybrids dubbed F7 and the one newcomer to the F1 ranks, Osella's FA1 was disastrously overweight and served principally to underline how far Formula One technology had recently progressed.

The turbo revolution continued to gain momentum in 1981, with the eventual appearance of Ferrari, BMW and Hart engines, the last two for Brabham and the new Toleman team respectively, and both in-line fours as opposed to the usual V6. Nevertheless, as Brabham developed the BMW engine for full time use in 1982, the team scored yet another Cosworth powered World Championship in 1981, with Piquet reversing the Williams-Brabham stranglehold. The Williams drivers, Reutemann and Jones, in that order won four Grands Prix (two each) while Piquet won three, FW07s to B and C specification and similar BT49s being simple developments of the previous cars.

Ferrari used two forced induction systems on their 126 cars in 1981, the Comprex pressure wave supercharger and the exhaust-driven KKK turbo-charger, the 126CX Comprex engine soon being dropped, however, in favour

Right: Brabham's problems at the introduction of their turbocharged BMW engine were somewhat different from those of Ferrari and Toleman, a typically workmanlike Gordon Murray chassis design being unable to show its worth with an initially unreliable engine

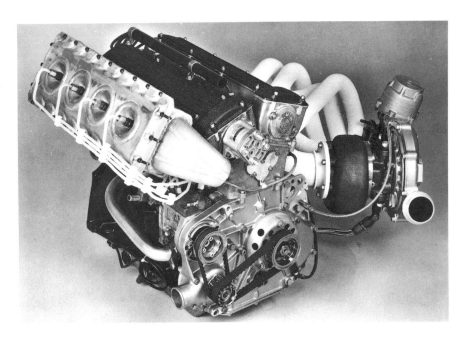

of the 126CK turbo version. Ferrari used a novel way of minimising turbine inertia induced throttle lag, allowing a rich overrun mixture to burn within the turbine housing, the combustion driving the compressor much like a gas turbine, quite independent of exhaust pressure. The turbine was therefore kept spinning even on closed or small throttle running and lag was minimised. The price was unreliability due to overheating of the turbine and its bearings and they eventually reverted to a more normal boost transfer system. The 126C won two races but that was largely due to Gilles Villeneuve as the turbo's 560 bhp was wasted on a very agricultural chassis.

Even from the beginning of testing, the BMW M12/13 turbos were at least in a decent chassis, Gordon Murray doing a characteristically neat adaption of the BT49 into the BMW powered BT50. The four-cylinder KKK turbocharged BMW engine had bore and stroke of 89.2 × 60 mm, or 1499 cc, and four relatively large valves per cylinder. Compared to most it was quite low revving, claiming (with typical German precision) 557 bhp at only 9500 rpm. Its one public outing, in practice for the British Grand Prix, suggested that it did indeed have a great deal of power.

The other four-cylinder turbo, Toleman's Hart 145T, was 1494 cc, 88 × 61.5 mm, used a Garrett AiResearch turbocharger instead of the otherwise universal KKK and offered 540 bhp (minimum) at 10,500 rpm. Again, its power was not in doubt but like Ferrari's it was rather wasted on the bulky and difficult TG181 chassis (designed by Rory Byrne and John Gentry). The car was variously nicknamed the Flying Pig, in deference to its handling, or the General Belgrano, a comparison with the unfortunate Argentine battle-ship . . .

Alfa Romeo had a V8 turbo engine on the drawing board, but they continued to rely on their 540 bhp, 1260 series V12, being joined in the V12 ranks by the latest Matra MS81 engine making another return with Ligier – successfully too, with two wins during the year and threatening several more. Its advertised 510 bhp may even have been somewhat conservative, for the beautifully engineered Talbot-Ligier JS17 was certainly no lightweight and the V12 was fairly thirsty.

1981 was also a busy year on the chassis engineering front, with new regulations dictating 6 cm ground clearance and an end to sliding skirts. Without the channelling effect of skirts, ground effect is largely lost, so a new approach was necessary. The ever innovative Gordon Murray found one answer – albeit exploiting a loophole and eventually spawning a breed of imitators which the drivers universally abhored. In that the 6 cm clearance could only be measured at rest, Murray contrived a soft, pneumatic suspension system on the Brabham which aerodynamic downforce at speed pushed into

a fully down position, at which time solid, vestigial 'skirts' ran close enough to the ground to approach the efficiency of the sliding skirt systems. The penalty was that once into the down position, suspension movement had to be minimised to maintain constant, minimum clearance and so the car ran astronomical spring rates – or, put another way, virtually solid suspension – subjecting drivers to a terrible pounding and making the cars *extremely* nervous on anything less than a perfect surface.

As FISA made little protest at the blatant rule bending, every team was soon obliged to imitate the Brabham system and before long cars even had driver controlled ride height systems and flexible (yet still fixed and therefore within the letter of the law) skirts with rubbing strips. A limit was eventually put on the dimensions, rigidity and fixing of the skirts but it really only served to make the cars even more rock hard.

There was one other attempt to achieve the same end but retain a degree of concern for the driver and that was Colin Chapman's 'twin-chassis' Lotus 88; the 'primary chassis' comprised the bodywork, sidepods, aerofoils and radiators, suspended on coil spring damper units at each wheel and intended to absorb aerodynamic loads while being unaffected by braking, cornering or acceleration loads. Those loads were fed to the 'secondary chassis' which comprised a monocoque, fuel tank, engine and gearbox and suspension, thereby isolating the driver from the need for constant aerodynamic trim and allowing him a degree of suspension movement. While accepting single chassis cars which blatantly ran in contact with the ground, FISA, after numerous and acrimonious protests, counter protests and technical tribunals, banned the 88 before it had a chance to prove its worth or otherwise.

The only other real technical innovation on the chassis front was John Barnard's beautifully neat McLaren MP4 whose monocoque was not rivetted or bonded from sheet metal but moulded in the extraordinarily light and strong carbon fibre. The car won at Silverstone and proved its strength in several very severe accidents.

With the return of Goodyear and the arrival of Pirelli (with Toleman),

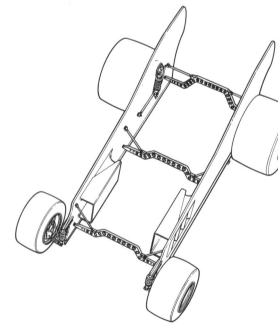

Top: the rules banning skirts but allowing the loophole of hydropneumatic suspension systems led to the ludicrous spectacle of cars like Carlos Reutemann's Williams running with enormous ground clearances such as here at low speeds but then hugging the ground at racing speeds

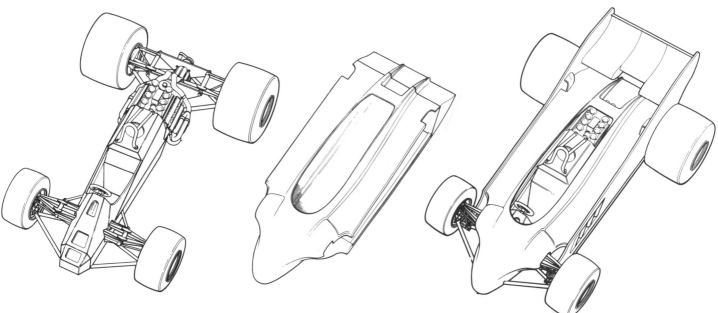

Above, left to right and top right: while FISA
tacitly accepted the patently illegal
hydropneumatic suspension cars, they banned
Colin Chapman's innovative, double chassis
Lotus 88 virtually before it ran

competition returned to the tyre scene after Goodyear's early season withdrawal but Michelin generally looked the better bet and Pirelli's steel belted
radials suffered not so much from compounding problems as from being
simply too heavy to allow competitively hard spring rates.

After 1981, 1982 was relatively calm once the early season controversy about
disposable ballast had been resolved. Unable to beat or even approach the
turbo runners in terms of power, the Cosworth users could only pursue their
weight advantage over the thirstier and bulkier turbos. Through the hideously
expensive use of exotic materials such as titanium and carbon fibre and the
equally exotic manufacturing methods which they imposed, the best of the
Cosworth teams, with the help of designs of exceptional engineering quality,

could now build cars substantially below the minimum weight limit, but how to use that advantage without breaking the rules? Well, the rules would bend before they would break and suddenly teams were exploiting the interpretation of the rule which allowed cars to be topped up with essential coolants after the race and before the weight check. The lighter cars now developed a need for water cooled brakes and as a rule of thumb the water in the cooling system generally weighed about as much as the car was shy of the weight limit. With the water quickly jettisoned in the approximate direction of the brakes, these cars could race underweight, giving a performance edge and easing the suspension problems. For once, FISA, protecting the interests of its closely

Above: from the middle of the 1982 season (starting at the British Grand Prix and seen here practising at the Italian Grand Prix) the Brabham team used (or when engines expired early prepared to use) tactical pit-stops. Faced with the dilemma of marginal fuel capacity for their thirsty BMW turbos, the team started the cars on half full tanks and soft tyres, theoretically allowing the drivers to build a big lead before pitting at roughly half distance for fuel and fresh rubber, preheated in an oven but still cool enough by racing standards to be a problem for a couple of laps. Given a chance the system showed some promise and by the beginning of 1983 many teams were copying it – even the Cosworth powered Williams. The more teams used the idea the less relevant it obviously became, FISA became increasingly concerned with the safety aspects and pit stops for fuel were due to be phased out by 1984

Left: the beautifully constructed Marlboro MP4 introduced carbon fibre monocoques, soon to be copied by virtually every team

aligned turbo and V12 teams, was quick to react and by mid-April the cheat was specifically banned.

With the arrival of Harvey Postlethwaite, Ferrari developed a 'modern', carbon fibre composite chassis to match the prodigious power of their latest turbo engine, with water injection and a relatively reliable 580 bhp (or probably more than 600 in short bursts during qualifying). Alas, Ferrari's dreadful misfortune made real assessment of the new car rather academic. The BMW turbo now began to race and showed terrific power coupled with appalling reliability, largely with the fuel system which often resulted in the BMW Brabhams making a spectacularly pyrotechnic departure. During the year

Right: with improving reliability from the Ferrari turbo engine, the carbon fibre and aluminium composite chassis of the 1982 Ferrari was seen by most as a potential champion in the hands of the brilliant Villeneuve but the car's worth was totally overshadowed by the team's dreadful run of luck. Ferrari did however win the Constructors' title

Brabham also introduced a tactical ploy which showed promise on the rare occasions when the cars lasted long enough to employ it. Starting on soft tyres and light fuel load, the Brabhams would endeavour to build a commanding lead before stopping for more fuel and fresh, soft tyres, preheated in an oven to speed their subsequent warmup. The cars were adapted with fast fuel fillers and the pit crews were impeccably rehearsed and equipped but the benefits were at best moot.

'Pull-rod' suspension, which operated in tension rather than compression and allowed for lighter and slimmer suspension arms without allowing unwanted bending spring effects (a Gordon Murray original idea) proliferated, as did the use of carbon fibre for anything from aerodynamic appendages to complete monocoques. Once early problems with pad compatibility and nearby component cooling had been overcome, carbon fibre brake discs, again pioneered by Brabham and offering a tremendous weight saving came to be seen more and more.

Yet in the end of course, the Championship went to a driver in a now 'conventional' car and with a Cosworth engine, although Ferrari, to their utmost credit, slavaged a worthy Constructor's Championship from this dreadful season. Rosberg and the Williams FW08 just might have represented the pinnacle of Cosworth achievement. For 1983, sweeping changes in the regulations, inspired by an urgent need to slow the cars through corners for safety's sake, banned skirts completely and introduced 'flat bottoms' to limit ground effect. At first it seemed that this new breed could be a great leveller, putting renewed emphasis on driver skill and engine response, giving the latest, short stroke, lightweight Cosworth, the DFY, a control advantage if not a power advantage, but it soon became apparent that power was still the name of the game and turbos would eventually rule the roost, albeit ultimately coupled to a fuel consumption formula.

After years of sprouting wings and squandering fuel, there was once more a fighting chance that this most specialised of vehicles would have a few lessons to be applied to its roadgoing counterparts. Once the turbo bandwagon started rolling, just about every car manufacturer soon jumped on it.

Below: in spite of the proliferation of the turbos, the Drivers' Championship went once again to a Cosworth-powered team and the Williams FW08, a simple design refined to the absolute state of the art

THE RACES: 1960-83

The change of formula in 1961 brought more than a change in the cars; it heralded a new hierarchy of drivers. The names which permeated the history of motor racing in the 1950s were gone and a new generation was born. The image of motor racing was changing and the sport's afficionados were finding a different breed of hero.

The first season of the new formula saw the first American World Champion, 34-year-old Phil Hill from Santa Monica. Hill, a member of the powerful Ferrari team, took the title when his German team mate, Wolfgang von Trips,

Below: by the 1962 season, British manufacturers had wiped out Ferrari's early lead in the 1½-litre formula, and Graham Hill was able to score his own and BRM's first championships. He is seen here in the championship-winning V8's four-cylinder predecessor during the 1961 Dutch Grand Prix, at Zandvoort

was killed at Monza. Hill won the Monza race, and also won at Spa – at 128.151 mph; von Trips had won at Zandvoort and at Aintree and Ferrari's 'rookie' driver, Giancarlo Baghetti, scooped a sensational debut win at Reims. the only break in Ferrari's monopoly came from the Lotuses of Moss – with Rob Walker's 18 – and Innes Ireland in the works 21. Moss scored spectacular victories, against the odds, in Monaco and Germany, through sheer driving skill; Ireland's first, and only, championship race win came at Watkins Glen, in the absence of the Ferraris. In the Principality, Moss led from lap fourteen onwards and had to use every ounce of his skill to fend off the works Ferraris of Hill and Ginther. He won by 3.6 secs, at an average speed of 70.70 mph, and shared fastest lap with second man Ginther, at 73.13 mph. In Germany, Moss gave everything to win by 21.8 secs from von Trips, at 92.34 mph.

The season was marred by the death of von Trips and fourteen spectators at Monza when, on the second lap, his and Jim Clark's cars touched at Vedano and the talented German's Ferrari was launched into the crowd. A happier statistic came from the Dutch Grand Prix, the first ever world championship race at which every starter finished without incident.

It had been a good start to the new formula for the Maranello cars but by 1962 the British teams had caught up some of their lost impetus and the season saw a sterling battle between Clark's Lotus and Graham Hill's BRM. The championship was eventually resolved at the very last round, in favour of Hill – who had taken four superb victories during the season in Holland, Germany, Italy and that final race in South Africa. Clark scored in Belgium, England and the United States and was within a few laps of winning his first world title when his engine failed.

The season started in Holland where Hill scored his own first Grand Prix win and BRM's second – at the same circuit where they opened their tally in 1959. Hill won at 95.44 mph from Lotus's new driver Trevor Taylor, who surprised many by his performance. John Surtees, making the switch from two to four wheels, in a Lola, had a lucky escape when a wishbone on the car broke at high speed.

One driver who was not so lucky in 1962 was Stirling Moss who crashed heavily and inexplicably during a non-championship race at Goodwood on Easter Monday. 32-year-old Moss was released, bleeding and partially paralysed, from his wrecked Lotus and, although he recovered to what would be regarded as full fitness by any other person, his racing career was over: the fine edge had gone forever from his judgement and reactions. Moss never did gain the world title he so thoroughly deserved, a mixture of national pride, when he drove sub-standard machinery simply because it was British, and wretched luck keeping that honour from him. He had risen from his first appearance at Prescott hill-climb, in a 500 cc Cooper on 9 May 1948, through almost every kind of racing, to be a works Formula One driver for Mercedes, Maserati, Vanwall and Connaught. He also drove BRMs, Lotuses, Coopers and many more. He was second in the World Championship for Drivers four times but he never won. The end of Moss's career severed a link with an earlier generation of drivers and left a space at the pinnacle of racing for someone else to fill.

The man who was to fill it was the young Scot who finished second in the 1962 championship, Jim Clark. Clark was born on 4 March 1936 and began his motoring career in the early 1950s, first in local rallies and then in circuit races. Early support from the Scottish Border Reivers team led Clark through saloon, Formula Junior, sports car and Formula Two racing, to a contract for Formula One with Lotus. In all his career, Clark never lost faith with Lotus and never drove for another Grand Prix team. Clark and Lotus were a combination whose story is woven into the web of racing for many years; he was a worthy successor to fill the void left by Moss.

Clark collected his first Grand Prix win at Spa in 1962, beating Graham Hill and Phil Hill into second and third places and averaging 131.89 mph in the process, with a fastest lap at 133.98 mph. The season saw the first championship victory for both Porsche and their lanky Californian driver, Dan Gurney, who inherited victory at Rouen when race leader Graham Hill's engine went off song twelve laps from home.

Top: before his death in a Formula Two race at Hockenheim in 1968, Jim Clark had dominated motor racing for several glorious years. His two World Championships, in 1963 and 1965, were gained with seemingly consummate ease and only mechanical misfortunes prevented him from claiming the title in other years. It became rare for Clark to be beaten in a straight confrontation in Grand Prix racing, mechanical failure notwithstanding; he was regarded as almost invincible

Above: Californian Dan Gurney was the mainstay of Porsche's first venture into Grand Prix racing; he gave the German team their first Grand Prix win at Rouen in 1962

Right: the master of Monaco at work – Graham Hill powers his BRM P56 through Casino Square on his way to victory and setting fastest lap during the 1963 Grand Prix. In the picture, he is pursued by John Surtees' Ferrari, a chase which lasted until the latter's goggles became covered with oil. By the end of his career, Hill had won the Monaco event five times

Below: Jim Clark led the 1963 Dutch Grand Prix from start to finish, lapping the whole field and setting the first 100mph lap record at the Zandvoort circuit. Clark's Lotus-Climax 25 was fitted with an air-deflector screen for the first time

The only other winner in 1962 was Bruce McLaren, who won the Monaco Grand Prix at an average speed of 70.46mph, after leader Graham Hill retired with no oil pressure. Phil Hill was just 1.3 seconds behind for Ferrari after making a tremendous effort to catch McLaren. 1963 was the year of 'the Flying Scot', Jim Clark. On his way to his first World Championship, Clark scored seven victories from the season's ten Grands Prix, with one second place, one third and a single retirement, in Monaco, to wrest the title from Graham Hill and BRM. Hill and his BRM team-mate Ritchie Ginther shared second place in the championship, albeit 25 points in arrears of Clark's perfect score of 54, from his best six results. The season began without Porsche, who had retired at the end of 1962. Their top driver, Gurney, joined the newly formed Brabham team, while the withdrawal of Lola from the scene sent John Surtees to Ferrari, alongside Willy Mairesse of Belgium. The Lolas did in fact appear again in 1963 in the colours of the Reg Parnell team and driven by Chris Amon, newly launched on a career to become notorious for its ill fortune.

With Clark retiring from a strong lead, when the gearbox of his Lotus broke on the 78th lap, Graham Hill scored the first of his famous series of Monaco victories in the opening round. At Spa, Clark scored the first of four consecutive 1963 victories at 114.1mph and by almost five minutes from Bruce McLaren's Cooper. The race was held in appalling conditions with thunderstorms sweeping the daunting Belgian circuit and it was sheer good fortune that none of many incidents had serious outcomes. After Spa, Clark simply ran away and hid from the opposition at the Dutch Grand Prix, lapping the entire field. Dan Gurney improved Brabham's standing by taking second place –

Left: after early leaders Brabham, Gurney, McLaren and Hill had dropped out, Jim Clark comfortably led the British Grand Prix of 1963, winning by a large margin from Surtees' Ferrari

Right: John Surtees looks pensive after his victory in the 1963 German Grand Prix. This was his first Grand Prix win, and he repeated the success in 1964, his World Championship year

Below: Richie Ginther's works BRM leads Jo Bonnier's Rob Walker-entered Cooper-Climax, Dan Gurney's Brabham and the debutant Chris Amon in Reg Parnell's Lola through the Zandvoort sand dunes in 1963. Ginther eventually finished fifth and Gurney second

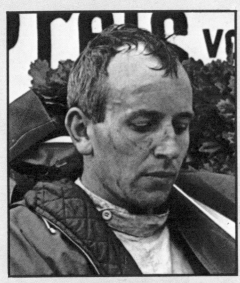

having scored an encouraging third in Belgium. Surtees raised Ferrari's spirits with a fighting third place, ahead of Innes Ireland's BRP BRM. Young Italian Ludovico Scarfiotti collected his first championship point for sixth place in this his first Grand Prix. Despite a continual misfire, Clark won at Reims, averaging 125.31 mph and collecting fastest lap at 131.14 mph in the process. Second place, a minute and five seconds behind, went to South African Tony Maggs in a Cooper and third went to Graham Hill – even counting a one minute penalty for a push start.

Clark's fourth successive victory was gained with consummate ease at Silverstone, followed home by a stirring battle for second place between Hill and Surtees, resolved on the last lap when Hill ran out of fuel to coast home third. Mike Hailwood followed in Surtees' footsteps, turning from two wheels to four for the first time at this race; he finished eighth.

It was Surtees who finally broke Clark's winning streak with a hard-won victory at the Nürburgring, with Clark bringing his ailing Lotus home second. Surtees' average speed was 95.83 mph and he set fastest lap at 96.8 mph. Clark was back to form in Italy and won from Ginther and McLaren after early leader

Surtees and his strongest challengers, Hill and Gurney, all retired. Clark drove a masterly race to finish third behind the BRMs of Hill and Ginther at Watkins Glen, having been left at the line with a flat battery. Clark's fastest lap of 111.14 mph was not enough to catch Hill who won at 109.91 mph. Clark rounded off a magnificent season with wins in the first ever Mexican Grand Prix and in South Africa. Brabhams were second in both races, Jack himself scoring in Mexico and Gurney in South Africa, a promising season for the team.

Clark's luck was not at its best in the 1964 season, which was one of the closest ever raced, being decided in favour of John Surtees at the final round in Mexico after a three-cornered fight with Hill and Clark. Surtees amply justified Ferrari's faith on his way to becoming the first ever man to win championships on both two and four wheels.

Hill and Ginther opened the season with another one-two finish at Monaco. Clark's Monaco gremlins struck again and he finished fourth behind his team-mate, Peter Arundell. Hailwood scored a championship point with sixth place in a BRM-powered Lotus. Clark scored his traditional easy victory at Zandvoort while Surtees showed his ever growing talent with a good second place.

Below : Dan Gurney's Brabham at the Nouveau Monde hairpin at Rouen, during the 1964 French Grand Prix. Gurney, who started from the middle of the front row of the grid, went on to score Brabham's first Grand Prix victory after Jim Clark retired from the lead of this race

Right : Jim Clark's Lotus-Climax 25 has just gone through the Monaco chicane, while Graham Hill's BRM P56 follows Bob Anderson's Brabham-Climax into the same bend. On the first lap, Clark had hit the straw bales on the exit from the chicane, breaking the anti-roll bar. His engine expired on lap 93, and Hill dominated this, the 1964 race. Ginther was second and Clark was classified fourth behind team-mate Arundell

Chris Amon finished fifth to score his first championship points, as did former motor cyclist Bob Anderson in sixth place. The Belgian race was again packed with drama and saw Clark take another victory at the one circuit which he openly hated. The victory was one of the luckiest of Clark's career; the Scot was lying fourth behind Gurney, Hill and McLaren with two laps to go when Gurney ran out of fuel and had none available in the Brabham pit. Hill took the lead only to go out with fuel pump trouble on the last lap and McLaren also ran out of fuel within sight of the finish, handing victory to a disbelieving Clark.

After so much promise, Gurney finally gave the Brabham team their first victory at Rouen, winning at 108.77 mph from Hill and Brabham himself who took fastest lap at 111.37 mph. At this stage in the season Surtees was way behind in the championship race with only a third of Clark's points total, but the German Grand Prix marked a turning point for the Italian team. Surtees scored another great Nürburgring victory from Hill, and Bandini's Ferrari. Surtees averaged 96.57 mph and set fastest lap at 98.3 mph. The meeting was marred by the death in practice of the Dutchman Count Carel Godin de Beaufort, a popular and dedicated privateer.

Austria's first championship Grand Prix was run at Zeltweg and won at 99.20 mph by Ferrari's Lorenzo Bandini, from Ginther and an inspired Bob Anderson in a private Brabham. Making his debut was a young Austrian who was to become the sport's first posthumous champion, Jochen Rindt. With most of the favourites, Rindt was on the list of retirements. Surtees won again at Monza in a thrilling slipstreaming battle at an average speed of 127.78 mph, with McLaren giving Cooper a rare high spot with second place. Graham Hill had gone no further than the start line in Italy due to clutch failure, but he kept his hopes of a second championship alive by winning at Watkins Glen from Surtees and Jo Siffert, who had a splendid outing with his Brabham.

All this left the championship open into the final round, with Surtees, Hill and Clark all in a position to win the title. Hill led with 39 points to Surtees' 34 and Clark's 30. With 9, 6, 4, 3, 2 and 1 point at stake for the first six places Clark had to win the race to take his second title. With Hill out of the race fairly early, Clark looked all set to take his second championship but, as in the South African race two seasons earlier, Clark was robbed almost within sight of the flag by engine trouble. In a classic example of team work, Bandini moved politely over to let Surtees through to second place, enough points to scoop the championship and a place in motor sport's history books.

The following year, 1965, was the final year of the very successful 1½-litre formula and it was dominated again by the man who had always been the one to beat, Jim Clark. Clark scored six more victories to add to his growing tally, at a time when the competition was stronger than ever. Clark won in South Africa, Belgium, France, Britain, Holland and Germany; Hill scored his Monaco hat trick and won at Watkins Glen and his young Scottish team-mate at BRM, Jackie Stewart marked himself as the greatest find for some years with several good performances culminating in victory in Italy. The final race of the formula saw a new make of car on the list of winners when Ritchie Ginther gave Honda a popular win in Mexico.

Hill's Monaco victory was a classic, achieved through pure skill and determination, after he had to go down the escape road at the chicane after 24 laps, to avoid Bob Anderson's Brabham. Hill gradually caught and passed the field to win a memorable race by just over a minute from Bandini's Ferrari and his own team-mate, Stewart, at an average speed of 74.30 mph. Hill's fastest lap was 76.72 mph. Clark and Gurney had both been missing from Monaco, driving for Team Lotus in the Indianapolis 500. Clark won. During the Monaco race, Paul Hawkins had a lucky escape when he crashed his Lotus 33 into the harbour, without injury!

Clark returned from America to score his fourth successive victory at Spa, again in atrocious conditions which kept visibility and lap speeds down. Clark's winning average was 117.16 mph and his fastest lap was 124.72 mph. The other 'Flying Scot', Stewart, was second, from McLaren, while Ginther gave Honda their first championship point with sixth place. The circus then moved on to a

Far left: Jim Clark, who won the Belgian Grand Prix four years running, is pictured here in June 1963. In the foul weather conditions which can so unexpectedly occur at Spa, Clark's Lotus Climax 25 leads Count Carel Godin de Beaufort's private four-cylinder Porsche, which eventually finished sixth. Team managers Rudd of BRM and Chapman of Lotus asked, in vain, for the race to be stopped. Only six cars finished

Left: Just before winning his sixth Grand Prix of the 1965 season, Jim Clark appears quietly confident. His Lotus 33 led the German Grand Prix from start to finish and thus clinched the Championship by half-season

Below: Yet another rain-soaked Spa-Franchorchamps, this time 1965, and Jackie Stewart drove an excellent race in his BRM P56 to finish second, 45 seconds behind Clark

new venue for the French Grand Prix, Clermont-Ferrand, a very difficult addition to the championship stage. Again it was Clark and Stewart who led the field, followed home by burly New Zealander Denny Hulme in a Brabham. They were Hulme's first points in the championship.

The British Grand Prix was at Silverstone and, in spite of a sick engine, Clark made no mistakes about winning, leading arch-rival Hill home by just 3.2 seconds. Clark used the four-valve engine at Silverstone and Surtees was at last given a flat-12 Ferrari to replace the V8 he had used until then. Clark scored another victory in Holland, after being pressed hard by Stewart, who finished only 8 seconds behind the maestro. Gurney was third, a further 5 seconds adrift with the Brabham. The Honda actually led for a few laps and Ginther eventually brought it into sixth place. Clark at last broke his Nürburgring duck with a splendid win in the German race from Hill and Gurney, while Jochen Rindt scored a good fourth place in his Cooper. Clark's winning average was 99.796 mph and his fastest lap 101.226 mph. His win clinched his second championship.

Stewart's championship winning days may have been a few years into the future, but he did not show it at Monza where he scored his first Grand Prix win from Hill in the other BRM. Even at this late stage in the 1½-litre formula there were plenty of revised cars to be seen, notably from Honda and Ferrari. Clark set fastest lap at 133.43 mph, before retiring on lap 63 with fuel pump problems; Stewart's winning average was 130.31 mph.

The final two races of the season, in the United States and Mexico, were without John Surtees, who had had a huge accident in a Can-Am race and was still seriously ill. The Ferraris were entrusted to Bandini, Rodriguez and local

Above: Jim Clark made a typical start at the 1965 United States GP at Watkins Glen where he is seen leading the pack from Hill, Ginther and Spence. Clark's hastily rebuilt engine broke a piston on lap 11 and the race was won by Hill's BRM with the Brabhams of Gurney and Jack Brabham second and third

Above right: Spa in 1966 saw the kind of race that every driver dreads. Fifteen cars started the first lap and only seven completed it; of the others seven were victims of the appalling conditions and Jim Clark's Lotus suffered an engine failure. The race was kept alive by this stirring battle between Surtees' Ferrari and Rindt's Cooper which was resolved in Surtees' favour, with the pair a whole lap ahead of Bandini in third place

star Bob Bondurant for the American race, but none of them could catch Graham Hill, who drove to his Watkins Glen hat trick at 107.98 mph, setting fastest lap at 115.16 mph on the way. Ginther wound up the 1½-litre years by giving the Honda team a well deserved win in Mexico by leading from flag to flag at 94.26 mph. Gurney set fastest lap with his Brabham, at 96.59 mph.

While the Japanese team celebrated their victory, everyone began to look ahead to the new 3-litre formula whose start was only months away.

The advent of the 3-litre formula was heralded as the 'Return of Power' and many foretold that it would bring forward a different type of driver to control the powerful new cars. These seers were only partly right, for although the drivers did change it was not their talent or determination that changed but rather their whole attitude to motor sport, which finally became a totally professional occupation with no place for the enthusiastic amateur of years gone by.

1966, the first years of the new rules, again caught the manufacturers in their natural state of unreadiness and it was Jackie Stewart who opened the scoring at Monaco with a 2.1-litre BRM. The race was one of attrition, with only four classified finishers from sixteen starters. Bandini was second and triple Monaco winner Hill was third, after racing with a slipping clutch. A fine day for BRM was completed by Bob Bondurant who brought his privately entered car home fourth. It was a rare highlight in a not very good year for BRM.

After Monaco all the other races went to full 3-litre cars, the next round, at Spa, being taken by Surtees in the V12 Ferrari from Rindt's Cooper-Maserati and Bandini in the second Ferrari. Surtees' winning average was 113.395 mph and he also set fastest lap at 121.91 mph, in a race again marred by the weather conditions and numerous accidents; no less than eight of the fifteen starters were eliminated on the first lap. Into fourth place came Jack Brabham in the new 3-litre Brabham-Repco, with which he was to win his third world title.

'Black Jack' opened his account with victory in the next round, at Reims, beating Mike Parkes' Ferrari by 9.5 seconds. Denny Hulme made it a convincing showing for the new Brabhams by bringing the other car home in third place, and Dan Gurney gave encouragement to the Eagle team with a fine fifth place. Brabham's winning average of 136.9 mph made this the fastest race ever run in France. Brabham continued his winning streak at Brands Hatch, leading Hulme to the flag by 9.6 seconds. Hill and Clark took the next two spots, albeit a long way in arrears with their smaller engined cars. The Ferraris missed the race through industrial problems. Jack collected his third win in a row in Holland with a hard fought victory, at 100.10 mph, over Hill and Clark – who led for much of the race before falling back with overheating. Brabham's fourth consecutive win, at the Nürburgring, virtually clinched the championship with three races remaining. He was pressed all the way in Germany by John Surtees, now driving for Cooper-Maserati and displaying all his old mastery of the Ring. Rindt, in another Cooper, was third and Surtees' fastest lap was 96.44 mph, compared with Brabham's winning average of 86.75 mph.

Ferrari fans had something to cheer in Italy when Ludovico Scarfiotti led team-mate Mike Parkes to a one-two triumph at Monza, following the demise of most of the regular front runners, including Ginther who was lucky to escape from a huge accident caused when his Honda threw a tyre tread at around 150 mph. While Brabham was confirmed as the new champion after Monza, despite his not finishing, Jim Clark brought a ray of light into an unhappy season by taking his BRM H16-engined Lotus to victory at Watkins Glen, scoring the engine's only Grand Prix win. The season finished in Mexico where John Surtees gave the Cooper-Maserati a well deserved win at the end of a season in which they had tried desperately hard with a basically poor car. Brabham and Hulme filled the next two places, ahead of Ginther's Honda and Gurney's Eagle. Already the new formula was bringing a host of new names to the winner's circle.

1967 started with another victory for Cooper and ended with another championship for the Brabham team, this time with Denny Hulme taking the title to New Zealand. It was a year of great strides in car design, and tragedy with Bandini's death in a terrible fiery accident at Monaco.

Pedro Rodriguez scored his first championship win with the Cooper-Maserati in South Africa after a sensational race, which looked as though it was going to be won by local hero John Love in an ancient Cooper-Climax before he ran short of fuel. Love was second and John Surtees, now driving for Honda, was a good third. Denny Hulme scored his first win in the tragic Monaco Grand Prix, from Graham Hill, who was making his debut alongside his old rival Clark in the Lotus camp. Chris Amon's magnificent third place on his first appearance with Ferrari was completely overshadowed by Bandini's accident on the 82nd lap. The talented Italian died a few days later from his terrible burns.

At Zandvoort, Lotus introduced the new 49, powered by the new Cosworth DFV engine. Hill claimed pole position but he retired from the race, leaving Clark to win in fine style at 104.49 mph, setting fastest lap on the way at 106.49 mph. It was a real *tour de force* for the team. Brabham and Hulme showed that they were not going to relinquish the championship without a fight, taking second and third places ahead of Amon's Ferrari. Dan Gurney put the Eagle on to the list of winners with a magnificent performance in Belgium where he averaged a sensational 145.74 mph to beat Stewart's H16 BRM by over a minute. Amon again came home third and the pace of the event can be judged by Gurney's fastest lap of 148.85 mph. Ferrari were lucky not to lose another driver when Parkes survived a huge first lap accident with no more than a broken arm and leg.

Brabham himself was back on top in France where the Grand Prix was held on the Bugatti circuit at Le Mans. Hulme finished second and both Lotuses retired, showing the gap in reliability between the two teams which would net Brabham's second championship, despite the Lotuses' undoubted speed.

Above left: the Dutch Grand Prix of 1968 was run in extremely wet conditions, and many drivers were caught out. One such was Jean-Pierre Beltoise, who spun his V12 Matra MS11 when lying second. After calling at the pits to have sand removed from the throttle slides, he rejoined the race, and re-took second place after a superb drive up from seventh place

Top: Jackie Stewart began racing in 1961 using a variety of borrowed sports cars, and in 1964 he drove Formula 3 Coopers for Ken Tyrrell, winning eleven of the thirteen races he entered. A full Formula One season with BRM in 1965 gave him third place in the Championship, but a bad accident at Spa in 1966 caused him to campaign vigorously for greater safety precautions. His long-standing rapport with Tyrrell paid off in 1969 when he took the Championship in Ken's Matra-Ford. Champion again in 1971 and 1973 driving Tyrrell-Fords, Jackie won a record 27 Grands Prix. He is now a businessman, but he and his wife Helen are still to be seen at the Grands Prix as Stewart is much in demand as a commentator

Top: Jackie Stewart at Kyalami during the 1969 South African Grand Prix, a race he won easily in the Ford-powered Matra. Soon after this the excessively high-mounted aerofoils were banned

Above left: Jacky Ickx's career began on motor cycles and he was Belgian Trials champion three years running. He was Belgian saloon car champion in 1965, and spotted by Ken Tyrrell, he won the European F2 Championship in 1967. Ickx drove for Ferrari in 1968, Brabham in 1969, and back with Ferrari was runner-up to Rindt in 1970. After a disjointed season in 1973, Jacky joined Lotus for two seasons. A man of very many interests outside the sport, he appeared happiest at the wheel of sports cars, having won Le Mans six times

Above: Mike Spence was a works Lotus driver from 1963 to 1966, then he drove for the Parnell team until 1968 when he joined BRM. In 1967 he and Phil Hill won the BOAC 500 miles at Brands Hatch in the Chaparral. He was killed at Indianapolis in 1968 in the Lotus 56 turbine car

Clark's Lotus did not let him down at Silverstone however and he scored his fifth British Grand Prix win in six attempts, 3.8 seconds ahead of Hulme and 14 seconds ahead of Amon. The gremlins hit Lotus again in Germany and Hulme and Brabham were again ready to pounce for the first two places. Hulme's winning average was 101.47 mph. The Formula One establishment was almost dealt a severe shock by young Belgian Jacky Ickx, who held fourth place in his Formula Two Matra before retiring.

Canada hosted her first Grand Prix in August and saw yet another one-two for Brabham and Hulme, from Gurney's Eagle.

The Monza race was sensational. After early problems, Clark drove the race of his life to retake the lead, only to lose it again on the last lap when he ran short of fuel. Surtees and Brabham swapped places all the way round that final tour until Surtees took the flag by just 0.2 seconds at an average of 140.5 mph. In making up a deficit of a whole lap Clark left the lap record at a staggering 145.3 mph. It was Lotus's turn to score first and second in the USA with Hill winning from Clark, whose suspension was rapidly falling apart! Hulme kept his sights on the title with third place, and finally resolved the battle by finishing in the same position in Mexico, behind Clark and Brabham. Clark's victory brought his total tally to 24, the same as that of Juan Manuel Fangio. Alas there was to be only one more.

The 1968 season lost all meaning to many people on 8 April when Jim Clark was killed in an inexplicable accident in a minor Formula Two race at Hockenheim in Germany. With Clark, motor racing lost one of its greatest-ever exponents and a true hero to hundreds of thousands of people. Once again there was a void to be filled at the top.

Clark's team-mate and greatest rival eased the burden, if only by the smallest amount, for Team Lotus, by taking the 49B to the title. On his way to his second championship, Hill won in Spain, Monaco and Mexico. Clark had given Lotus another victory in the opening race of the season in South Africa taking his number of wins to the quarter century – one more than Fangio. Lotus were given another memorable victory when Jo Siffert won the British Grand Prix at an average speed of 104.83 mph in a Lotus 49B entered privately by Rob Walker. The other winners of the season were Bruce McLaren, scoring his first victory in his own car at Spa (at a remarkable 147.14 mph), Jackie Stewart with the Ford-engined Matra in Holland, Germany and the USA, Denny Hulme – now McLaren mounted – in Italy and Canada, and Jacky Ickx at Rouen. Rouen was marred by the death of Jo Schlesser, giving the air-cooled V8 Honda its debut. Mike Spence and Ludovico Scarfiotti were also victims of their cruel sport, the former dying at Indianapolis and the latter in practice for a hill-climb. What did emerge from 1968 was that if any driver might be a future heir to Clark's crown it was his countryman, Stewart, who shone out of a galaxy of new talent which was taking over from the old brigade.

After finishing second to Hill in 1968, Stewart took his first title in the

Right: Lorenzo Bandini made his competition debut in 1957 and became a works Ferrari driver in 1963. A promising career, which included wins at Le Mans in 1963 and in the Austrian Grand Prix in 1964, was tragically cut short in 1967: while chasing Denny Hulme at Monaco, he crashed at the chicane on the 82nd lap and was trapped in his blazing car. He was released and flown to hospital, but died three days later

Far right: Hulme drove brilliantly at Monaco in 1967 to win by a whole lap from Graham Hill. He is seen here leading Bruce McLaren, who took his McLaren-BRM to a creditable fourth place after a pit stop to change the battery

Below: on his way to his third World Championship, in 1966, Jack Brabham won at the Nürburgring after a monumental battle with John Surtees and Jochen Rindt – both in Cooper-Maseratis

following year with a series of magnificent performances with the Ken Tyrrell entered Matra-Ford. With Cooper, Eagle and Honda all withdrawing from the fray, and Brabham building Ford-powered cars for the first time, the championship became virtually a straight fight between Ford and Ferrari, BRM's fortunes being at a fairly low ebb and Matra's own V12 project still being in need of much development. Driver changes too were a new element in the struggle, with new found advertising revenue tempting several stars to new seats. Rindt left Brabham to join Hill at Lotus and was replaced by Ickx, while Surtees made a brief flirtation with the troubled BRM team.

Stewart started the season in style at Kyalami for the South African Grand Prix. He led from start to finish to beat his former team-mate, and reigning champion, Hill, into second place. The Brabham team suffered problems at Kyalami with their large, high-mounted aerofoils and in the next race, at Barcelona's Montjuich Park, the problem came to an ugly head when Hill and Rindt were lucky to survive major accidents directly attributable to the devices. The newly installed Armco barriers – for whose use Jackie Stewart had become a vociferous and much criticised campaigner – earned their keep on that day by keeping the errant Lotuses out of the packed crowds. Stewart himself took a lucky win in the race after early leader Amon again fell victim to his appalling fortune, his Ferrari engine digesting its bearings after 34 laps.

The new, wingless, look was enforced by new regulations coming into force – during practice – at Monaco but it didn't stop Graham Hill from taking his fifth victory at the demanding circuit. Piers Courage enhanced his reputation with a stirring second place in Frank Williams' privately entered Brabham and Siffert brought the Walker Lotus home third. Hill's winning average was 80.18 mph and Stewart confirmed that his sights were on the title by taking fastest lap at 82.67 mph before retiring.

The next three races, in Holland, France – at Clermont Ferrand – and Great Britain, saw three clear cut victories for Stewart. After Rindt dropped out, Stewart beat Siffert to the flag in Holland; he led his team-mate Beltoise home to a classic one-two victory in France, averaging 97.71 mph and at Silverstone he drove Beltoise's car, after wrecking his own in a practice accident. It did not deter him from a running battle with Rindt which was resolved when the new low-mounted wing on Rindt's Lotus came adrift, vindicating the new rules by the absence of spectacular consequences. Rindt eventually finished fourth behind Ickx and McLaren. Four-wheel-drive cars from Lotus and McLaren had very disappointing outings.

Ickx scored a classic win for Brabham at the Nürburgring after hounding Stewart for many laps. His fastest lap on the road to a 108.43 mph victory was 110.13 mph. American ace Mario Andretti drove one of the works Lotuses, but lasted only as long as the first lap. Stewart clinched the title in an epic slip-streaming battle at Monza in which 0.2 seconds covered the first four finishers. The order was Stewart, Rindt, Beltoise and McLaren. Stewart averaged

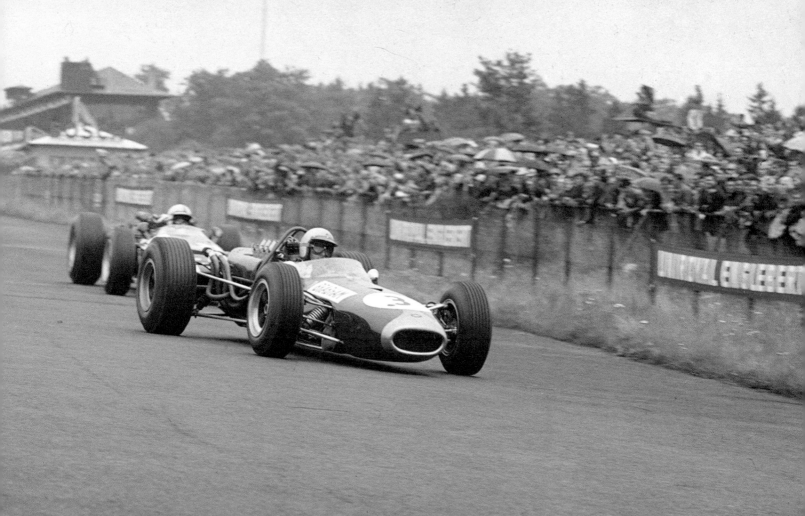

Above: Jochen Rindt's Lotus 49B on its way to victory in the 1969 United States Grand Prix and the 200,000 dollars prize fund.

Left: Winner Rindt and his close friend Piers Courage share the spoils of victory after the US Grand Prix. Courage came second in Frank William's Brabham BT26A

Above right: Bruce McLaren won New Zealand's 'Driver to Europe' award in 1958, and at age 22 had won the 1959 US Grand Prix. He was a pioneer of the Can-Am sports car championship as well as Le Mans winner in 1966. His cars virtually monopolised Can-Am until 1971, and Bruce won the 1968 Belgian GP in his own car. Sadly, McLaren was killed in 1970 while testing his latest Can-Am car, but his name has lived on in several subsequent World Championship-winning cars

146.96 mph and Beltoise put the lap record over 150 mph, to 150.96 mph. Ickx won again in Canada, after a coming together with Stewart in the early stages had eliminated the Scot. Black Jack backed up his young team-mate with a popular second place ahead of Rindt.

In the USA, Rindt showed that Stewart may not have been the only heir to Clark's crown by scoring the victory that he had threatened for so long. He finished 46.99 seconds ahead of Piers Courage followed two laps later by Surtees, giving the BRM its best result of the season. Graham Hill had a terrible accident in the closing stages of the race, breaking both legs when he was flung from his cartwheeling Lotus. It was only sheer determination that brought Hill back to the grids for the opening round of 1970. The one race that he missed, Mexico 1969, was a triumph for Hulme over Ickx's Brabham, but the championship was already Stewart's by a clear 26 points from Ickx.

1970 was a black year for the sport with the championship being awarded posthumously for the first time. The champion who did not live to receive his acclaim was Jochen Rindt. As well as the death of Rindt the sport was rocked by the loss of Bruce McLaren, killed at Goodwood while testing a Can-Am sports car, and Piers Courage, who perished in his burning de Tomaso after crashing heavily at Zandvoort.

Ickx returned to Ferrari, and the World Champion found himself equipped with one of the new March cars to start the season, while Matra now had their own cars for Beltoise and Henry Pescarolo.

Brabham won the season opener in South Africa, with Hill earning the hardest point of his career for sixth place, in his comeback with the Rob Walker team. Stewart gave heart to newcomers, March, with a flag-to-flag win in Spain, at Jarama. McLaren was second, a lap down, and Andretti completed a great day for March with third place; Hill was fourth. Ickx's Ferrari and Oliver's BRM were totally destroyed in a fiery accident from which they were lucky to escape intact.

Monaco will be remembered as a race where Jack Brabham made one of his rare mistakes to let Rindt, who was hounding him all the way, slip through on the last corner. Pescarolo drove well to bring the new Matra home in third place. Rodriguez brought a smile back to the glum faces from Bourne by giving BRM a rare win at Spa, by just over a second from Amon's March. Beltoise rewarded Matra with another third place at the ultra-fast Belgian circuit, which Amon had lapped at 152.07 mph in his chase of Rodriguez, who averaged 149.94 mph for the race.

Zandvoort saw the debut of a new Lotus, the 72, and like Clark with the 49 Rindt made no mistake at all in winning the race. It brought him little joy though, his great friend Courage was no longer alive to share it. Stewart gave March another second place from the Ferraris of Ickx and Regazzoni, making a promising debut. Rindt's sequence of mid-season triumphs, at Clermont Ferrand, Brands Hatch and Hockenheim, gave him an unassailable lead in the

title race. The British race saw a near replay of the Monaco finish, with Brabham this time running out of fuel almost within sight of the line to let Rindt through. Post race protests over the height of the Lotus's wing were eventually rejected and Jochen celebrated his third successive win. A new face joined the Lotus team that day, a young Brazilian by the name of Emerson Fittipaldi whose steady drive to eighth place gave little clue to the future that lay ahead of him. Hockenheim saw Rindt's last Grand Prix win, by 0.7 seconds from Ickx's Ferrari after a race long duel. Rindt averaged 123.90 mph and Ickx's consolation was fastest lap at 126.02 mph. Fittipaldi was fourth and a promising French newcomer, François Cevert, was seventh in a March.

Ickx and Regazzoni gave notice of a Ferrari revival by taking the first two places in Austria, where Rindt lost the chance to win in front of his home crowd due to engine failure.

After Rindt's death at Monza during practice, the race was of academic interest. All the other Lotus entries, works and private, were withdrawn – both out of respect for Rindt and respect for the possibility that a mechanical failure had caused the accident. It was a pity that a fine victory, in his first season, by Regazzoni should have been so overshadowed. The lap speed at Monza was again over 150 mph, Regazzoni turning in one lap at 150.96 mph and the whole distance at 147.07 mph. The authorities began to look seriously at the circuit's future. Victories by Ickx in Canada and Mexico, and by Fittipaldi in America were not enough to wrest the title from Jochen and no one begrudged him his posthumous triumph.

The March drivers had not been without their successes in 1970, with Stewart scoring one win, and at least one of the cars being well placed in most

Top: Niki Lauda's first Grand Prix was in his native Austria in 1971 with a March 711. He retired after only 20 laps with handling problems and did not race in Grands Prix again until 1972. In 1975 at the age of 26 he won the World Championship for Ferrari, taking the title from Ford-powered cars for the first time since 1967

Above: 1971 saw François Cevert, with the guidance of team-mate Jackie Stewart and manager Ken Tyrrell, mature into a fast and consistent competitor. He is seen here in the French Grand Prix, at Paul Ricard, where he finished second to Stewart to complete a great day for the French-financed Tyrrell team. Parisian born Cevert was killed at Watkins Glen in practice for the final race of the 1973 championship. He was then 29

Top: motor racing can be a cruel sport and one of its cruellest blows was the death of Jochen Rindt in practice for the Italian Grand Prix at Monza in 1970: his death left the sport with its first posthumous World Champion. The 28-year-old Austrian was widely regarded as one of the all time great drivers and his loss was a great tragedy

Above: with the possible exception of the drivers, the most important part of a motor racing team is the team manager; perhaps the most respected manager in the business is Ken Tyrrell. Tyrrell is a former driver himself and his business as a timber merchant earned him the nickname 'Chopper'. It was Tyrrell who 'discovered' the young Jackie Stewart and developed his talents to world championship class. When the March 701 which he was running for Stewart in 1970 left doubts over its potential Tyrrell entered the ranks of the car constructors. His cars were immediately front runners and have stayed that way ever since

races, but Ken Tyrrell had long wanted more control of his own team and, early in 1970, he had introduced Tyrrell 001. With the latest Tyrrells, Stewart and his new team-mate, Cevert, were to have a remarkable season in 1971.

The year got off to a bad start even before the season started, when Ferrari's Italian rising star, Ignazio Giunti, was killed in a sports car race in Argentina. Jean-Pierre Beltoise was rather hastily held by the organisers to be culpable, and lost his licence for much of the year. Ferrari started the season proper on a happier note when their American ex-patriot-Italian, Mario Andretti, scored a sensational first Grand Prix win, by 20.9 seconds from Stewart. Regazzoni with the other Ferrari was third, ahead of Reine Wisell's Lotus.

Stewart opened his 1971 account – and Tyrrell's Grand Prix score – in Spain, where he beat Ickx's Ferrari by just 3.4 seconds after a race-long struggle. His 97.19mph win was his third Spanish victory in a row. He followed it up with a start to finish win in Monaco, but that day it was second man Peterson who caused the sensation by driving a brilliant race in the works March 711 to beat Ickx and Siffert – the latter now in a BRM. Graham Hill had joined the Brabham team with Jack's retirement at the end of 1970, but he was out of luck at his beloved Monaco, writing off his BT34 on only the second lap. Stewart was off form at a very wet Zandvoort, but Ickx and Rodriguez put on a great display of their wet weather skills to finish first and second, in that order, Rodriguez giving the BRM team a needed lift. Regazzoni was third and Peterson fourth. Emerson Fittipaldi was out of commission following a road accident and Dave Walker, deputising, crashed both a 72 in practice and the debutante turbine Lotus in the race.

The French Grand Prix had yet another new home, at the Circuit Paul Ricard near Marseilles, a new purpose built circuit which met with mixed feelings from the purists. Stewart obviously liked the place though, disappearing into the distance with Cevert in pursuit to give the French-financed team a great day, in front of a partisan crowd. Emerson showed that his brief absence had taken away none of his fire, with a brilliant drive to third place less than six seconds behind Cevert. Ferrari and the works March team could not boast a finisher between them.

Stewart did not take long to overhaul the leading pair of Ferraris at Silverstone to score another comfortable victory, with Peterson recording another fine second place; Fittipaldi was third and again no Ferraris finished. From England, the circus moved to Germany, where the Tyrrell twins were first and second again, Stewart leading Cevert home by 30.1 seconds at 114.46mph, although Cevert took fastest lap at 116.07mph. Regazzoni and Andretti in Ferrari 312 B2s filled the next two places and Peterson was fifth. When Stewart ignominiously crashed out of the Austrian Grand Prix he was consoled by the fact that Ickx's failure to score in the race had handed him his second championship on a plate. The race was won in style by Jo Siffert, for BRM, who needed a morale booster after the death of Rodriguez in a minor sports car race a week before the British race. The rising stars had a good day with Fittipaldi second, Tim Schenken – in a Brabham – third, and Reine Wisell fourth. Not-so-new boy Graham Hill had a better day than of late with the 'lobster claw' Brabham, to finish fifth. A young Austrian in a rented March retired with handling trouble, his name was Niki Lauda and it was his first Grand Prix. The Ferraris both retired again and for once so did the Tyrrells.

The traditional Monza slipstreamer was won after a momentous struggle by BRM's new signing, Peter Gethin. Gethin, Peterson, Cevert, Hailwood (in a Surtees TS9) and Howden Ganley (in a BRM) finished in that order and with just 0.61 seconds covering all five. Chris Amon was sixth and had looked like winning until his cruel luck struck again and he lost his visor a few laps from home. The winning average was 150.76mph and Pescarolo's fastest lap, for March, was 153.49mph. The Canadian race ran only 64 of its scheduled 80 laps, due to bad weather conditions, and when the flag was hung out Stewart was first beneath it for the sixth time of the season, with Peterson again following him home and Mark Donohue in a privately entered McLaren M19A taking a popular third place. Cevert completed a happy season for Tyrrell by scoring his first win in the final round at Watkins Glen, the richest race on the

calendar. Siffert was second and Peterson was third, to claim the runner-up spot in the championship. This was Siffert's last Grand Prix, the season ending as it had begun, with tragedy in a minor race, when 'Seppi' was killed at Brands Hatch in a race to celebrate Stewart's victory.

After two seasons of tragedy, 1972 was free of incident and Lotus came out of the shadows to score another world title, through Emerson Fittipaldi, who, at 25, was the sport's youngest ever champion. The Brazilian took the championship in style with wins at Jarama, Nivelles (in Belgium), Brands Hatch, the Österreichring and Monza. He was second at Kyalami and Clermont Ferrand and third in Monaco, to win by a handsome margin. Emerson's nearest rival was Stewart, who won the opening round as the championship returned to the Argentine for the first time in twelve years, plus the French, Canadian and American races. Denny Hulme won in South Africa, Jacky Ickx won at the Nürburgring and Jean-Pierre Beltoise scored a memorable triumph for BRM at an extremely wet Monaco. Stewart, in taking second place in the championship, revealed some of the pressure of modern racing when he had to miss the Belgian Grand Prix through stomach ulcer problems. Chris Amon looked all set for his first ever win at Clermont Ferrand before a puncture stole his glory. Carlos Reutemann was a new name on the grids and impressed many people with very fast performances in his Brabham, scoring pole position at his first ever Grand Prix, appropriately in his native Argentina. With a new World Champion and a promising new star, the South Americans again had something to shout about in motor racing.

1973 was a year symptomatic of the modern trend of racing, with as much competition off the tracks – mostly concerning money – as on. Fortunately the quality of the racing diverted the public eye from the more unseemly side of things and it was another vintage championship year, though one again tainted by tragedy.

The first race, in Argentina, saw Ronnie Peterson alongside Fittipaldi in the black and gold Lotus 72Ds and the reigning champion won the race after Regazzoni, Cevert and Stewart had problems ahead of him. Regazzoni was newly ensconced at BRM and was sensational in practice, giving the team their first pole position since 1971. He led for 29 laps before overheating tyres forced him out. Fittipaldi won again in his native Brazil, at 114.88 mph and the stage looked set for him to retain his title. Stewart thought otherwise and followed up second place in Brazil and third in the Argentine (behind Cevert) with his first win of the season in South Africa. It was a meeting of high drama; Stewart had crashed in practice, local man Jody Scheckter shared the front row with McLaren team-mate Hulme (who used the new M23 to give him his first ever pole position) and Mike Hailwood earned himself a George Medal during the race for a heroic rescue of Regazzoni from his blazing BRM. George Follmer also survived all the dramas to give the new Shadow team their first point.

The Spanish Grand Prix was back to the round the houses circuit at Mont-

Above: keeping it in the family at the French Grand Prix, at Paul Ricard, in 1973 are the Fittipaldi brothers, with Emerson's Lotus 72 ahead of Wilson's Brabham

Above left: while Denny Hulme, with the new McLaren M23, claimed his first ever pole position at the 1973 South African Grand Prix, local hero Jody Scheckter put his older McLaren M19 onto the front row too. Scheckter led the race for several laps, with his McLaren team-mate Peter Revson on his tail as seen here, but his race ended with a blown engine. An inspired Jackie Stewart took the lead on the seventh lap and beat Revson into second place. The race was marred by an accident in the opening stages in which Clay Regazzoni was trapped in his blazing car. The Swiss was rescued by Mike Hailwood, whose Surtees had also been involved in the accident, and Hailwood was later awarded a George Medal for his bravery

Left: Jo Siffert will be remembered as a driver who always gave his utmost. He started racing on motor cycles in his native Switzerland and graduated to cars in 1960. In 1968 he scored a memorable Grand Prix victory at Brands Hatch with Rob Walker's privately entered Lotus 49B. He only won one other Grand Prix, in Austria in 1971, but his reputation as a driver of the enormously powerful Porsche 917 sports cars made him a man to respect. At the end of the 1971 season a race was organised at Brands Hatch to celebrate Jackie Stewart's World Championship. During the race Siffert's BRM crashed heavily and burst into flames. Inadequately equipped marshals were unable to release Siffert and he perished in the blazing car

juich and the drivers must have been glad of the new deformable structures on the cars, which became mandatory at this race. Peterson was again on pole, but the race went to Fittipaldi after Peterson, Hulme, Cevert and Stewart were all sidelined. Emerson's 97.86mph win gave Lotus their 50th Grand Prix victory. Emerson's win was a close thing as he had a tyre deflating over the closing laps, and Cevert, recovering after a puncture of his own, drove as hard as he knew how in his efforts to take the lead. Follmer brought his Shadow home in third place.

Politics reared their head at the Belgian Grand Prix, which was transferred from Nivelles to Zolder. The newly resurfaced track began to break up during practice and for a while it looked as though the race might be cancelled. An idea of the conditions can be gained from the fact that Peterson, having gained pole position, crashed twice during the race-day warm up and again in the race. He was not alone: as car after car left the circuit, Stewart and Cevert pounded through to a one-two, from Fittipaldi. There were plenty of statistics to note at Monaco: Graham Hill was making his 150th Grand Prix appearance and Stewart was aiming for the 25th win of his meteoric career. He collected it, too, beating Fittipaldi by 1.3 seconds at an average of 80.96mph. Making his debut in the race at the wheel of the flamboyant Hesketh team's March 731 was James Hunt. His engine blew up five laps from home, while he was lying sixth and silencing many critics.

Sweden was a new country to be added to the championship trail and all eyes at Anderstorp were naturally on Peterson. From pole position he led until less than two laps from home, when a deflating tyre forced him to give way to Denny Hulme who had stormed through the field in his McLaren M23 after early problems. McLaren's new boy, Jody Scheckter, sprung some surprises in France, leading from the flag and disputing the lead until he collided with Fittipaldi, eliminating them both. On his 40th attempt, Peterson won his first Grand Prix, by 40.92 seconds from Cevert; Hunt scored his first point at his second attempt with sixth place.

The British Grand Prix, at Silverstone, saw one of the biggest accidents of all time when, at the end of the first lap, Scheckter – lying fourth – lost control coming onto the start-finish straight from the very fast right hander, Woodcote. He bounced off the pit wall and into the pack, which was soon reduced to so much wreckage. The only injuries amidst the mechanical carnage were to Scheckter's ego and Andrea de Adamich's ankle. The race was restarted after a long delay and was no less of a sensation with Peter Revson winning from Peterson, Hulme and Hunt. 3.4 seconds covered the four of them and Revson's average speed was 131.75mph. Hunt pleased his local crowd with fastest lap, at 134.06mph.

The sense of security lent by the efficiency of the new deformable structures in the Silverstone melée was shattered at Zandvoort. Roger Williamson, in only his second Grand Prix with Tom Wheatcroft's March, crashed heavily on lap eight and the car burst into flames. Although David Purley tried heroically to rescue Williamson – virtually unaided by the marshals – the promising young Englishman perished. Stewart went on to win his 26th Grand Prix, from Cevert, but there were no celebrations, only bitterness.

Stewart and Cevert pulverised the opposition at the Nürburgring, finishing 1.6 seconds apart and a long way ahead of third man Ickx, who was making a 'guest' appearance with McLarens. The winning average was 116.82mph and fastest lap went to an inspired Carlos Pace at 118.43mph. Peterson won in Austria, from Stewart, after Fittipaldi had retired only five laps from victory. Ronnie won again at Monza, with Emerson second, but Stewart, who drove a magnificent race to finish fourth after a puncture, clinched his third championship. The Canadian race was won by Peter Revson in total confusion after rain forced pit stops for tyre changes and an accident brought the newly introduced pace car out to slow the action. Unfortunately, it came out in front of the wrong car and the race degenerated into a shambles.

What should have been the crowning of a magnificent career for Stewart with his 100th and last Grand Prix at Watkins Glen was completely over-shadowed by the death of Cevert in practice. The Tyrrell team withdrew,

Stewart announced his retirement a week later as Champion, and Peterson won the race from a hard charging and very impressive Hunt.

Stewart's retirement again left a throne to be filled and the sport was now so competitive that no single driver could fill it. 1974 began with doubts over the very future of the sport, brought on by the energy crisis of the winter months. Out of the gloom came one of the most exciting championships ever. With Stewart gone, drivers began a major reshuffle of their services. Fittipaldi went to McLaren, Ickx to Lotus, Lauda to Ferrari and Regazzoni *back* to Ferrari; Revson joined Shadow and Ken Tyrrell set out to rebuild his team with Jody Scheckter and Frenchman Patrick Depailler.

At last, the domination of the Cosworth DFV was being challenged by Ferrari's flat-12. Reutemann, leading his home Grand Prix in Argentina had his own fuel crisis one and a half laps from home and handed victory to Denny Hulme, followed by the Ferraris of Lauda and Regazzoni. Fittipaldi scored his first win for his new team in front of his home crowd in Brazil after a duel with Peterson. The race was shortened to forty laps after a sudden cloudburst. Regazzoni's second place for Ferrari put them on top of the title table.

Below: Ronnie Peterson's John Player Special-Lotus 72 leads team-mate Emerson Fittipaldi and Jacky Ickx's Ferrari past the Monza pits during the 1973 Italian Grand Prix. Peterson was out to win, and did not repeat his gesture of the preceding Austrian Grand Prix of waving Fittipaldi past for maximum points in order to retain the Championship. Meanwhile, Stewart, who could not know what the Lotus tactics would be, was having the drive of his life, storming from twentieth to fourth place after a puncture. This was enough to guarantee him the Championship, so Peterson's race victory was vindicated

Below: Carlos Reutemann's Brabham sandwiched between the Ferraris of Regazzoni and Lauda at the start of the 1974 South African Grand Prix, and *inset,* a delighted Lole after his victory. It had been four years since Jack Brabham had won the same race in a Brabham, and Carlos was the first Argentinian to win a Grand Prix since Fangio in 1957

The South African Grand Prix was put back into the calendar at the end of March, having been cancelled during the winter. It seemed that there was something to be happy about after all, but it was all forgotten when Peter Revson's Shadow crashed head on into the barriers during practice, killing the very popular American instantly. The race saw the introduction of the new John Player Specials, or Lotuses by any other name, but it was an inauspicious debut, with the type 76s eliminating each other on the first lap. Lauda started the race from pole but the glory went to Reutemann who gained his first win and the first for Brabham for four years. Into a sensational second came Beltoise with the new BRM P201.

Ferrari finally came in from the cold with a magnificent one-two finish at Jarama after a race turned topsy turvy by rain. Ronnie Peterson had a more encouraging outing with the Lotus 76, now running with a conventional clutch. He started from the front row and roared away in the lead with Ickx backing him up in third place but when the rains came the Lotus pit work was shambolic while Ferrari's was exemplary; Lauda won his first Grand Prix at an average speed of 88.48mph. Fittipaldi took victory at Nivelles by the narrowest of

margins (0.35 seconds) from Lauda, after driving the race of his life. It put him into the lead of the championship by one point.

In Monaco, Lotus reverted to using the 72Es and Peterson showed that there was life in the old cars yet by claiming victory in a race which saw almost everyone, including Ronnie, fall off at some stage. His average speed was 80.74 mph and he took fastest lap at 83.42 mph. With this win in the bag, Lotus went to Sweden full of confidence but the establishment was stood on its ear by the new Tyrrell twins who filled the front row of the grid and finished first and second in the race, with Scheckter beating Depailler by 0.38 seconds. James Hunt was now equipped with Hesketh's own car and gave it its first points with a fine third place, while Graham Hill with a Lola was sixth; Scheckter's win made him the sixth different winner from the first seven rounds! Ferrari steamrollered all the Ford opposition at Zandvoort with Lauda winning his second race of the season from Regazzoni, while Fittipaldi and Hailwood in McLarens headed the vain chase by the 'Formula Ford' cars.

Notions that the reign of the DFV was over were firmly quashed when Peterson led home Lauda and Regazzoni at Dijon, the fifteenth new home of

Below left : Niki Lauda was desperately unlucky in the 1974 British Grand Prix at Brands Hatch when his Ferrari suffered a deflating rear tyre only six laps from the finish. Lauda, who had been leading, rushed into the pits for a new tyre, but he was prevented from rejoining the race by a course car and the many officials, mechanics and personnel who had gathered at the end of the pit road to watch the finish. Lauda was classified ninth, and his protest that he could have taken fifth place was rejected, although the FIA later awarded him two championship points

Right : Jody Scheckter took the lead of the 1974 British Grand Prix after Lauda's puncture and went on to win. Scheckter is pictured with the John Player girls about to be taken on his lap of honour. He left Tyrrell at the close of the 1976 season and he gave the Wolf Team an auspicious debut by winning the 1977 Argentine Grand Prix

the French Grand Prix. Lauda thus went to Brands Hatch with a four point lead in the championship. After leading all the way from Scheckter's Tyrrell 007, the flying Ferrari became one of many to fall victim of a puncture. Lauda struggled on, falling to third place by the closing stages. With only two laps to go, the tyre had disintegrated completely and Lauda was forced into the pits. By the time the new wheel was on, Scheckter was well on his way to the flag and the pit exit road was so crowded that Lauda was unable to rejoin the race. It was not until two months later that a tribunal awarded him fifth place. Ferrari honour was restored at the Nürburgring where Regazzoni was uncatchable. Lauda was eliminated in the season's sixth first-lap accident – a sure sign of the extraordinary intensity of the competition. Scheckter set fastest lap at 118.49 mph on his way to second place and Reutemann was third. Mike Hailwood's career came to a sad and premature end at Pflanzgarten when he landed all

awry and smashed into the barriers, severely damaging his legs. Reutemann won his second race of the season in Austria, heading Hulme and Hunt by a healthy margin.

Regazzoni's fifth place sent him to Italy with a five point lead over Scheckter in the championship and the kind of support that comes only to Ferrari at Monza. Alas, both Maranello cars were sidelined by engine failures and Peterson went on to win from Fittipaldi – by 0.8 seconds. Fittipaldi won in Canada with Regazzoni finishing second which resulted in the amazing situation of those two drivers going to the last round at Watkins Glen with 52 points each. Scheckter, with 45 points, also had a mathematical chance of winning. It turned into something of an anticlimax. Reutemann disappeared into the distance while Regazzoni fought unpredictable handling back in ninth place and Scheckter dropped out when a fuel pipe broke. Fittipaldi's fifth place was unspectacular but enough to earn him his second championship in one of the most closely fought series ever. Once again, the end of the series was overshadowed by tragedy. Helmuth Koinigg was killed when his Surtees ploughed under a guard rail on lap nine.

The DFV engine's incredible run of success was finally halted in 1975 when Ferrari put everything right at the same time to take the championship away from the Ford-powered cars for the first time since 1967. Niki Lauda applied all his single minded determination to winning the title and win it he did. Ferrari started the season with the latest 312B3 cars but they were soundly beaten in the opening round in Argentina by Fittipaldi and by Hunt – with the Hesketh 308; Regazzoni was third and Lauda sixth. Jarier had been sensationally quick in practice to put the new Shadow DN5 on pole but the car broke on the warm up lap and did not start. Carlos Pace was the second Brazilian race winner in two events when he delighted everyone by storming home first in Brazil. His Brabham BT44B led home compatriot Fittipaldi's McLaren M23 by 5.79 seconds; Jarier had led with ease before the Shadow again failed.

Right: the Armco barriers were in such a poor state of neglect at Barcelona's Montjuich Park circuit prior to the 1975 Grand Prix that the team mechanics were forced to do what they could to rebuild them. Even Ken Tyrrell lent a hand, but it was not enough to prevent a tragedy when Rolf Stommelen's Hill-Lola crashed, fatally injuring three officials and a spectator

Below left: Emerson Fittipaldi's McLaren M23 won the Argentine Grand Prix of 1975 after Reutemann and Hunt had dropped back

Below right: Jean-Pierre Jarier astonished everyone by setting pole position time for the Argentinian and Brazilian Grands Prix in 1975. Such promise was unfulfilled, however, for the Shadow broke a crown-wheel before the Buenos Aires race, and a metering unit failed when Jarier was in the lead at Interlagos

South Africa saw the debut of the Ferrari 312T, with transverse gearbox, which was to end Ford's domination. It was not to happen in this race, however, for Scheckter became the second 'home' winner of the season by beating Reutemann into second place.

The Spanish race started with arguments and ended with tragedy. On arriving at Barcelona's Montjuich Park, the teams took one look at the shoddily erected safety barriers and said 'no way!'. After much wrangling and work by the teams themselves, the race was grudgingly staged – albeit without Fittipaldi, whose principles were more important to him than his contract and who withdrew. Tragically, the Embassy-Hill-Lola of Rolf Stommelen, which had inherited the lead as others fell by the wayside, crashed heavily on the 25th lap, seriously injuring the driver and hurling debris over the barriers which killed three officials and a photographer. The race was stopped four laps later and Jochen Mass was declared the winner for McLaren and awarded half points. Lella Lombardi of Italy came home in sixth place with her March 751 to give a rare break in the total male domination of Grand Prix racing and collected half a point. It was not, however, a weekend for celebration.

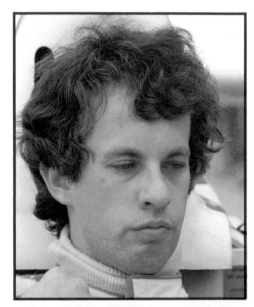

Above: Graham Hill retired from race-driving in
1975, but his team was on the threshold of success
when Hill and his young protégé, Tony Brise,
were killed in a tragic air crash at the end of the
year. Four team members died with them and
the team was disbanded

Below: Tony Brise drove a fine race at Sweden's Anderstorp circuit to take sixth place. He might have finished higher had his Embassy Hill GH1 not been jammed in fourth gear

Left: Emerson Fittipaldi at the Rascasse hairpin during the 1975 Monaco Grand Prix. The Brazilian, seen leading Mark Donohue's Penske PC1, finished second after a race interrupted by tyre changes when the wet track dried out

Monaco, with some similarity to Montjuich as a true road circuit, was obviously in the public eye and happily it was a classic race with no squabbles or major incidents. The organisers made great efforts to make the race safe by limiting the grid to 18 cars, but this prevented Graham Hill from qualifying on the circuit of his greatest triumphs. Lauda gave the new Ferrari its first win at 75.55 mph after a race dominated by the weather and pit stops. Fittipaldi was second, 2.78 seconds adrift. The race was shortened by three laps as the rain came down again and whether Emerson might have caught Lauda's ailing Ferrari remained a matter for conjecture. It did not seem to trouble Lauda unduly as he reeled off the laps to win in Belgium and again in Sweden after a rousing battle with Reutemann who came home second. One of the most impressive performances in Sweden came from young Tony Brise in the new Hill GH 1: he finished sixth. His promise was lost to the world when he was killed with Hill himself and other team members in a plane crash in November 1975 at Hendon.

The Dutch Grand Prix was again influenced by tyre changes: James Hunt judged the time for a change to slicks to perfection on a rapidly drying track

Far right: this is how the 1975 John Player British Grand Prix ended, when twelve cars, including most of the leaders were eliminated on the 56th lap. The race had been dogged by foul weather, necessitating as many as four tyre-changes, act conditions became so bad at Club corner that most of the drivers crashed into the catch fencing. The race was abandoned after Emerson Fittipaldi had completed the 56th lap, but it took three days for the official finishing order to be established

Centre: it was a sad day for motor racing when Mark Donohue died. One of the nicest people in his profession, he was fatally injured in a crash while practising for the 1975 Austrian Grand Prix. An experienced development engineer, Donohue had been Trans-Am Champion in 1968, 1969 and 1970 in Roger Penske's Camaro, Can-Am Champion in a Porsche 917 in 1973 and Indianapolis winner in 1972 and he was hoping for Grand Prix success

Below: World Champion in 1972 with Lotus and in 1974 with McLaren, Emerson Fittipaldi finished the 1975 season second in the points standings. He did not enjoy the same success in 1976, driving for his brother's Copersucar-backed team

and his pit crew were ultra quick. James went back out and built up a commanding lead before the others read the signs and then fought a magnificent running battle for many laps as Lauda reeled in his advantage. He beat the Ferrari by 1.06 seconds to give the Hesketh team a well deserved win. The French Grand Prix at Paul Ricard saw the status quo restored, with Lauda turning the tables to beat Hunt by 1.59 seconds at 116.60 mph. Mario Andretti brought the Parnelli VPJ-4 into fifth place. The British Grand Prix was at Silverstone and again the weather decided the outcome. A deluge of rain on the 56th lap sent car after car crashing into the barriers, leaving Emerson Fittipaldi – who had called at the pits while everyone else was slithering off – as the winner.

Reutemann showed his skill at the Nürburgring to win at 117.73 mph from a very surprising Jacques Laffite in Frank Williams' Williams FW04. A host of punctures and mechanical failures decimated the field. The Austrian Grand Prix was wet. Race day was marred by an accident in unofficial practice which was to cost the life of Mark Donohue, driver of the Penske PC1. The race itself was shortened by rain once again and the winner was surprised and delighted.

Vittorio Brambilla had driven magnificently to give March their first ever works win. In his enthusiasm he spun and knocked the nose off the car only yards past the flag.

Lauda's third place behind Regazzoni and Fittipaldi at Monza was enough to wrest the title for Ferrari and give the Italian crowd their greatest day in many years. James Hunt debuted the Hesketh 308C and finished fifth. With chicanes now slowing down the cars and breaking up the slipstreaming bunches, the race average was 135.48 mph and Regazzoni's fastest lap 138.87 mph. Lauda celebrated his championship in the United States with his fifth win of the season. The race had a sour note when Regazzoni held up Fittipaldi's challenge to Lauda by putting his Ferrari between them. Regazzoni was eventually black flagged and fists flew in the pits between the Ferrari team and the organisers. It was not a very decorous end to a season of fine achievement.

1976 was the season to end all seasons in terms of political wranglings, with the results being decided as much by the rule books as on the circuits. Fortunately, it was also a season with plenty of close racing and several new cars to enliven the scene. The main feature of the year, on the circuits, was the terrific struggle between Hunt and Lauda. Hunt actually took the chequered flag first at seven races, in Spain, France, Great Britain, Germany, Holland, Canada and at the US Grand Prix East at Watkins Glen. Lauda scored four first places, in Brazil, South Africa, Belgium and Monaco but the second half of his season was badly affected by his accident in Germany which almost cost him his life. Five other drivers put themselves onto the list of winners in 1976, Regazzoni at the US Grand Prix West, Scheckter in Sweden, John Watson in Austria, Peterson in Italy and Mario Andretti at Mount Fuji in Japan where Hunt finally clinched his title.

The season opened with three victories in succession for Ferrari; Lauda beat Depailler in Brazil and Hunt, by a mere 1.3 seconds, in South Africa; then Regazzoni made amends for his display in the last American race by winning the first US Grand Prix West at the newly laid out 'round the houses' circuit in Long Beach, California. Lauda was second there and Hunt was pushed out of the race by Patrick Depailler, driving the Tyrrell 007 while the six wheeler was being developed. The protests started to flow after Hunt won the Spanish Grand Prix at Jarama by 20.97 seconds from Lauda. Hunt's McLaren M23 was found after the race to be marginally over the maximum allowable width and, although the team protested that the discrepancy was due to manufacturing tolerances in the rear tyres, Hunt was excluded from the results. Laffite's Ligier-Matra JS5 was also excluded from twelfth place for an alleged wing infringement; both teams appealed.

Lauda went on to score two successive victories at Zolder and Monaco; at Zolder, he was followed home by Regazzoni and Laffite, and in Monaco by Scheckter.

The Swedish race was a historic one. After Mario Andretti, with the new Lotus 77, had started from the front row and led for the first 45 laps, unaware of a one minute penalty for a jumped start, his engine blew up allowing Scheckter and Depailler to coast home to an easy one-two finish with the two six-wheeled Tyrrell P34s; Lauda was third and Hunt was fifth. James Hunt 'won' two races within 24 hours at Paul Ricard in France. As well as beating Patrick Depailler on the road, he learned that his appeal over the Spanish result had been upheld and that he was reinstated as winner. To add to James's joy, Lauda failed to score in France, retiring with a broken engine.

His satisfaction was to be short lived, however, and the British Grand Prix, at Brands Hatch, was to result in more wrangles. After a first corner shunt caused by Regazzoni's over enthusiasm, the race was re-started, but it was contended that Hunt, among others, had not completed the first lap under his own power and should be excluded. He was allowed to restart and went on to win by almost a minute from Lauda's ailing Ferrari and Sheckter. The race was later taken away from Hunt after a series of appeals by Ferrari and the points awarded to Lauda which made Hunt's championship position look bleak both mathematically and psychologically.

Although Hunt had troubles they were nothing compared to what awaited

Below left: John Watson from Belfast scored his first well deserved Grand Prix win at the Österreichring in the Penske, but despite this, the American team withdrew at the end of 1976

Far left top: rated by many as the fastest Grand Prix driver of the 1970s, Ronnie Peterson spent three years with March before driving for John Player Team Lotus from 1973 to early 1976. His eighth Grand Prix victory came at Monza in 1976 at the wheel of a March 762. He rejoined Lotus in 1978 enjoying great success until his tragic fatal accident at Monza

Below: the race at the rain-soaked Mount Fuji circuit put Mario Andretti and Lotus back in the winner's circle. Andretti had rejoined Lotus in 1976 after a spell with the Parnelli team and became World Champion in 1978

Lauda at the Nürburgring. The race was stopped after rain had swept the circuit to allow the drivers to change tyres if they wished. After the restart, Lauda was quite far down the field and trying hard to catch the leaders. His Ferrari crashed in flames and he was fortunate that several following drivers stopped or were involved in the accident and were able to pull him from the blazing wreckage, which was some way from the nearest marshals. Even so, his life hung in the balance for a considerable time and his future looked bleak. With Lauda in hospital, no Ferraris were sent to Austria and John Watson won his first Grand Prix, after years of promise, with the Penske PC4.

When it seemed that Lauda might make a miraculous comeback before the end of the season, Ferrari relented and sent Regazzoni to Holland where he finished under a second behind a very 'on form' Hunt; it was just one year since Hunt's first Grand Prix win at the same circuit with the Hesketh.

Italy saw Lauda make a miraculous return and, although Hunt was openly pleased that Niki was back to fight the title, he was barracked by the crowd and sent to the back of the grid, with Watson and Mass, for allegedly using fuel of more than the permitted octane ratings. It was a decision made on very

dubious evidence and effectively robbed Hunt of all chance of a good result. In his efforts to come to terms with the leaders, he crashed, without personal harm, on lap 12. The race was won by Ronnie Peterson who gave both himself and the March team a much needed morale booster.

The circus now moved on to Canada and the United States, East – or Watkins Glen where Hunt knew he had to win to pull back some of the lead which Lauda still clung to. In both races, he did everything that was necessary to score two superb victories and go to the final round, in Japan, with a reasonable chance of winning the title. Lauda had scored a courageous fourth place in his comeback at Monza and, despite obvious problems, he was a magnificent third at the Glen. It seemed that he was not going to give up the championship without a fight.

As things turned out, that assumption was wrong and, as the rain swept Mount Fuji circuit where Japan was hosting her first Grand Prix and getting a thrilling finale for her money, Lauda made one of the most courageous decisions of his life in deciding not to race. After a few brief moments of exploring the circuit, Niki came to the conclusion that the conditions were simply not fit for him to race under, troubled as he was by problems with his eyelids, burned at Nürburgring. As he climbed from his car, the race went on in truly appalling conditions which were tailor made for a huge accident. The accident did not come, though, and the circuit even began to dry a little. Hunt, who had charged away into a commanding lead – intent on winning the title in style – tried desperately to preserve his wet-weather tyres but with only five laps to go and having lost the lead to Mario Andretti his left front tyre deflated. He rushed into the pits where the McLaren mechanics changed all four wheels with amazing rapidity and stormed out again knowing only that he had to make up several places. Those last few laps saw Hunt give the performance of his life to pull back to third place behind Andretti and Depailler and to take the title by a single point from Lauda. It was quite some time before James could be convinced that he was really World Champion.

It was a remarkable ending to a season which would have been dismissed as incredible had it been written as a film script but then motor racing sometimes can be much larger than life.

Below: it took James Hunt only three seasons to become World Champion – from a flamboyant beginning with Lord Hesketh's March in 1973 and with the same team's Harvey Postlethwaite designed cars until he took over Fittipaldi's seat at McLaren for 1976. An excellent third place at Mount Fuji clinched the title for Hunt after a very hard-fought season

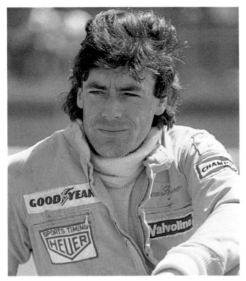

Top: Jody Scheckter enjoyed a fairy-tale start with the brand new Wolf WR1 at the Argentine GP in 1977. The debutant Wolf demonstrated the reliability that distinguished it throughout the season, even at the hands of a hard driver like Jody

Above: Welsh driver Tom Pryce in pensive mood. His death at Kyalami in 1977 was one of those particularly unfortunate and needless accidents that periodically mar the sport.

Above right: Pryce's Shadow DN8 in action at Buenos Aires during the very hot Argentine Grand Prix. Unlike many cars, the Shadow did not succumb to the heat, although it ran a rather undistinguished race, finishing out of the points

While 1977 never repeated the high drama of the previous year, it was nonetheless a see-saw season which saw eight Grand Prix winners and a very open run for the title. It was much less tainted by political in-fighting but there were inevitable rumblings about the scoring system when it was realised that the champion had won fewer races than the man who was placed third.

After Japan, Niki Lauda might well have been written off as a championship challenger but in the end it seemed almost inevitable when he regained his coveted title. He won in South Africa, Germany and Holland, but his championship was earned more through dogged insistence on finishing in the points than on a need to win at all costs; to Lauda the championship was all important, the races relatively incidental. Mario Andretti seemed intent on winning races at whatever cost and the occasional impetuous moment helped snatch the championship from his grasp. In spite of this and a spate of Cosworth 'development' engine failures, Andretti won at Long Beach and in Spain, France and Italy, yet he did not even take the runner-up spot to Lauda; that went to Scheckter, who had left the struggling Tyrrell team and put his faith in Walter Wolf Racing – as their sole driver.

Scheckter opened the season in fairy-tale style, taking the debutant Wolf WR1 to victory in Argentina. His was not the fastest car in Buenos Aires but as the intense heat took its toll of cars and drivers he outlasted the opposition. A strong military presence and volatile political situation added tension to the stifling heat and when the fire extinguisher bottle on Andretti's Lotus exploded during practice (at very high speed, in front of the pits) there were mutterings of terrorist bombs. Hunt, on pole position with the latest M23, was one of four leaders, the others being the winner and the much improved

Brabham-Alfas of John Watson and Carlos Pace. Hunt and Watson fell foul of suspension failures while Pace succumbed to the heat, surrendering the lead to Scheckter just six laps from home.

Speculation about rivalry between Lauda and his new team-mate, Carlos Reutemann, was fuelled when the latter scored a convincing first win for the team in Brazil. Hunt was on pole again but, after a storming start, local hero Pace led for six laps before being caught out by the crumbling track – forfeiting his nose cone to the pursuing McLaren. As the track surface began to break up in the heat, eight cars came to grief on one corner alone. From thirteenth on the grid Lauda avoided the mayhem to snatch third place, behind Hunt and ahead of a delighted Emerson Fittipaldi who at last seemed to be making progress with the home grown FD04.

Lauda retorted by winning at Kyalami, but his win was not to be fêted as the race was marred by the death of Welshman Tom Pryce and a young South African marshal. Ironically, an incident involving Pryce's new Shadow team-mate precipitated the disaster. On lap twenty, Renzo Zorzi pulled off the pits straight with a dead engine. As he walked away, leaking fuel flared up briefly, sending Zorzi back to activate the car's extinguisher. As the flames fizzled out two marshals, one carrying a heavy extinguisher, ran across the track to the Shadow. The unencumbered one made it but the other was hit head on by Pryce who was probably killed instantly. The car continued out of control along the straight until it clipped the Armco, collected Laffite's Ligier and crashed headlong into the barriers. It was a needless end to a career which had the utmost promise. Pryce started racing with a Formula Ford car, won in a newspaper competition. He progressed to Formula Three and trounced the opposition in the prestigious Monaco race in 1974, earning himself a Formula One contract with Shadow. He won only one Formula One race, the Race of Champions, at Brands Hatch, in 1975. That his unbounded enthusiasm and abundant talent should never be rewarded was a sad blow.

Two weeks later Carlos Pace died in a flying accident in his native Brazil. He had never lost faith in the difficult Brabham-Alfa and his death was a major setback to the team just as it seemed he had transformed the car into a winner.

As always, the circus recovered from its too oft felt sense of loss and returned to the fray with a stirring, three-cornered, flag-to-flag battle at Long Beach. Having avoided a first corner barging match involving Hunt, Reutemann, Watson and Brambilla, Jody Scheckter demonstrated the Wolf's worth. For 75 of the eighty laps he held off determined challenges from Andretti (the Lotus 78 now sufficiently reliable to show its pace) and Lauda,

but now he was fighting the effects of a slowly deflating right front tyre. On lap 76 he could hold off his pursuers no longer and both Andretti and Lauda slipped past. At the end less than five seconds covered the three and Lauda had left the lap record for the increasingly well respected waterfront circuit at 87.87 mph.

Andretti made it two in a row with a demoralising walkover in Spain, where he sat on pole by the margin of .72 seconds. A very on-form Carlos Reutemann was sixteen seconds adrift at the end. The only remote threat to the Lotus came from Jacques Laffite who had the Ligier JS7-Matra flying to be second on the grid and set fastest lap, at a record 94.24 mph. Laffite lost over a lap early in the race but fought back from nineteenth place to seventh – just outside the points. Third place for Scheckter put him into an outright lead in the championship as Lauda missed the race, having cracked a rib (without apparent reason) during practice.

Andretti's hat trick was scotched in Monaco by an absolutely stunning performance from Scheckter which, coincidentally, brought up the hundredth win for the ubiquitous Cosworth engine. Lauda missed his Monaco hat-trick by less than a second in beating Reutemann into third place. A race long battle between Andretti and Jochen Mass finally went to the McLaren driver and the final point went to new Shadow team leader Alan Jones.

Belgium showed again the superiority of the Lotus 78. Andretti was on pole by a demoralising 1.54 seconds from Monaco pole man John Watson but in dismal conditions the two collided in the chicane on the first lap and went no further. As the weather went from wet to dry to wet six drivers led: Scheckter, Watson, Mass, Brambilla, Lauda and Gunnar Nilsson. Having outbraked Lauda on lap fifty, it was Nilsson who led them home. Lauda was second and Ronnie Peterson gave Tyrrell a rare moment for celebration by wrestling the six-wheeler into third place.

Sadly, Zolder was to be Nilsson's only Grand Prix win. He began experiencing health problems and early in 1978 it was learned that he was suffering from cancer. He never drove for the Arrows team for which he had signed for 1978. In October the 28-year-old Swede died in a London hospital. He had taken Formula Three and Formula Atlantic by storm but instead of the world title which many predicted, his monument became the Gunnar Nilsson Cancer Treatment Campaign.

Andretti was one of the few who did not rejoice in Jacques Laffite's all-French win in Sweden; Andretti led for all but the last two laps when a fuel metering fault finally resulted in the inevitable fuel shortage.

The tables were turned two weeks later at Dijon where Andretti was

forced to settle for second place to John Watson's Brabham until almost within sight of the flag when it was Watson's turn to run out of fuel!

By this time in the season there were so many entries for most races that organisers were making life very hard for privateers who, on occasion, had to resort to legal action even to gain the right to practice. For the British Grand Prix, at Silverstone, the organisers set aside a separate 'pre-qualifying' session to determine which of the many second string entries would go forward to qualifying proper. During this session David Purley survived what was later billed as racing's most severe non-fatal accident, when his Lec went straight on at Becketts, hitting the barriers at about 110 mph. Sticking throttles were to blame. It was a happier weekend for James Hunt who (having put the M26 on the front row and led briefly at Dijon) at last scored his first win of the season. Watson again led much of the race before succumbing to fuel feed problems and Lauda cruised home second, to extend his lead in the championship.

He extended it still further with a sweet victory, just one year after his accident, in the German Grand Prix – now transferred from Nürburgring to Hockenheim.

In Austria Alan Jones drove the Shadow magnificently in poor conditions to haul himself to second place behind James Hunt and was delighted to inherit a well deserved first Grand Prix win when Hunt's engine expired eleven laps from home. Yet again Niki Lauda stayed clear of everyone else's problems to take home six points from second place, stretching his lead to sixteen points....

At Zandvoort he virtually sewed up his second title by overhauling and just staying ahead of Laffite's very quick Ligier. Andretti threw away all hopes of challenging Lauda in an early incident with Hunt when both laid claim to the same piece of road.

With his sixth second place of the season, this time behind an uncatchable Mario Andretti, Lauda put the championship beyond all doubt at Monza and finished his season with a cool drive to fourth place in the wet US Grand Prix behind Hunt, Andretti and Scheckter. Thereafter he earned few friends by

Right: Alan Jones enjoying practice for the 1977 Austrian Grand Prix, a race he went on to win

Below right: Jacques Laffite only managed to give the beautifully built Ligier JS7, with its distinctive sounding V12 engine, one victory, here at Anderstorp in the 1977 Swedish GP

Below: the immensely likeable Gunnar Nilsson's promising career was cut short by cancer. The action shot of Nilsson's Lotus 78 is from the 1977 Belgian Grand Prix. Although this was to be Gunnar's only Grand Prix victory it was a particularly impressive one earned through great skill in poor conditions.

taking no further part in the championship after Ferrari had co-opted young Gilles Villeneuve into the team for the Canadian and Japanese races. Lauda expressed his feelings by heading for Brabham with his faithful mechanic, Ermanno Cuoghi, in tow. . . .

Scheckter scored his third win in Walter Wolf's adopted country, Canada, and no doubt reflected on what could so easily have been a first time championship but for a disastrous loss of form in mid-season. James Hunt too, no doubt, thought back to the previous season as he won the Japanese Grand Prix at Fuji. Hunt's results for the season did not do true justice to his title defence for he led many races and was inevitably competitive but dogged by cruel luck. The Fuji race was marred by a dreadful accident involving Gilles Villeneuve's Ferrari which cartwheeled off the end of the straight after hitting Peterson's Tyrrell and killed two onlookers standing in a prohibited area. Villeneuve was unhurt and as third place man Patrick Depailler climbed alone onto the victory rostrum the circus tramped wearily home for a short rest after a long and not always happy season.

Anyone who thought Andretti the moral victor in 1977 needed no recourse to semantics at the end of 1978, for Mario won the title in convincing fashion. He won six Grands Prix – Argentina, Belgium, Spain, France, Germany and Holland – and crossed the line first in one more – Italy. Such was the superiority of the Lotuses that his only serious challenger was his team mate. Ronnie Peterson was employed by Lotus as number two driver and although he won in South Africa and Austria (with Andretti out of contention) he dutifully maintained that role, finishing second to Andretti on four occasions.

Come Monza, only Ronnie had a mathematical chance of challenging Andretti, but by the next morning Peterson was dead, the victim of a fiery accident as the cars funnelled into the first chicane.

Reutemann, now Ferrari's number one, took obvious pleasure in beating Niki Lauda into fourth spot in the championship. He won in Brazil, Long Beach, Great Britain and at Watkins Glen, while Lauda's wins in Sweden and Italy were both tinged by controversy. First-time winners picked up the re-

maining crumbs; Patrick Depailler's Monaco victory ended years of near misses, but when Gilles Villeneuve won in Canada he had not had to wait quite so long.

Andretti, with the Lotus 78, won easily from pole position in Argentina, with Lauda a distant second for Brabham; Depailler rewarded Tyrrell with an encouraging third place in the new 008. In Rio only half the 22 starters survived in the fierce heat, and none could catch Reutemann's Ferrari; his win looked easy as Andretti dropped back with gearbox problems and Fittipaldi came home second, ahead of Lauda. In South Africa the final laps were dominated by Peterson and Depailler, almost side by side on the final circuit until Peterson was first through the esses and then home.

At Long Beach the star of the show was Alan Jones in the Williams FW06, but in the end he dropped out with fuel problems and Reutemann scored again for Ferrari; Jones, however, took the lap record. From there the circus moved to Monaco, a classic race with a finish no one could have predicted. Pole man Reutemann threw it all away at the start, getting away slowly and puncturing a tyre. Watson stormed into the lead but then, under intense pressure from Depailler, overcooked his brakes and dropped out. Lauda took the lap record, at 83.57mph, but Depailler at last put himself on the winner's rostrum. In Belgium, Andretti gave the Lotus 79 the best possible debut with pole position and a flag to flag win, followed by his team-mate Peterson, and then they repeated their performances in Spain.

In Sweden there was controversy when the Brabham team's BT46 appeared with an engine-driven fan to suck air from underneath the car. Lauda simply drove the car into the distance, with Patrese second in the equally controversial Arrows. There were protests of course and, although the FIA (Fédération Internationale de l'Automobile) subsequently declared the Brabham illegal, the result stood. Andretti and Peterson were now first and second in the points table, and they repeated their performance in the French and Dutch GPs, with

Below: Brabham designer Gordon Murray's use of the rear-mounted fan to glue the Brabham BT 46 to the road was only allowed to have one moment of glory before it was outlawed, here at the 1978 Swedish GP. Lauda easily showed the way home to second man Patrese. Had Grand Prix development progressed along this road, there was talk of drivers needing g suits to protect them from cornering forces

Right: a variation on 1978's theme of Lotus 1-2 was seen in the opening races of the 1979 season. Here in Argentina, Jacques Laffite's Ligier leads the sister car of Patrick Depailler. The ground-effect JS11 Ligier with Cosworth instead of Matra power was immediately competitive, Laffite wining both South American GPs

Below right: Gilles Villeneuve driving a racing car the only way he knew how: right on the limit. Here the French-Canadian demonstrates his style at Montreal

Above: after a promising début with McLaren, Gilles Villeneuve really shone with Ferrari, even when the cars were no match for his prodigious talent

Andretti also winning the German GP and Peterson taking the Austrian. Tragically the Dutch GP was to be Peterson's last race, for at Monza there was a multiple pile-up at the first chicane. Hunt's McLaren was pushed into Peterson's Lotus, which ran across the track into the barriers at enormous speed and burst into flame. He was critically injured and later died.

The last two races of the season were sombre formalities. As Reutemann crossed the line to win the US GP, from Alan Jones in the Williams, he gave a derisory salute to the Ferrari pit which left them in no doubt as to his feelings about his imminent departure to Lotus, but Ferrari's faith in Gilles Villeneuve was rewarded when he took his first GP of the season in Montreal. After that everyone went home to think of ways of challenging the flying Lotuses, which had taken the Constructors' Cup with 86 points, followed by Ferrari with 58. The order of drivers was Andretti, Peterson, Reutemann, Lauda, Depailler, and Watson.

During winter testing it became apparent that the Ligier team, with a switch to Cosworth engines and a ground-effects chassis, had found the answer; Laffite won the Argentina and Brazilian GPs, with team-mate Depailler second in the latter race. At Kyalami, for the South African GP, the tables were turned with the Ferraris of Villeneuve and Jody Scheckter coming home first and second, proving one of the main precepts of motor racing – you may be winning today, but someone will always find a better idea. In Spain it was the Ligier of Depailler once again, but the Belgian and Monaco GPs were taken by Scheckter and his flying Ferrari. The latter race marked the end of the road for former World Champion James Hunt, who retired his uncompetitive Wolf on the first lap and then announced his own retirement, frustrated by the changing emphasis from driver skill to machinery.

On home ground, Renault at last fulfilled their promise and rewarded the vast investment of the previous two years. Frenchman Jean-Pierre Jabouille won the French GP in a French car on French Michelins. France was for the

French but Britain was for the British, and at Silverstone Frank Williams, so long the frustrated underdog, enjoyed victory as Regazzoni roared home over 24 seconds ahead of René Arnoux's Renault.

The next Williams win was in the German GP, in which Jones was absolutely untouchable, despite a slowly deflating and rapidly chunking rear tyre, and he was followed by Regazzoni to make Williams' first 1-2. Williams was the team of the moment, and Jones came first in the next two GPs, the Austrian and Dutch, and then, after the Ferraris of Scheckter and Villeneuve finished 1-2 in the Italian GP, won again in the Canadian. In the last GP of the season, at Watkins Glen, Villeneuve won for Ferrari, with Arnoux's Renault in second place. The season was Ferrari's, with Scheckter and Villeneuve leading the Drivers' Championship and Ferrari far ahead in the Constructors' Championship, with 113 points to Williams' 75. Whichever way you looked at it, Scheckter was a worthy champion, and the rapidly changing fortunes of the sport were highlighted by Mario Andretti's lowly 10th equal, with just 14 points for a season's dogged effort centred around the uncompetitive Lotus 80.

One driver who thought the effort no longer worth it was another former champion, Niki Lauda. He practised the new and very promising Brabham Cosworth in Canada, and having done so announced that he was retiring from the sport forthwith. He left to develop his airline business, making the classic comment that he was no longer interested in driving around in circles.

1980 was the year of skirts, turbos, and arguments about who should control the sport. Right from the start it was apparent that Williams' designer, Patrick Head, had developed the sliding skirt ground-effect concept of the FW07 sufficiently to keep the technological lead, and it was to be Williams' season. Alan Jones took the Argentine, French, British, Canadian and American GPs, with second places in the Belgian, Austrian and Italian GPs. The German GP, held at the unloved Hockenheim, was run under the appalling shadow of Patrick Depailler's death in a testing accident. His Alfa Romeo crashed, inexplicably, into unprotected barriers at the end of the very fast straight. The race saw a change of fortune for Ligier; for once, Laffite not only led convincingly but survived to win, albeit with a little luck. Both Renaults suffered valve breakages while running away with the lead and Alan Jones lost the lead with a puncture.

René Arnoux and his Renault took the honours in Brazil, his first GP win, and he made it two in a row with the South African, where the thin air of

Above: having broken their duck in 1979, things looked promising for Renault in 1980 with the fast but erratic René Arnoux behind the wheel. He won successive races in Brazil and South Africa but reliability problems later scuppered championship hopes

Below: even with a ground-effect chassis, Alan Jones could still throw his car around, as he demonstrates here at Long Beach

Kyalami favoured the turbo engines, but, although the Renaults continued to be fast, they also proved to be embarrassingly fragile. At the US Grand Prix at Long Beach, Nelson Piquet added his name to the list of GP winners for the first time. This race sadly marked the end of Clay Regazzoni's career. He survived a terrible accident when his Ensign's brake pedal broke as he approached the hairpin, resulting in an accident which left him with paralysed legs. Piquet went on to win the Dutch and Italian GPs in his Brabham, as well as coming second to Jones in the British GP. At season's end Jones was World Champion, followed by Piquet, Reutemann, Laffite, Pironi, and Arnoux. In the Constructors' Championship the Williams team was streets ahead, with 120 points to Ligier's 66. Ferrari, the '79 winners, had had a disastrous year, and came 10th, with just 8 points. It had been a season marked by arguments, especially at the Spanish Grand Prix, which the President of FISA (Fédération Internationale du Sport Automobile), Jean-Marie Balestre, had attempted to stop because of unpaid fines by several drivers who had been penalised by FISA for not attending briefings before the Belgian and Monaco races.

Right: the Ferraris of Villeneuve and Scheckter head towards a 1-2 at Long Beach in 1979. Depailler follows in his Ligier, ahead of Mario Andretti's Lotus, Hunt's Wolf, and Jarier's Tyrrell

Below: Jean-Pierre Jabouille was with the Renault turbo programme right from the start, but it was two years before he notched up his and his team's first win

The battle between FISA and FOCA (Formula One Constructors' Association) was dragged into 1981 with FISA unwilling to backtrack on its revised regulations and FOCA refusing to concede an ounce of commercial muscle. The so-called 'grandee' teams, principally the technically autonomous Ferrari, Renault and Alfa Romeo, all aligned with FISA, partly because the revised regulations would favour turbos and V12s, and partly for political expediency. In February, with the threat of a split remaining, FISA declared the

approaching South African GP illegal. Reutemann won the race but for the first time since 1966 the GP carried no championship points.

At Long Beach the cars complied with the regulations, without skirts and with a nominal 6cm ground clearance. Alan Jones opened his defence as he had clinched his previous championship, with a near-faultless win. After that race Frank Williams reiterated that Reutemann was his number two driver and should move over for Jones if the need arose, but in the rain-soaked Brazilian GP Reutemann led Jones, and, although the pit crew hung out the 'JONES-REUT' board, Reutemann stayed put and won.

In Argentina it was Piquet's turn, with Reutemann second, and Piquet did it again at the first San Marino GP, when Reutemann came third. At Zolder, for the Belgian GP, rain brought a mercifully premature end to a miserable weekend, which saw a mechanic fall between the wheels of Reutemann's moving car in a crowded pit lane during practice, and then an Arrows mechanic injured on the grid at the start of the race. Incredibly, the race continued until Pironi took the initiative and forced a halt. From the restart Reutemann won as Jones spun out of the lead.

In Monaco Villeneuve gave the V6 Ferrari turbo its first win when Jones began to slow with a mysterious misfire, and he won again in the Spanish GP. The British GP was a fairy-tale result for John Watson in his McLaren, the win his first since Austria in 1976. He was helped by a spinning Villeneuve taking out Jones, by Piquet crashing and both Renaults going out with engine failure.

The German GP saw Nelson Piquet win for Brabham, followed by Prost in the Renault turbo. In Austria it was Laffite's turn to win, followed by Arnoux and Piquet, and then came high drama in Holland as Reutemann and Laffite, fighting for fourth place, eliminated each other when Reutemann made for a nonexistent gap. Try as he might, Jones could not prevent the power of the Renault giving Prost a well-earned win. Prost won again at Monza, followed by Jones and Reutemann, the latter inheriting Piquet's place when he dropped out on the last lap with a blown engine. John Watson's fortunes had been on the wane since Silverstone, but luck was with him when he survived a violent accident which left his car all over the track.

The Canadian GP was held in appallingly wet conditions. Jones tried a bit too hard and spun off. Laffite won, followed by Watson and Villeneuve. Reutemann simply gave up. With the championship his for the taking, he still could not rise above his moods; with a perfect car he was magnificent, with anything less he was abject.

Next came the Caesar's Palace GP in Las Vegas. In practice Reutemann was devastating and the outcome looked settled; in the race he did not even fight as Piquet cruised past into sixth place and gained the vital points. The race was won by Jones, followed by Prost and Giacomelli's Alfa, with Reutemann a forgotten eighth and Piquet the new World Champion by one point.

1982 was another year of controversy over rule bending, of all but undrivable cars and tragedy. During practice for the Belgian GP in May, Villeneuve, going all out for pole position, drove over the back of Jochen Mass' March and cartwheeled to destruction; Villeneuve died a few hours later. Riccardo Paletti died in a start-line accident in Canada and Pironi was badly injured at Hockenheim.

Above: John Watson with the impressive McLaren MP4 at Monaco. This car formed the basis of McLaren's resurgence of form in the 1980s, both with Cosworth and TAG turbo power

Right: anyone who thought that modern Grand Prix cars cornered on rails should have been watching Jean-Pierre Jarier with the Candy Tyrrell in the wet at Zolder in 1980

Below left: considering the dreadful handling and seemingly inevitable tyre problems with the Ferrari 312T4s, it was just as well that Gilles Villeneuve simply did not know how to give up. Here at Monaco he salvaged fifth place while his team mate Scheckter threw in the towel, so bad was the car

Frank Williams started the season with Keke Rosberg and a seemingly revivified Reutemann; although Rosberg had failed to score a single point with the Fittipaldi team in 1981, Williams saw the Finn with uncanny car control as an obvious successor to Jones.

Once again the season got off to a shaky start as the South African GP endured a drivers' strike over clauses in the Super Licence form which restricted their transfer between teams and generally required them to toe the FISA line. A settlement of sorts was negotiated and then the race began; it proved to be a Renault *tour de force*, won by Prost, with Reutemann's Williams second and then Arnoux in the other Renault. Prost took the Brazilian GP, but only after winners Piquet and Rosberg were disqualified because their cars had over-exploited a loophole in the weight regulations.

Long Beach was full of surprises. De Cesaris' Alfa took pole but spun away the lead on a crumbling track and allowed Lauda his first Grand Prix win since coming out of retirement; Rosberg, charging hard, took second place.

At Imola the majority of FOCA teams stayed away in protest at the Brazilian disqualifications, and Pironi, against team orders, overtook a furious Villeneuve to give a Ferrari 1-2. This, sadly, was to be Villeneuve's last race, and at Zolder Watson won, robbing long-time leader Rosberg two laps from home as the Williams destroyed its tyres.

If Zolder was tragedy, Monaco was farce. With rain falling steadily and three laps to go, Prost, leading comfortably, crashed heavily. Patrese inherited the lead with his Brabham BT49 only to throw it away on the penultimate lap. Pironi then took over until he suffered electrical failure in the tunnel. De Cesaris might have taken the lead but he ran out of petrol, and then Daly, in his second race for Williams, could have won if he had not smashed his gearbox on the barriers. A Lotus 1-2 suddenly seemed possible, but then Patrese was running again to take the chequered flag and what he only later realised was his first Grand Prix win.

At Detroit it was Watson, Eddie Cheever, and Pironi who took the honours, Watson having carved his way from 13th to first, the opposition destroyed to an extent rarely seen. In Canada, where Paletti was so tragically killed, it was a triumph for Brabham, with Piquet and Patrese giving the team a 1-2 victory.

The Dutch GP was an encouraging win for Pironi and Ferrari, and at Brands Hatch the Ferraris of Pironi and Tambay came second and third behind Lauda's McLaren. In France, René Arnoux and Alain Prost cruised to a comfortable Renault 1-2, ahead of the two Ferrari turbos.

At Hockenheim, with Pironi hospitalised after a practice accident which ended his career, the championship fight devolved to Rosberg, Watson, Prost,

Above: during the 1981 season Ken Tyrrell spotted the potential of Italian Michele Alboreto and signed him up for 1982. His foresight was rewarded when Michele won here in Las Vegas

Below: Derek Warwick hounded the eventual second-place man Pironi at Brands before being forced to retire

Right: in 1982, for the first time since Mike Hawthorn won the World Championship in 1958 the champion won only one Grand Prix. However, that was more a reflection of the competitiveness of the racing than the ability of Finnish star Keke Rosberg, seen here after winning the 'Swiss' GP at Dijon in his Williams – his first Grand Prix victory

and Lauda. In Germany, Tambay won, giving Ferrari a morale-boosting victory, but the Austrian GP was dominated by a last-lap duel between Rosberg and the Lotus of Italian Elio de Angelis, the latter holding the Finn at bay to win by the narrowest margin then ever seen in Grand Prix racing – a mere 500th of a second.

At Dijon-Prenois, for the 'Swiss' GP, Rosberg won his first Grand Prix, followed by Prost and Lauda. At Monza, Ferrari were back to full strength, with Tambay being joined by former World Champion Mario Andretti. In the event, a sticking throttle held him back and he had to be content with a third place behind Arnoux's untouchable Renault and a very on-form Tambay. By this stage, Rosberg could have clinched the title with a single point, but while running sixth he lost the wing of his Williams, leaving Watson in fourth place and with an outside chance of taking the championship.

The finale was again at Caesar's Palace Hotel in Las Vegas, on a circuit as artificial as the city's tinsel glamour. This race was really between Rosberg and Watson. Watson had to win, but, after a skilful drive to recover from a lowly 12th place, he was beaten fair and square by the young Italian who had been impressive all year, Michele Alboreto. Rosberg, by finishing a careful and calculated fifth, clinched his first World Championship title to bring a little cheer to the end of a dreadful season.

CHAPTER 5

THE STATE OF THE ART

THE CARS AND THE RACES 1983-87

The FISA governing body gave very short notice of slapping their 'flat-bottom' restriction on to all Formula One cars with effect from the first race of 1983. The announcement was made without warning on 3 November 1982, giving only three months' grace before the opening race of the new season, in Brazil. Many teams had already invested heavily in the next logical stage of underwing chassis development, only to find this investment blown out the window overnight by the governing body's decree. One of the greatest investments had been made by McLaren International, who had commissioned the Porsche-produced TAG V6 turbo engine along compact lines packaged especially to modern ground-effect car requirements. As it happened, McLaren's brilliant chief engineer John Barnard was able to adapt his concept adequately to the new flat-bottomed regime, one which his fast and supremely reliable products would eventually dominate.

Meanwhile, most teams believed that their opposition would begin the new season with stopgap cars, fitting regulation body-width flat undertrays to existing ground-effect chassis. Odd men out in this general concensus were Gordon Murray and David North, technical brains behind the Brabham team. When the new ruling was announced only three months before the 1983 Brazilian GP, they promptly scrapped their planned BT51 ground-effects design and began instead with a clean sheet of paper to produce the needle-nosed

Right: having shown the potential of the Toleman-Hart at the previous year's British Grand Prix, Derek Warwick looked forward to an even better 1983 with team-mate Bruno Giacomelli. Although Warwick always qualified his flat-bottomed car, his best results were a brace of fourth places

Below: in 1983 Williams sorely missed turbo power but could always rely on their new World Champion to give 100%. When wet conditions demanded the best car control, Keke was there. At Spa he was quick, at Monaco he demoralised the rest of the field

spearhead-shaped Brabham-BMW BT52, tailor-made to the new requirements.

Such commitment paid off brilliantly. As the new season began at Rio, Nelson Piquet flashed his brand-new BT52 past Keke Rosberg's interim flat-bottomed Williams FW08C to take an early lead, and then held his advantage to the finish, giving the startling new Brabham-BMW a debut victory. Williams attempted in-race refuelling for the first time, but the filler neck on Rosberg's car failed, causing a brief but dramatic pit fire and leaving the Finn with no chance of improving on second place. He was then disqualified for having been push-started after that pit fire. This presented second place – and its two extra championship points – to Niki Lauda's McLaren-Cosworth MP4/1.

The US GP (West) followed at Long Beach, a staggering event in which the McLarens suffered terribly during practice (qualifying a woeful 22-23 on the grid) but then adopted a brilliant race set-up on their Michelin tyres to enable John Watson to win easily with team-mate Lauda second! Tambay's Ferrari and Rosberg's Williams meanwhile had collided while duelling for the lead. 'Wattie' took first place on lap 45 of the scheduled 75, and only René Arnoux's third-placed Ferrari remained on the same lap as the McLarens at the finish. Who said the Cosworth DFV was dead?

The minor Race of Champions followed at Brands Hatch, American Tyrrell driver Danny Sullivan enjoying a brief blaze of glory in a thin field as Rosberg's blistered-tyred Williams beat him by just half a second. Retired former World Champion Alan Jones staged a brief comeback in an Arrows A6, and came third.

The French GP was run early that season, as round three of the championship at Ricard on 17 April. Renault were determined to excel on home soil and Prost made no mistake on Michelin tyres which showed great superiority over Goodyear that day. The similarly shod Brabham-BMWs matched Renault power but not their handling, Piquet finishing a distant second ahead of Renault number two Eddie Cheever. The Williams pair of Rosberg and Laffite drove their hearts out to finish 1-2 in the 'Cosworth Class' of 3-litre naturally aspirated cars and 5-6 overall. It was not a good day for McLaren.

At Imola the spear-nosed Brabham BT52s looked set to dominate. Piquet slammed his car on pole position only to stall as the green light came on. This allowed Arnoux to lead briefly for Ferrari before Patrese tore by in his BT52. He was barracked by the Italian crowd for displacing their beloved Ferrari, but made his scheduled refuelling and tyre-change stop still ahead. Strangely for the well drilled Brabham team, the stop was slow, and Riccardo rejoined second but managed to catch the leader and retake the lead, only to slide off and crash heavily on the next corner. Tambay emerged leading for Ferrari to score an immensely popular home win from Prost. Now the non-turbocharged cars were being outclassed even on the slower circuits . . . but not all. The slowest of them all, Monaco, followed on 15 May, and Rosberg made the most of the rain to win in his Williams-Cosworth FW08C from Piquet, Prost, and Tambay in turbo cars, then Sullivan's Tyrrell 011 fifth. A Williams 1-2 had seemed on the cards until Jacques Laffite's FW08C broke its gearbox.

The modified Spa-Francorchamps circuit hosted the Belgian GP for the first time in 13 years, the following weekend. Horsepower still told there, and Andrea de Cesaris shone briefly with his Alfa Romeo 183T V8 turbo by taking pole position and leading until injection failure with 15 laps to go. This handed Prost and Renault their second victory of the season, Piquet fell from second to fifth after losing fifth gear and the Williams cars' consistency paid minor dividends with a 5-6 finish, albeit 1-2 in the Cosworth Class.

The Detroit GP saw Brabham quietly plan to run non-stop through the Motown race only for Piquet's BT52 to suffer a puncture when leading with 10 laps to go. Michele Alboreto had been quietly making progress through the field in his Tyrrell-Cosworth 011, profiting from trouble afflicting others, and lo and behold he won, beating the similar Cosworth-engined cars of Rosberg and Watson, with Piquet salvaging fourth place in the turbo Brabham, Laffite fifth, and Nigel Mansell's usually outclassed Lotus 92 sixth.

Above: Alain Prost strokes his Renault RE40 to an easy victory at Spa-Francorchamps in 1983 after the surprising Alfas faltered mid-race. Alain went on to challenge for the championship only to lose out to Nelson Piquet in the last race of the season

Cars powered by the Cosworth-Ford DFV had been lucky to fill five of the top six places on Ford's home ground but this was to be the power unit's 155th and last World Championship GP victory.

Montreal's island circuit one week later saw the turbos re-established by a faultless Ferrari win for Arnoux, who lost the lead only briefly during his pit-stop; Cheever's Renault was second and Tambay's Ferrari third. Prost suffered a down-on-power engine and a puncture, restricting his Renault to fifth place, and Watson's McLaren was back in the points (at last), with sixth.

Arnoux ripped around Silverstone in a staggering time of 1 minute 9.462 seconds to put his brand-new Ferrari 126C3 on pole position for the British GP. He and team-mate Tambay led for 20 laps until their Goodyear tyres lost grip. Prost's Renault RE40 – the definitive '83 flat-bottomed model – inherited victory, with Piquet second also enjoying Michelin's tyre dominance.

However, the story of the race was the change wrought to Team Lotus fortunes by new French chief engineer Gerard Ducarouge's completely re-vised Type 94T cars using Renault turbo V6 engines. Both Elio de Angelis and Nigel Mansell revelled in the new cars' handling in practice, and the latter finished fourth in his home GP, the equipe's best result for ages. Honda returned to Formula One with an F2-based turbo V6 engine installed in Stefan Johansson's thinly financed Spirit 201, while Lauda's McLaren won the Cosworth Class . . . in sixth place.

The fast turbo circuits pack the latter end of the season, and in the German GP at Hockenheim, Tambay's Ferrari led for two laps then team-mate Arnoux took over for the rest of the way apart from his pit stop. Piquet lost second place when a fuel filter bowl cracked just three laps from the end and his Brabham-BMW caught fire. Cheever's Renault broke its fuel pump drive and gave the de Cesaris Alfa 183T second place, which was the Italian marque's best result in modern Formula One. Prost was handicapped by the loss of fifth gear to finish only fourth, while Lauda's fifth-on-the-road McLaren MP4/1 was disqualified for reversing in the pit lane after overshooting its pit-stop marks. This elevated team-mate Watson to fifth, beating Laffite's Williams for Cosworth Class honours.

Ferrari dominated qualifying in Austria, Tambay taking pole and leading until baulked by Jarier's Ligier, which allowed Arnoux to rip by. Arnoux's gearbox then began to fail, enabling Prost to sneak ahead to win for Renault with Piquet third. By this stage of the season, McLaren had clearly the most effective Cosworth-powered package, and Lauda won the class on his home ground, but only sixth overall.

Back home at Woking, McLaren International at last had an interim TAG turbo V6-engined car, the MP4/1E, ready for Niki to drive in the next race – the Dutch GP at Zandvoort. Its presence there seemed to inspire John Watson – still with Cosworth power in his sister car. Arnoux's Ferrari won from 10th on the grid, Tambay came back from an awful start to finish second, while Prost and Piquet had been disputing the lead before colliding on lap 42. 'Wattie' rampaged home third in the old McLaren, and Lauda enjoyed a brief but promising debut in the team's turbo hack. For the following race, at Monza, Watson would also have TAG Turbo power, so Zandvoort had seen McLaren's Cosworth swansong, and their fourth consecutive 'victory' among the non-turbo cars.

At this stage in the season, Prost led the Drivers' Championship but Piquet was threatening, although his chances of closing the gap at Monza seemed threatened by his own team-mate Patrese when the Italian qualified his BT52 on pole position! He seemed disinclined to move over for his team leader in the race, so many observers wondered if his car's massive engine failure after only three laps was entirely providential. . . .

Prost's Renault then suffered turbo failure, wrecking his chance of adding to his points tally, and Piquet won easily from Arnoux, Cheever, Tambay, de Angelis, and an elated Derek Warwick, scoring his first points in the Hart 4-cylinder turbo-engined Toleman TG183B. This was the first Grand Prix in which the first six places were filled by turbocharged cars. Both turbo McLarens suffered teething troubles.

A European GP was organised at Brands Hatch, where Ferrari's hopes of championship honours for either Arnoux or Tambay exploded in a complete debacle, René struggling home ninth having ruined his tyres and Patrick crashing due to brake failure when fourth. De Angelis put his Lotus-Renault 94T on pole but collided with the forceful Patrese in an early duel for the lead, while Warwick shone again, until his Toleman's onboard extinguisher discharged accidentally, dropping him to fifth. Overall, Piquet was uncatchable, winning his second consecutive Grand Prix, from Prost and Mansell.

So the championship lay clearly between Prost and Piquet with Tambay having a very slim outside chance into the final round at Kyalami, South Africa, on 15 October. Piquet's car started very light with a tiny fuel load, built an early lead from Patrese, stopped early to refuel and to fit conservative hard Michelin tyres and then stroked comfortably home to a safe third-place finish, while Patrese won easily from de Cesaris' Alfa. Prost lost fourth place and the title with turbo failure on lap 35, and Lauda showed the great potential of the TAG Turbo engine by soaring into second place and looking set to threaten Patrese's lead before his engine-management-system electrics vibrated apart. Piquet's third-place finish clinched him the Drivers' title, while Ferrari just saved the Constructors' crown, and there was consolation for Warwick's now reliable Toleman which finished fourth ahead of Rosberg's brand-new Wil-

liams-Honda FW09. This car, along with its sister driven by Jacques Laffite, had gone exceptionally well in its practice debut giving warning of Honda turbo power to come.

The late-season championship-winning charge by Nelson Piquet and the Brabham-BMWs caused some controversy. Renault especially became suspicious of the specially brewed high-toluene heavy fuel which they used, made by BASF Chemicals in Germany. Renault personnel maintain to this day that Piquet's late-season 1983 fuel bent the rules, and that the governing body swept incontrovertible evidence to this effect under the carpet. However, BMW maintained that their fuel rating was acceptable within the rules, while others took note and turned to their fuel suppliers for brewing assistance.

Fuel value would be vital in the new 1984 season, as FISA now slashed permitted tank capacity from 250 litres to just 220 and banned in-race refuelling. This economy component of the regulations would have a profound effect, for hitherto cars had carried sufficient fuel – and had been allowed to top up the level mid-race – to enable them to cascade fuel through their engines to achieve internal cooling, in order to sustain artificially high turbo boost pressures. This now became impossible. Teams did their best to slip around the regulations by hyper-cooling their fuel – thereby causing it to contract greatly and so occupy smaller volume – before filling the 220-litre tanks just prior to the start!

Right: for 1984 Alain Prost joined McLaren, where he was team-mate to Niki Lauda (below). The two friends dominated the season, the Austrian taking the title by the slimmest of margins

Another very significant factor shaping the coming 1984 season was that Goodyear had changed from bias-ply tyre construction to radial ply to maintain better tyre profiles and thereby flat-bottom-car ride heights, and this instantly put the giant American company in touch with Michelin, the contemporary masters of the art.

All engine suppliers paid enormous attention to fuel economy, and Porsche's TAG Turbo engine for McLaren – being the most modern in Formula One – had a head start which McLaren's star drivers (Lauda now being joined by Alain Prost to replace John Watson) could exploit to the full.

John Barnard designed all-new MP4/2 tailor-made turbo cars for the new season, and amazingly only four of them would be used in an historic dominance of quite epic proportions. The cars won no less than 12 of the 16 GPs comprising the 1984 World Championship series, Prost winning seven of them and Lauda the other five. Niki drove the same car, McLaren-TAG Turbo MP4/2-1, in every race that season, and it was his having a better placings record than Prost which eventually gave him the world title by a nerve-tingling half-point in the final Portuguese GP at Estoril on 21 October. Why half a point? Because the rain-swept Monaco GP had been stopped at 31 laps instead of the scheduled 78 'on safety grounds', and Prost's first place there was consequently accorded only half-points: four-and-a-half for the win instead of the customary nine.

McLaren's threat became clear in the opening race of 1984 at Rio on 25 March, where 220-litre fuel economy had everybody worried and nearly all drivers were forced to ease off purely to survive race distance, yet Prost managed to win with fuel to spare! Michele Alboreto had just joined Ferrari from Tyrrell, and his new 126C4 spun from the lead on lap 12, enabling Lauda's MP4/2 TAG Turbo to take over until a lap 38 electrical failure. Warwick – replacing Prost at Renault – inherited the lead until his front suspension failed due to an earlier nudge from Lauda, so Prost hit the front.

Back at Kyalami on 7 April, the new McLarens utterly dominated with a brilliant race set-up despite Prost having to race Lauda's spare car at the last moment. It was not properly adjusted to his needs, but he put in a superb drive from the back of the field to complete a stunning team 1-2 behind the victorious Austrian.

The Belgian GP at Zolder saw poor fuel wreck practice for BMW and TAG, with pistons burning and engines exploding. This helped Alboreto to his first Ferrari pole position. Rosberg's Williams-Honda shot into third place after a bad start at the price of running out of fuel on the last lap, while Alboreto won handsomely from Warwick's Renault RE50, Ferrari team-mate Arnoux, Rosberg, and de Angelis' Lotus 95T. This was the first Grand Prix win for an Italian Ferrari driver since Monza 1966.

In May at Imola, McLaren-TAG re-established themselves after the Belgian hiccup, Prost leading from the start. At Dijon the first Renault pole in almost a year, taken by ex-Ferrari driver Patrick Tambay, still left Lauda winning for McLaren after the apparently dominant Prost had been delayed by a loose wheel. Monaco saw teeming rain and a fortuitous win for Prost as the red flag came out after Mansell had thrown his leading Lotus into the barrier, while new boy Ayrton Senna's Toleman was lapping quicker than the McLaren and closing fast.

The McLaren steamroller was then halted briefly in Canada, where Piquet won superbly in his latest Brabham-BMW BT53, ahead of the now familiar McLaren pair. This time, Lauda headed Prost. In Detroit, Piquet won again – in his spare BT53. McLaren's effort looked to be falling apart, as the inaugural – and as it happened one-off – Dallas GP fell to Keke Rosberg's wildly handling Williams-Honda after the opposition gradually dropped out.

Back home, McLaren got their MP4/2s back on song and won the final seven consecutive GPs of the season, the British (Lauda), German (Prost from Lauda), Austrian (Lauda), Dutch (Prost from Lauda), Italian (Lauda), European at Nürburgring (Prost) and Portuguese (Prost from Lauda) to settle both Drivers' and Constructors' Championships in staggering style. There were problems along the way, but McLaren's problems were at least all curable,

Left: Ayrton Senna stormed on to the Grand Prix scene with Toleman and quickly established a reputation as the fastest driver of all when he transferred to Lotus

Below: a fine chassis, a strong and reliable engine and the driving talents of the clinically precise Lauda, combined to secure the 1984 World Championship. However, not even the greatest can ignore a nose spoiler coming adrift, as here at Spa

Left: racing engines used to be quite crude and cumbersome devices, but this Renault V6 is as intricate as a Swiss wristwatch. The detailing on this 1500cc, 24-valve, four-cam, twin-turbo power unit would have impressed NASA a few years before. When Renault entered F1 again in 1977, they were running little over 550bhp; by the time they bowed out in 1986 they were producing well over twice that figure

Right: before an abortive switch to Alfa power for 1987, Guy Ligier's team was one of three using Renault engines. In spite of veteran Jacques Laffite's pace the cars never quite matched the similarly propelled Lotus challengers

Below right: the motive power behind McLaren's success has been the TAG Turbo. Built by Porsche, the engine was funded by Mansour Ojjeh's *Techniques d'Avant Garde* company, while McLaren's John Barnard had overall technical control. The engine was built from the start to fit perfectly into his MP4 chassis

Below: the profile of a modern F1 car. Michele Alboreto sitting at the sharp end of his 156/85 Ferrari. Alboreto managed a couple of wins in 1985 and led the Drivers' Championship for most of the season. In the end, however, he had to give best (like everybody else) to Alain Prost

unlike the more intractable types of dilemma afflicting most of the opposition teams.

For 1985, the planned move to reduce race-distance fuel allowance to 195 litres was postponed, the current 220-litre limitation being extended instead for a further season. During 1984, high-download rear winglets had appeared on the cars' rear wings just abaft the rear axle line. These were now outlawed, the whole of the rear wing structure having to remain within the 100cm span limit. Intensive engine and fuel developments promoted massive power increases, especially in qualifying, when fuel economy did not matter, and, although McLaren managed to keep their edge for much of the year, it was the Williams-Honda team which came very much on song at the end of the season.

Patrick Head, chief engineer of the Williams team, had developed new moulded carbon-composite monocoque chassis for the new year's Honda-powered FW10 cars to be driven by Rosberg and new recruit Mansell. Meanwhile, Ayrton Senna had taken Nigel's old Lotus seat alongside Elio de Angelis.

Alain Prost won the opening Brazilian GP at Rio for McLaren in the latest MP4/2B turbo car while Ferrari showed some resurgence with Alboreto's latest model 156 second and Arnoux's fourth. But Arnoux was dropped by Ferrari immediately after this race and replaced by the young Swede Stefan Johansson.

Senna showed his value by scoring his maiden win in terrible weather conditions at Estoril (Lotus' first GP victory since Austria in 1982), while both Prost and Rosberg crashed in the torrential rain. The Frenchman then came back to win the San Marino GP at Imola for McLaren, only to be disqualified as his car – which had run out of fuel on the cooling-off lap – was found to be underweight at post-race scrutineering. This was a catastrophe for McLaren, victory going instead to a bemused de Angelis and Team Lotus! Senna had dominated in the latest Lotus-Renault 97T, only to run out of fuel with four of the 60 laps to go; Johansson had then inherited the lead for Ferrari in only his second drive for them, but his tanks ran dry too, leaving Prost to finish first but consequently to be disqualified. It was Elio's lucky day....

Senna led again at Monaco until his Renault's engine broke on lap 13, and Prost got the best of a battle with Alboreto's Ferrari when the Italian slid off on oil spilled by a spectacular Piquet/Patrese collision. Prost won legally this time,

although his MP4/2B was still uncomfortably close to that minimum weight limit. However, at this point in the season, de Angelis led the Drivers' Championship.

The first visit to Spa for the scheduled Belgian GP was abortive as 'green' track resurfacing broke up and the meeting was abandoned until later in the season. In Canada there was the first Ferrari 1-2 since Zandvoort '83, as Alboreto won from Johansson and Prost, but Williams had a new series Honda engine and Rosberg finished threateningly in fourth place. He fulfilled this promise in Detroit, winning handsomely from the two Ferraris, Johansson ahead of Alboreto this time, and then at Ricard in the French GP Piquet's Pirelli-tyred Brabham-BMW BT54 scored a sensational surprise victory from Rosberg and Prost.

Lauda's McLaren season was being riven by mechanical failure and retirement – as was Ayrton Senna's – while Prost's finishing record was as good as ever, but he was not winning. At Silverstone, he put this right in the British GP. At the Nürburgring in the German GP he was a close second to Alboreto's victorious Ferrari, and in Austria he won as Honda engine bottom-

Above left: after a début spell with Lotus, Nigel Mansell switched to the Williams-Honda Grand Prix team where he ran alongside first Keke Rosberg and then Nelson Piquet. He emerged as a driver of the very highest talent with a determination that was second to none

Above: Nigel Mansell pressing on with his 1986 Williams-Honda FW11. Honda's re-entry into Grand Prix racing started off timidly with Spirit and then transferred to Williams. Initially, their engines were peaky and almost undriveable, but they had developed into the ones to beat by 1986

end failures shattered Williams' hopes. Prost and Alboreto headed the Drivers' table, and Ferrari led McLaren in the Constructors' table by 17 points.

McLaren's fortunes improved with a Dutch GP 1-2 result, but Prost's suffered as he was beaten by Lauda in a dramatic wheel-locking battle. Ferrari's engine power seemed to be eclipsed at Monza where Prost won after Rosberg's dominant Williams-Honda broke its engine, and both Prost and McLaren went to the head of their respective championship tables.

The delayed Belgian GP was finally run at Spa on 15 September, Senna winning from Mansell's Williams-Honda with Prost third. Then came the final three races of the season, the European GP at Brands Hatch, South African at Kyalami, and the inaugural Australian GP at Adelaide, and Williams won them all, Mansell taking the first two to break convincingly his long-standing duck, and Rosberg the last of them in his Williams-team swansong before replacing the again-retiring Lauda at McLaren for 1986.

Still, Prost finished fourth at Brands to clinch his first Drivers' Championship after so many near-misses, and his third place at Kyalami gave

McLaren-TAG Turbo their second consecutive Constructors' Championship title.

For 1986, permitted fuel was cut to 195 litres, making economy engineering, race tune, and onboard pace computers even more vital.

Piquet took Rosberg's old place at Williams, Senna headed Team Lotus and de Angelis took Piquet's old place. Renault had withdrawn from competition after their terrible '85 season, leaving Derek Warwick without a drive until, tragically, de Angelis died after a testing accident at Ricard, and Brabham invited Warwick to replace him for the rest of the season. However, Brabham-BMW's star had well and truly dimmed, and their latest lowline BT55 car with its lay-down turbo engine proved a complete flop.

Williams were rocked by the road accident which befell Frank Williams paralysing him below the shoulders. However, Piquet dominated the Brazilian GP, the new Williams-Honda FW11 cars were taking up where the previous season's FW10s had left off. Renault were well represented by their V6 engines in Lotus, Ligier, and Tyrrell chassis, which finished 2-3-4-5 in the capable hands of Senna (Lotus), Laffite and Arnoux (Ligier), and Brundle (Tyrrell).

Senna then tipped the scales by beating Nigel Mansell's Williams-Honda by a fleeting 0.014 seconds at Jerez to win the revived Spanish GP, with Prost and Rosberg 3-4 in McLaren's latest MP4/2C cars.

At Imola, Senna was blindingly fast in Gerard Ducarouge's latest Lotus-Renault 98T until hub bearing failure stopped him, leaving Prost to win from Piquet's Williams with Gerhard Berger's Benetton-BMW third.

Monaco saw an old-style McLaren 1-2, Prost winning from Rosberg, then Senna and Mansell, but in Belgium Nigel was back into his winning stride for Williams-Honda, making the most of an early Prost delay in a first-corner collision which left his McLaren bent amidships, despite which the brilliant Frenchman still finished sixth and set fastest lap at 148mph.

Montreal fell to Mansell from Prost's McLaren and Piquet, with Rosberg fourth. In Detroit, the cards fell Senna's way and he bounced back to win after both Williams-Hondas struck trouble. Veteran Jacques Laffite's Ligier-Renault JS27 finished second. Prost third and Alboreto fourth in the latest Ferrari F1/86.

The Williams bandwagon was rolling again in the French GP at Ricard where Mansell beat Prost, Piquet, and Rosberg in a carbon copy of the Canadian result. At Brands Hatch for the British GP, Mansell and Piquet completed a Williams-Honda 1-2 demonstration on merit – not team orders – beating Prost into third place again. In Germany Piquet made it three in a row for Williams, beating Senna and Mansell.

At this point, Mansell led the Drivers' Championship with 51 points to Prost's 44 and Senna's 42, while Williams were well clear in the Constructors' Cup competition, with 89 points to McLaren's 63.

A new Hungarian GP had been instituted and there Piquet won again, the Williams team's fourth consecutive win and their seventh of the season. Second was Senna – watching his fuel read-out in frustrated agony on the last lap and unable to attack – and third Mansell.

In Austria, both Williams cars, and Senna's Lotus and Rosberg's McLaren all failed dramatically, leaving Prost to win by a clear lap from Alboreto's Ferrari. Piquet came back at Monza, notching Williams-Honda's eighth victory of the year in an FW11 1-2 finish ahead of the troubled Mansell. In Portugal Mansell won superbly, Williams-Honda's ninth victory of the year, but Prost finished second and Piquet third.

On 12 October, the Mexican GP was revived. Both Williams-Hondas suffered terrible tyre problems, and Gerhard Berger notched a sensational maiden victory for the Benetton-BMW team. Significantly for the championship, Prost was second again, and Piquet and Mansell could salvage only a 4-5 finish. Now Mansell led on 70 points with Prost lying second on 64 points, and Piquet third with 63. Each could still win the Drivers' Championship in the final round, the Australian GP at Adelaide on 26 October.

Below: even though the Renault power unit was generally outclassed in 1986, the combination of Ducarouge's fine Lotus chassis and the blistering speed of driver Ayrton Senna made Team Lotus a force to be reckoned with. The team invariably dominated practice, and despite reliability problems, at times the Brazilian still managed to head the field

There Mansell took pole position, and did everything right in the race as Rosberg led with Piquet, Mansell and Prost behind. Prost had a puncture and changed to fresh tyres, then tyre failures suddenly beset his rivals.

First Rosberg's leading McLaren shredded its right-rear tyre. He thought the thumping and bumping signified engine failure, so he switched off and abandoned his last Grand Prix before retirement. Mansell took the lead within a lap, only for the circumferential band in his left-rear tyre to part, triggering a high-speed exit from the race. Piquet had to change his tyres. Prost was left with a clear run to win race and championship, and so became the first driver since Jack Brabham in 1959-60 to achieve two consecutive world titles, by two points from Mansell and three from Piquet.

It was the third time in three seasons that a McLaren International driver had been World Champion, but Williams-Honda took the Constructors' Championship to end a spectacular season of Grand Prix racing.

There were several changes in Formula One for 1987. For a start, Michelin and Pirelli withdrew giving Goodyear an unwanted monopoly, which led to a decision to supply standard 'control' tyres for each race, tailored to suit

the leading teams.

FISA attempted to reduce speeds by restricting turbocharger boost to 4 bars or less for the 1.5-litre cars and by introducing a new 3.5-litre naturally aspirated class. 'Pop-off' valves were issued at each race by FISA engineers, set to keep boost down to 4 bars or less. In theory, this should have reduced non-economy-conscious qualifying speeds, but in practice the teams largely circumvented the restriction by fitting larger turbochargers that blew the gas in quicker than the pop-offs could dump it. Thus qualifying speeds rose ever higher.

To satisfy 3.5-litre demand, Cosworth quickly developed an enlarged, 570BHP, version of the famous DFV series, now known as the DFZ. FISA ruled that any switch away from turbo power would be irrevocable, in theory to prevent teams from choosing their engines to suit different circuits. But in fact this was an irrelevance, since the turbo cars were as dominant as ever throughout the season.

The season opened in Brazil on 12 April with the two Williams-Honda FW11Bs of Mansell and Piquet on the front row of the grid, ahead of Senna's similarly powered – and now actively suspended – Lotus 99T. Prost's McLaren-Tag Turbo MP4/3 started fifth but in the race he moved relentlessly towards the front, taking the lead before his first pit stop and then losing it only briefly, despite a second tyre change. Piquet finished a distant second and Mansell sixth, both Williams cars suffering from overheating.

Round two was the San Marino GP at Imola. Piquet non-started after an almighty shunt during qualifying, apparently due to tyre failure on the Williams, which was destroyed. Goodyear replaced their entire stock overnight but the meeting continued without the miraculously unharmed Brazilian.

Senna qualified handsomely on pole, from Mansell, Prost, Teo Fabi's strong Benetton and Berger and Alboreto on row three in the Ferrari F1/87s with their 90-degree V6 turbos, as introduced at Rio. Nigel Mansell won, his only problem as he beat Senna by almost half a minute, being lost wheel balance weights. Alboreto salvaged third on home soil beating Johansson's McLaren into fourth.

Two weeks later, at Spa-Francorchamps for the Belgian GP, Mansell and Piquet qualified 1-2 for Williams. On the second race lap, Tyrrell driver Philippe Streiff crashed, cannoned back off the barrier and was torpedoed by team-mate Jonathan Palmer. The race was stopped.

At the restart, Senna and Mansell quickly collided and spun off into the sand-traps. Senna was stuck fast, but Mansell continued for a further seventeen laps with a damaged undertray. Later Mansell assaulted Senna in the Lotus garage for an incident which most observers concluded was his own fault. With these two out of it, Prost coolly headed Johansson home in a McLaren 1-2, the little French 'Professor' equalling Jackie Stewart's fourteen-year-old record of 27 Championship GP wins.

In Monaco on 31 May, Mansell took pole position, but after thirty race laps his Williams lost turbo boost. Senna inherited the lead and victory, with Piquet a distant second after Prost's TAG engine exploded with two laps to run. Berger led a Ferrari 3-4 and Palmer scored his maiden Championship points in the Tyrrell DG/016 – the first 'atmospheric' car home.

Three weeks later, in Detroit, Mansell was on pole yet again, but in the race developed leg cramps and so finished a distant fifth. However, Senna paced himself for a valuable Lotus victory, while Piquet recovered brilliantly after an early puncture to finish second in a Brazilian 1-2.

The French Grand Prix, held at Ricard-Castellet on 5 July, saw Prost alongside Mansell's regular pole slot, but the race belonged to the two Williams drivers, between whom little love was lost. Mansell demolished Piquet in a crushing Williams 1-2. Prost's ailing McLaren scraped third and Senna took an off-the-pace fourth. Senna now led the Championship by one point from Prost, then Piquet and Mansell.

A week later, the British GP at Silverstone was a war between Mansell and

Above: for 1986 Brabham revamped their Grand Prix contender and turned it into the racing 'skateboard', the BT 56. With the driver lying virtually prone and the BMW turbo engine canted over, the car's height was reduced for better air penetration. However, problems with chassis rigidity and poor engine pick-up plagued the season, and Derek Warwick had to cope with a new 7-speed gearbox as well

Right: Nelson Piquet, the 1987 World Champion. His leadership of the championship race could not be challenged once Mansell had crashed out (injuring his back) during practice for the Japanese Grand Prix

Piquet. This was set up in qualifying, with Nelson on pole, and confirmed in a sensational race which saw the Englishman snatch a last-minute victory in real win-or-bust style. Senna and Nakajima finished 3-4, so Honda engines were utterly dominant.

Piquet won both the German and Hungarian GPs when Mansell's pole-winning car had to withdraw. Piquet had now opened up a good lead over Senna and Mansell in the championship.

Just for a change, the Austrian Grand Prix, on 16 August, saw Piquet pip Mansell for pole, but the order was reversed for the race result. The much-improved and very fast Benetton-Fords of Fabi and Boutsen came next.

At Monza, on 6 September, Piquet took pole position again, with an active-suspension Williams, but he lost the race lead to Senna, who gambled on finishing the race without changing tyres. He very nearly made it, too, but spun off, returning the lead – and victory – to Piquet, with Senna second and Mansell a disappointed third. Piquet now had 63 points, Senna 49 and Mansell 43.

The Portuguese GP saw a Ferrari revival, with Gerhard Berger notching up Maranello's first pole position in years. A first-corner shunt caused the race to be interrupted. The restart saw Berger lead brilliantly until two laps from home when, sorely pressed by Prost's McLaren, he spun his Ferrari. Alain was through to score his 28th GP victory – at last breaking Jackie Stewart's long-standing record – and Berger finished second, with Piquet a distant third.

Piquet and Mansell headed the grid for the Spanish GP. It was a hectic race behind Mansell, who led at the end of lap one. Senna defended a non-stop second place for 62 spectacular laps before giving way to Prost, who took second, Johansson and a sub-standard Piquet.

Round 14 was in Mexico on 18 October. Mansell was on pole, alongside Berger, and was determined to make Piquet race for the coveted title, but Arrows driver Derek Warwick suffered – and survived – a heavy mid-race crash, which caused the event to be red-flagged and restarted. Mansell won on aggregate from Piquet, who was controversially second after an early incident which apparently led to a push-start from enthusiastic marshals. Now one or other of the Williams-Honda drivers was assured of the Championship: Piquet was on 73 points, Mansell on 61.

The Japanese GP, at Honda's own Suzuka circuit, brought the season's climax, but failed to stick to the script. During practice, Mansell crashed his Williams, damaged his back and was out for the remainder of the season. At that dramatic instant of impact, Piquet became 1987 World Champion.

Four drivers qualified faster than Piquet and the quickest Honda-powered car: Berger, on pole, from Prost, Boutsen and Alboreto. In the race, Prost punctured a tyre on lap two, while Berger drove brilliantly throughout to notch Ferrari's first win since Nurburgring '85. Senna just pipped Johansson for second and Alboreto was fourth to complete a great comeback day for Maranello.

Only the Australian GP remained at Adelaide on 15 November. Berger again won brilliantly from Alboreto. Senna was disqualified from second for a brake-cooling infringement and Piquet retired, as did Patrese, who replaced the injured Mansell.

Piquet was confirmed as 1987 World Champion, while Williams-Honda took the Constructors' Championship with a crushing 137 points to McLaren's 76, Lotus's 64 and Ferrari's 53. Palmer finished first in the 3.5-litre class Jim Clark Trophy, while Tyrrell-Cosworth won the Colin Chapman Trophy for 3.5-litre-car constructors.

The participants all looked forward to a 1988 season of 2.5-bar turbo boost and 150-litre fuel limits, prior to a complete turbo ban coming in 1989. As the season opened, the turbos were still on top, but their advantage was reduced. More excitement was yet to come . . .

287

Nichols, Steve 284
Nilsson, Gunnar 257, 258
Nixon, St John 45
North, David 268
Norton/Rolls-Royce 143
Nunn, Mo 200, 210
Nurburgring 179, 182, 183
Nuvolari, Tazio 83, 84, 86, 103, 105, 105, 108, 109, 109, 110, 111, 114, 115, 115, 116, 117, 118, 120, 131, 153, 158

Oliver, Mike 140, 235
Opel 15, 16, 51, 57
Opel, Fritz von 16
OSCA 126, 126, 136
Osmont 41

Pace, Carlos 239, 244, 256
Packard 48
Paletti, Ricardo 264, 266
Palmer, Johnathan 284, 285
Panhard 30, 31, 34, 36, 39, 40, 41, 43, 44, 47, 48
Panhard & Levassor, 7, 9, 11, 15, 28, 31, 33, 35, 36, 37, 43
Paris-Amsterdam race 34, 48
Paris-Berlin race 38, 41, 48
Paris-Bordeaux-Paris contest 7, 9, 33, 34, 36, 48
Paris-Boulogne race 35
Paris-Dieppe race 34
Paris-Lyons race 36
Paris-Madrid race 7, 12, 28, 31, 40, 43, 44, 48
Paris-Nice-La Turbie race 34
Paris-Rouen trial 7, 31, 35
Paris-Trouville race 34, 36
Paris-Vienna race 39, 41, 43, 48
Parkes, Mike 185, 229, 230
Parnell, Reg 155, 163, 166, 167, 169, 170, 182, 221
Patrese, Riccardo 260, 266, 270, 272, 279
Pau Grand Prix 170
Pau Week of Speed 43
Penske PC4 205
Perdisa 141
Pescarolo, Henry 235, 237
Peterson, Ronnie 237, 238, 239, 240, 240, 241, 242, 244, 251, 251, 254, 257, 259, 260, 261
Petit Journal, Le 31
Peugeot 7, 9, 12, 13, 16, 19, 21, 22, 24, 31, 33, 34, 35, 56, 57, 58, 60
Peugeot Frères 34
Philippe, Maurice 192, 208, 209
Phönix 11 9
Piccard-Pictet 57
Pietch, Paul 169
Pilbeam, Mike 182, 205
Pinson 43
Pintacuda, Carlo 117
Piquet, Nelson 211, 212, 263, 264, 265, 266, 270, 271, 272, 272, 274, 277, 279, 282, 283, 284, 285
Pirelli 146, 214, 284
Pironi, Didier 263, 264, 266
Pomeroy, Laurence 31
Poore, Dennis 170
Pope-Toledo 48
Pop, Victor 31
Porsche 150, 180, 182
Porsche, Dr Ferdinand 84, 89, 99
Porter, Leslie 45
Postlethwaite, Dr Harvey 197, 201, 209, 217, 254
Pousselet 31
Prost, Alain 264, 266, 267, 270, 271, 271, 272, 274, 275, 275, 276, 277, 279, 280, 281, 282, 283, 284, 285, 285
Pryce, Tom 255, 256
Purley, David 204, 205, 239, 258

Quantin 31

Race of Champions 270
Railton, Reid 90
Ramponi 71, 81
Raph 153
Regazzoni, Clay 206, 235, 236, 237, 238,

239, 241, 242, 243, 244, 251, 251, 253, 262, 263
Renault 28, 39, 41, 49, 50, 51, 203, 204, 211, 271, 276, 278, 282
Renault, Louis 39, 41, 44, 46
Renault, Marcel 6, 39, 41, 45
Repco 418 189
Resta, Dario 56, 909
Reutemann, Carlos 206, 212, 214, 238, 240, 241, 243, 244, 245, 256, 257, 257, 259, 260, 261, 263, 264, 266
Reventlow, Lance 152
Revson, Peter 239, 239, 241
Richard-Brasier 47, 49, 53
Rigal 56, 56
Rigolly, Louis 46
Riley Six 84
Rindt, Jochen 192, 193, 226, 228, 229, 232, 232, 235, 235, 236, 237
Rodriguez, Pedro 228, 230, 235, 237
Rolland-Pilain 56, 65, 66, 68, 93
Rosberg, Keke 218, 266, 267, 267, 270, 276, 277, 279, 280, 281, 282, 283
Rose, Gerald 25
Rosemeyer, Bernd 116, 116, 117, 118
Rosenberger, Adolf 89
Rosier, Louis 162, 163, 165, 169
Roussat 31
Rudd 227
Rudge-Whitworth 62

S and M Simplex 48
Salamano, Carlo 96, 97, 99
Salleron 47, 47
Salmson 78, 82
Salzer 20, 57
Sanesi 154, 158, 161, 167
Scarfiotti, Ludovico 185, 223, 230, 231
Scheckter, Jody 201, 208, 209, 210, 238, 239, 242, 242, 243, 244, 245, 251, 255, 256, 257, 257, 258, 261, 262, 263, 263
Schenken, Tim 237
Schlesser, Jo 190, 231
Schneider 57
Seaman, Dick 81, 86, 90, 117, 118, 118, 120
Segrave, Sir Henry 66, 72, 78, 93, 96, 102
Sénéchal, Robert 102, 109
Senna, Ayrton 277, 279, 280, 281, 282, 282, 284, 285
Serafini 166
Serpollet steamer 34, 39, 44
Shadow 197, 198, 204, 206, 212, 255
Sieler, Max 89
Siffert, Jo 231, 237, 238, 239
Silverstone 172
Sivocci 96
Sizaire-Naudin 55
Smallman, Andy 198
Snoeck-Bolide 36
Sommer, Raymond 153, 154, 160
Southgate, Tony 197, 207
Spa Francorchamps 173
Spence, Mike 228, 231, 231
Spirit 201, 271
Spyker 27
Stacey, Alan 175
STD 62, 76, 93, 96
Stead 40
Stewart, Jackie 186, 187, 190, 192, 193, 195, 197, 226, 227, 228, 229, 230, 231, 231, 232, 235, 236, 237, 238, 239, 240
Stocks, J.W. 45
Stommelen, Rolf 244, 245
Stuck 84
Stuck, Hans 113, 115, 117
Sullivan, Danny 270
Sunbeam 22, 23, 27, 28, 28, 31, 56, 57, 60, 62, 66, 67, 68, 71, 72, 72, 73, 74, 76, 79 82
Surtees, John 175, 182, 189, 193, 205, 208, 220, 221, 222, 223, 225, 226, 228, 229, 230, 231, 232
Szisz, Francois 49, 50, 50, 53

Talbot 33, 62, 123
Talbot-Darracq 62, 64, 67, 67, 76, 82, 83, 97
Talbot-Lago 109
Tambay, Patrick 266, 267, 270, 271, 272, 277
Targa Florio race 12, 22, 49, 90, 94, 103, 108, 110, 110
Taruffi 165, 170

Tauranac, Ron 182, 208
Taylor, Geoffrey 126
Taylor, Henry 175
Taylor, Trevor 220
Teste 34, 43, 48
Theodore 208
Thery, Leon 35, 47
'Thin Wall Special' 139, 140
Thomas, J.G. Parry 79, 136
Thomas, René 59, 60, 90, 93
Toleman 212, 212, 272
Tracy 48
Trintignant, Maurice 154, 170
Trossi, Count 112, 121, 154, 155, 158, 161
Trucco 15
Turin circuit 154, 156
Tyrrell, Ken 190, 193, 195, 197, 230, 232, 236, 237, 237, 244, 251
Tyrrell 148, 192, 197, 201, 205, 208, 209, 270

Ugolini 173
Uhlenhaut, Rudolf 89, 146

Vanderbilt Cup 47, 48
Vanderbilt Trophy 118
Vanderbilt, W.K. Jnr 43, 48
Vandervell, Tony 140, 143, 173, 174
Vanwall 139, 140, 143, 143, 144, 147, 149, 150, 173, 174, 179
Varenne 31
Varzi, Achille 105, 105, 107, 107, 108, 109, 110, 110, 112, 113, 114, 115, 116, 117, 154
Vauxhall 56, 57
Vauxhall Prince Henry 27
Vauxhall TT 67
Vauxhall Villiers Supercharged Special 68, 68
Vehicle Dynamics Programme 202
Villeneuve, Gilles 210, 212, 217, 259, 260, 261, 261, 262, 263, 264, 266
Villoresi brothers 120, 128, 153, 160, 161, 166, 167, 170, 170, 172
Viscaya, Pierre de 94, 94
Voisin 68, 94
Volkswagen 88
von Brauchitsch, Manfred 56, 113, 117, 118, 120, 121
von Delius 117
von Eberhorst, Professor 89
von Trips, Wolfgang 'Taffy' 219

Wagner, Louis 20, 52, 52, 57, 62, 71, 89, 93, 102
Walker, Dave 237
Walker, Peter 169
Walker, Rob 149, 166, 175, 178, 180, 220, 222, 232, 235
Wanderer 89
Warwick, Derek 266, 268, 272, 276, 282, 285
Watkins, Glen 180
Watson, John 204, 251, 253, 253, 256, 257, 258, 260, 261, 264, 264, 266, 267, 270, 271, 272, 275
Werner, Dr 89
Weslake, Harry 186
Wheatcroft, Tom 239
Whitehead, Peter 126, 162
Wilcox, Howdy 90, 94
Williams, Frank 198, 199, 206, 208, 210, 211, 214, 218, 249, 251, 262, 264, 266, 270, 274, 279, 282, 283, 284, 285
Williamson, Roger 239
Wilton 36
Wimille, Jean-Pierre 103, 116, 154, 155, 158
Wolf, Walter 212, 259
Wolf 201, 208, 209, 255, 255
Wolseley 44
Woods, Aubrey 186

Yeoman/Credit Team 103

Zborowski, Count Eliot 43, 44
Zborowski, Count Louis 75, 93, 94
Zori, Renzo 256
Zuccarelli 55